Text Processing
in Java

Text Processing

in Java

Mitzi Morris

Colloquial Media
New York
2014

Text Processing in Java
Copyright © Mitzi Morris 2014
Colloquial Media, Inc.

ISBN 978-0-9882087-2-8

http://colloquial.com/text-processing-java

Contents

Preface

This book explains the basics of text processing in Java. Java provides an extensive set of tools for manipulating character-based data, including byte-to-character conversion, input and output streams, and high-level methods such as regular expressions. This book assumes you are familiar with basic coding in a language such as Java, but that you may not be familiar with low-level representations of bytes and integers, the representation and manipulation of strings, or how to write non-greedy regular expressions based on Unicode.

The presentation here will be hands-on. You should be comfortable reading short and relatively simple Java programs. The specific aspects of Java coding relating to text processing, such as streaming I/O, character decoding, string representations, and regular expression processing, are discussed in depth. We also go into some detail on web technologies for transporting text via HTTP, and parsing and generating XML, HTML and JSON. Open-source software dependencies include the International Components for Unicode (ICU) library and Apache Lucene and Solr. We provide a warm-up chapter on using the various tools required for effective software development including text editors, version control, and the Ant build system for Java. The last two chapters cover the use of the Apache Lucene search library and the Apache Solr search server.

This book grew out of the book *Natural Language Processing with LingPipe*, which was written by my husband Bob Carpenter. Bob realized that building robust, scalable applictions with LingPipe requires a solid grasp of the fundamentals of encoding, decoding, and processing character data in Java. He wrote draft versions of the first four chapters and suggested that I turn them into this book. I am forever grateful for his help, feedback, encouragement, and love.

Mitzi Morris
New York
January 20, 2014

Text Processing
in Java

Chapter 1

Getting Started

The canonical first program in Java (and many other programming languages) is "hello world."

```
public class HelloWorld {
    public static void main(String[] args) {
        System.out.println("Hello, World!");
    }
}
```

This is a very simple example of text processing but not a trivial one. The Java program generates text characters and sends them to an output device, in this example, the terminal. What is necessary in order to generate and display text in a language other than English? How do we greet the world in Japanese?

The HTML equivalent of our "hello world" program is the file HelloWorld.html containing the following HTML:

```
<html><body>  Hello, World! </body></html>
```

A Java program that creates this file interacts directly with the file system and indirectly with the web server and web browser. How do we generate a web page that says "Hello World" in Japanese? What is required for the Japanese characters to display correctly in the browser? How do we process a set of web pages that includes HelloWorld.html so that a search for the word "hello" will return this page as one of the results?

We answer these questions with a series of small, self-contained example programs that report the state of the data before, during, and/or after processing. We provide the source code, data, and scripts to run them as well as instructions for setting up your tools and displays. These programs can be reused and expended to provide diagnostics over inputs, outputs, and intermediate results of text processing.

1

Being able to process text data correctly and efficiently is a prerequisite for building robust, scalable natural language processing (NLP) applications. NLP applications over text data include recognizing the language(s) used; breaking the text into constituent sentences, phrases, and words; and indexing the text for search. There is considerable overlap between text processing and NLP. For example, breaking a stream of text into a series of words requires knowing which language or languages are used in that text and what alphabet, punctuation symbols, and writing conventions are used by each of these languages. We show how to do several of these tasks using existing open-source Java libraries.

If you are building a new NLP application, this book will help you make it both general and efficient. If you are working with an existing NLP tool kit, this book will show you how to do the necessary data munging to bridge the gap between your data and the API of the tool kit.

In the next few chapters we cover the fundamental Java classes and packages used to processes text data, starting with bytes, characters, and strings, proceeding to the packages `java.io` and `java.util.regex`, which handle I/O and regular expressions, respectively. Then we cover sending data via HTTP and common web data formats. These chapters can serve either as tutorials or as reference material, and the demo programs for each chapter can be used as diagnostic tools to examine texts and intermediate results of processing. We include a case study that uses all of these packages to transform text from an idiosyncratic format to XML. We conclude with chapters on Lucene and Solr, the Apache search engine and search server written in Java, two extremely powerful and popular tools for large-scale NLP applications.

1.1   The Tools We Use

First we'll take some time to explain the tools we'll be using or that you might want to use for program development. After describing and motivating our choice of each tool, we'll provide downloading and installation instructions. Not all of these tools are needed to run every example.

We favor the *printf debugging* technique, whereby trace statements are used to record the flow of processing. This technique takes its name from the `printf` statement in C. In Java, we rely on the `System.out.println` method, as in the `HelloWorld.java` example above.

We use a Unix-like command-line shell to present and run our examples via the Apache Ant build tool, in keeping with our own development practices. We also discuss the most popular integrated development environment (IDE) tools for Java that can be used instead of the shell to view and run the examples. If you're already writing and running Java programs using these tools, you may skip to section 1.3, which covers how to configure and troubleshoot your development environment so that multilingual text data display correctly.

1.1.1 Unix Shell Tools

In this book, we use the so-called "Bourne Again Shell" (bash) for Unix-style commands. Bash is the default shell in Linux, Mac OS X, and Cygwin on Windows, and it is also available for Solaris.

There are several terminal programs for the Linux desktop. On the Mac, we use the Terminal.app found in Applications/Utilities.

If you're working on a Windows machine, we recommend the Cygwin suite of Unix command-line tools for Windows. Cygwin is released under version 2 of the GNU Public License (GPLv2), with terms outlined here:

```
http://cygwin.com/license.html
```

It's also available with a commercial license. Cygwin can be downloaded and installed through Cygwin's home page:

```
http://www.cygwin.com/
```

The `setup.exe` program is small. When you run it, it goes out over the internet to find the packages from registered mirrors. It then lists all the packages available. You can install some or all of them. You can just run the setup program again to update or install new packages; it'll show you what version of what's already installed.

It might also be easier to list what Cygwin doesn't support. We use it mainly for running Unix-like commands in Windows, including pipes, find, grep, (bash) shell support, tar and gzip, wget, aspell, which, and so on. We also use its implementation of the Subversion and CVS version control systems. We do not install emacs or TeX through Cygwin. These packages are indexed under various categories in Cygwin, such as Web, Net, Devel, and Base.

Although it's possible to get Python, Perl, Emacs, TeX and LaTeX, and so on, we typically install these packages directly rather than as part of Cygwin.

Archive and Compression Tools

In order to unpack data and library distributions, you need to be able to run the `tar` archiving tool, as well as the unpacking commands `unzip` and `gunizp`. These may be installed as part of Cygwin on Windows.

1.1.2 Version Control

If you don't live in some kind of version control environment, you should. Not only can you keep track of your own code across multiple sites and/or users but also you can keep up-to-date with other projects under version control, such as the LingPipe sandbox, and projects hosted by open source hosting services such as GitHub, SourceForge or Google Code.

We are currently using Git, which is used by the Linux developers. Git is a very powerful distributed revision and source code control system. It is free and open-source. Software and documentation is found on the official Git home page:

```
http://gitscm.com/
```

1.1.3   Text Editors

In order to generate code, HTML, and reports, you will need to be able to edit text. We like to work in the Emacs text editor, because of its configurability. It's as close as you'll get to an IDE in a simple text editor.

Spaces, Not Tabs

To make code portable, we highly recommend using spaces instead of tabs. Yes, it takes up a bit more space, but it's worth it. We follow Sun's coding standard for Java, so we use four spaces for a tab. This is a bit easier to read but wastes more horizontal space.

(GNU) Emacs

We use the GNU Emacs distribution of Emacs, which is available from its home page:

```
http://www.gnu.org/software/emacs/
```

It's standard on most Unix and Linux distributions and Mac OS X; for Windows, there is a zipped binary distribution in a subdirectory of the main distribution that only needs to be unpacked in order to be run. We've had problems with the Cygwin-based installations in terms of their font integration. And we've also not been able to configure XEmacs for Unicode, which is the main reason for our preference for GNU Emacs.

We like to work with the Lucida Console font, which is distributed with Windows; it's the font used for code examples in this book. It also supports a wide range of non-Roman fonts. You can change the font by pulling down the `Options` menu and selecting the `Set Default Font...` item to pop up a dialog box. Then use the `Save Options` item in the same menu to save it. It'll show you where it saved a file called `.emacs`, which you will need to edit for the next customizations.

In order to configure GNU Emacs to run UTF-8, you need to add the following text to your `.emacs` file:[1]

```
(prefer-coding-system 'utf-8)
(set-default-coding-systems 'utf-8)
(set-terminal-coding-system 'utf-8)
(set-keyboard-coding-system 'utf-8)
(setq default-buffer-file-coding-system 'utf-8)
(setq x-select-request-type
    '(UTF8_STRING COMPOUND_TEXT TEXT STRING))
(set-clipboard-coding-system 'utf-16le-dos)
```

The requisite commands to force tabs to be replaced with spaces in Java files are:

```
(defun java-mode-untabify ()
  (save-excursion
    (goto-char (point-min))
    (if (search-forward "t" nil t)
        (untabify (1- (point)) (point-max))))
  nil)

(add-hook 'java-mode-hook
      '(lambda ()
          (make-local-variable 'write-contents-hooks)
          (add-hook 'write-contents-hooks 'java-mode-untabify)))

(setq indent-tabs-mode nil)
```

Aquamacs

Aquamacs is an Emacs text editor for Mac OS X. It is based on GNU Emacs from the GNU project but with a user interface (UI) that is designed to conform with Mac OS X UI standard. It is available from:

`http://aquamacs.org`

To customize Aquamacs as described above, instead of editing your `.emacs` file, you need to edit the file

~/Library/Preferences/Aquamacs Emacs/Preferences.el

---

[1] The UTF-8 instructions are from the Sacrificial Rabbit blog entry `http://blog.jonnay.net/archives/820-Emacs-and-UTF-8-Encoding.html`, downloaded 4 August 2010.

1.1.4   Java Standard Edition 7

The presentation here assumes the reader has a basic working knowledge of the Java programming language. We will focus on a few aspects of Java that are particularly crucial for processing textual language data, such as character and string representations, input and output streams and character encodings, regular expressions, parsing HTML and XML markup, and data interchange protocols.

This book is based on the latest currently supported standard edition of the Java platform (Java SE), which is version 7. You will need the Java development kit (JDK) in order to compile Java programs. A java virtual machine (JVM) is required to execute compiled Java programs. A Java runtime environment (JRE) contains platform-specific support and integration for a JVM and often interfaces to web browsers for applet support.

Java is available for the Windows, Mac, Linux, and Solaris operating systems in both 32-bit and 64-bit versions. The 64-bit version is required to allocate JVMs with heaps larger than 1.5 or 2 gigabytes (the exact maximum for 32-bit Java depends on the platform). Java is updated regularly, and it's worth having the latest version. Updates include bug fixes and often include performance enhancements, some of which can be quite substantial.

All supported versions of Java for all platforms can be downloaded from:

```
http://oracle.com/technetwork/java/javase/downloads
```

This page also contains licensing information as well as downloads of Java demos, samples, and co-bundled NetBeans IDE.

Java must be added to the operating system's executables path so that the shell commands and other packages such as Ant can find it.

We have to manage multiple versions of Java, so typically we will define an environment variable JAVA_HOME and add ${JAVA_HOME}/bin (Unix) or %JAVA_HOME%\bin (Windows) to the PATH environment variable (or its equivalent for your operating system). We then set JAVA_HOME to either JAVA_1_5, JAVA_1_6, or JAVA_1_7 depending on use case. Note that JAVA_HOME is one level above Java's bin directory containing the executable Java commands.

You can test whether you can run Java with the following command, which should produce similar results:

```
> java -version
java version "1.7.0_10"
Java(TM) SE Runtime Environment (build 1.7.0_10-b18)
Java HotSpot(TM) 64-Bit Server VM (build 23.6-b04, mixed mode)
```

Similarly, you can test for the Java compiler version, using:

```
> javac -version
javac 1.7.0_10
```

Java Source

The OpenJDK project creates and distributes an open-source reference implementation of Java SE 7 in collaboration with Oracle, IBM, and the major Linux distributions. The source code for Java SE 7, as well as Java SE 6, is available for download from:

```
http://download.java.net/openjdk/jdk7/
```

The source is subject to yet another license, the Java Research License, available at:

```
http://www.java.net/jrl.csp
```

The source provides a fantastic set of examples of how to design, code, and document Java programs. We especially recommend studying the source for strings, I/O, and collections. Further, like all source, it provides a definitive answer to the questions of what a particular piece of code does and how it does it. This can be useful for understanding deeper issues such as thread safety, equality and hashing, efficiency, and memory usage.

1.1.5 Ant

We present examples for compilation and for running programs using the Apache Ant build tool. Ant has three key features that make it well suited for expository purposes. First, it's portable across all the platforms that support Java. Second, it provides clear XML representations for core Java concepts such as classpaths and command-line arguments. Third, invoking a target in Ant directly executes the dependent targets and then all of the commands in the target. Thus, we find Ant builds easier to follow than those using the classic Unix build tool Make or its modern incarnation Apache Maven, both of which attempt to resolve dependencies among targets and determine whether targets are up-to-date before executing them.

Although we're not attempting to teach Ant, we'll walk through a basic Ant build file later in this chapter to give you at least a reading knowledge of Ant. If you're using an IDE such as Eclipse or NetBeans, you can import Ant build files directly to create a project.

You can test whether Ant is installed with:

```
> ant -version
Apache Ant(TM) version 1.9.0 compiled on March 5 2013
```

Installing and Configuring Ant

If Ant is not already installed on your machine, you can download one of the binary distributions from apache.org.

Ant is an Apache project and it is subject to the Apache license:

    http://ant.apache.org/license.html

Ant is available from:

    http://ant.apache.org/

You need only one of the binary distributions, which will look like
apache-ant-*version*-bin.tar.gz.
    First, you need to unpack the distribution. We like directory structures with
release names, which is how Ant unpacks, using top-level directory names such
as apache-ant-1.9.0. Then, you need to put the bin subdirectory of the top-
level directory into the PATH environment variable so that Ant may be executed
from the command line.
    Ant itself runs as a Java process. For Linux, Cygwin, and Windows Ant re-
quires the JAVA_HOME environment variable to be set to the path above the
bin directory containing the Java executables. Ant's installation instructions
suggest setting the ANT_HOME directory in the same way and then adding it
to your PATH environment variable, but it's not necessary unless you will be
scripting calls to Ant.
    In order to use Ant for many of the examples in this book, it
is necessary to set the ANT_OPTS environment variable and specify the
file encoding used by Ant when sending program output to the terminal. Most of the examples in this book use the UTF-8 file encoding, so the setting ANT_OPTS="-Dfile.encoding=UTF-8" is appropriate,
as is ANT_OPTS="-Dfile.encoding=Latin1", for reasons explained in section 3.10.
    Ant build files may be imported directly into either the Eclipse or NetBeans
IDEs (see below for a description of these).

1.1.6   Integrated Development Environment

Many people prefer to write (and compile and debug) code in an integrated
development environment (IDE). IDEs offer advantages such as automatic
method, class and constant completion, easily configurable text formatting,
stepwise debuggers, and automated tools for code generation and refactoring.
The two most popular IDEs for Java are Eclipse and NetBeans.

Eclipse IDE

Eclipse provides a full range of code checking, auto-completion and code generation, and debugging facilities. Eclipse is an open-source project with a wide
range of additional tools available as plug-ins. It also has modules for languages other than Java, such as C++ and PHP.
    The full set of Eclipse downloads is listed on the following page:

`http://download.eclipse.org/eclipse/downloads/`

You'll want to make sure you choose the one compatible with the JDK you are using. Though originally a Windows-based system, Eclipse has been ported to Mac OS X (though Carbon) and Linux.

Eclipse is released under the Eclipse Public License (EPL), a slightly modified version of the Common Public License (CPL) from IBM, the full text of which is available from:

`http://www.eclipse.org/legal/epl-v10.html`

NetBeans IDE

Unlike Eclipse, the NetBeans IDE is written entirely in Java. Thus, it's possible to run it under Windows, Linux, Solaris Unix, and Mac OS X. There are also a wide range of plug-ins available for NetBeans.

NetBeans is free and may be downloaded from its home page:

`http://netbeans.org/`

Its licensing is rather complex, being released under a dual license consisting of the Common Development and Distribution License (CDDL) and version 2 of the GNU Public License version 2 (GPLv2). Full details are at:

`http://netbeans.org/about/legal/license.html`

1.1.7 Example Programs, Data, and Jar Files Used in This Book

The example programs from this book are freely available from GitHub. The homepage for this repository is:

`https://github.com/colloquial/javabook`

Links on the page allow you to clone this repository. If you're not using Git, you can download the contents of the repository as a zip archive from:

`https://github.com/colloquial/javabook/archive/master.zip`

The repository contains all of the source code and Ant build files for the examples in this book and the third-party jar files that they depend on as well as two datasets used for the Lucene and Solr examples. The size of the zip file is 21.8 MB, as many of the jar files are rather large.

The distribution is organized into two top-level directories called `src` and `data`. The `src` directory is organized into one directory per chapter. The name of each directory corresponds to the subject of the chapter, e.g., the directory `src/io` contains all examples from chapter 3 on input and output in Java. Each of these directories contains a `build.xml` file that can be used to compile and run the example programs. If third-party jar files are needed, they are found in a subdirectory named `lib`.

1.2   "Hello World" Example

In this section, we provide a very simple "hello world" program and use Ant to compile and run it.

1.2.1   Running the Example

To the extent we are able, we'll start each discussion with an example of how to run examples. This is pretty easy for the "hello world" example. As with all of our examples, we begin by changing directories into the directory containing the example. The top-level directory is called `javabook` or `javabook-master`, depending on whether the archive was cloned with git or downloaded as a zip file. We then execute the change directory (`cd`) command to move into the subdirectory `javabook/src/intro`:

```
> cd src/intro
```

Note that we have italicized the commands issued by the user. We use the command `ls` to list the contents of the directory:

```
> ls
build.xml demo.properties src
```

We use Ant to run the demo. Ant uses the file `build.xml` as its build file. An Ant build file contains zero or more targets elements. We start by invoking the `hello` target:

```
> ant hello
```

Ant prints out the full path names of all files it uses and creates. We've used (...) to indicate the full path to the current working directory. The Ant output is:

```
Buildfile: (...)/build.xml

jar:
    [mkdir] Created dir: (...)/build/classes
    [javac] Compiling 3 source files to (...)/build/classes
     [jar] Building jar: (...)/build/intro-1.0.jar

hello:
    [java] Hello, World!

BUILD SUCCESSFUL
Total time: 2 seconds
```

First, Ant echoes the name of the build file. When Ant is invoked without specifying a particular build file, it uses the `build.xml` in the directory from which it was called, as is the case here, where the build file is `build.xml`.

Reading down the left side of the output, you see the targets that are invoked. The first target invoked is the `jar` target, and the second target is the `hello` target. The targets are left aligned and followed by semicolons. A target consists of an ordered list of dependent targets to invoke before the current target and an ordered list of tasks to execute after the dependent targets are invoked.

Under the targets, you see the particular tasks that the target executes. These are indented, square bracketed, and right aligned. The `jar` target invokes three tasks, `mkdir`, `javac`, and `jar`. The `hello` target invokes one task, `java`. All of the output for each task is shown after the task name. If there is more than one line of output, the name of the task is repeated.

In this example, the `mkdir` task makes a new directory, here the `build/classes` directory. The `javac` task runs the Java compiler, here compiling a single source file into the newly created directory. The `jar` task builds the Java library into the build subdirectory `build` in file `intro-4.0.jar`. Moving onto the `hello` target, the `java` task runs a command-line Java program, in this case printing the output of the "hello world" program.

The reason the `jar` target was invoked was because the `hello` target was defined to depend on the `jar` target. Ant invokes all dependent targets (recursively) before the invoked target.

Finally, Ant reports that the build was successful and reports the amount of time taken. In the future, we will usually show only the output of the Java program executed and not all of the output from the compilation steps. To save more space, we also remove the `[java]` tag on the task. Under this scheme, the `hello` target invocation would be displayed in this book as:

```
> ant hello
Hello, World!
```

1.2.2 `HelloWorld` Code Walkthrough

The code for the "hello world" program is in the file `HelloWorld.java` in the source code subdirectory. The path to this file is:

```
javabook/src/intro/src/com/colloquial/intro/HelloWorld.java
```

Throughout the book, the files are organized this way, under the top-level `src` directory, then the name of the chapter (here `intro`), followed by `src`, followed by the path to the actual program. We follow the Java convention of placing files in a directory structure that mirrors their package structure, so the remaining part of the path is `com/colloquial/intro/HelloWorld.java`. The contents of the `HelloWorld.java` program file are:

```
public class HelloWorld {
    public static void main(String[] args) {
        System.out.println("Hello, World!");
    }
}
```

As usual for Java programs, the first thing in the file is the package declaration, here `com.colloquial.intro`; note how it matches the end of the path to the file, `com/colloquial/intro`. Next is the class definition, `HelloWorld`, which matches the name of the file, `HelloWorld.java`.

When a Java class is invoked from the command line (or equivalently through Ant), it must implement a static method with a signature like the one shown. Specifically, the method must be named `main`, must take a single string array argument of type `String[]`, must not have a return value (i.e., return type `void`), and must be declared to be both public and static using the `public` and `static` modifiers. The method may optionally throw any kind of exception.

The body of the program here just prints `Hello World` to the system output. As usual, Java provides a handle to the system output through the public static variable `out` of type `java.io.PrintStream` in the `java.lang.System` class.

1.2.3 Hello with Arguments

Often we need to supply arguments to programs from the command line. Our second demo `HelloName` takes two command-line arguments to provide a customized greeting. The easiest way to do this with Ant is by setting the properties on the command line.

```
> ant -Dfirst=Mr. -Dlast=Phelps hello-name
Hello, Mr. Phelps!
```

`HelloName` varies from `HelloWorld` in the body of its `main()` method.

```
public class HelloName {

    public static void main(String[] args) {
        String first = args[0];
        String last = args[1];
        System.out.printf("Hello, %s %s!\n",first,last);
```

Each argument to a program corresponds to a named property, here `first` and `last`. In general, properties are specified -D*key*=*val*.[2] As a convention, we

---

[2]Depending on your shell, this may also require varying amounts of quoting and/or escaping special characters. For example, keys or values with spaces typically require double quotes on Windows.

assign the command-line arguments read from the array `args` to a sequence of named variables. We then use these same names in the Ant properties (see section 1.4.3).

1.3 Multilingual Text Example

The examples in this book draw on languages from around the world. In order to run these examples from the command line, both the terminal window and Ant must be configured properly. The demo class `ConfigTest` writes several letters and symbols outside of the basic range of ASCII text to the terminal.

Because the `ConfigTest` program writes UTF-8 encoded data to the terminal, the terminal's character encoding property should be set to UTF-8 via the Settings or Preferences panel. Ant captures the program output and sends it to the terminal; therefore, we need to tell Ant what character encoding to use as well. The shell environment variable ANT_OPTS has as its value the configuration information we need to pass in to Ant. We can set this property in the bash `.profile` or directly in the shell via the command:

```
> export ANT_OPTS="-Dfile.encoding=UTF-8"
```

The Ant target `test` compiles and runs this program.

```
> ant test
```

Figure 1.1 shows the results of `ConfigTest` when both the terminal and Ant have been configured for UTF-8, running on a MacBook Air that has the Latin, Cyrillic, and Hangul fonts installed. Figure 1.2 shows the results of `ConfigTest` when the ANT_OPTS environment is set to ASCII. Here Ant replaces all the non-ASCII characters with a question mark. Figure 1.3 shows the results of `ConfigTest` when the ANT_OPTS environment variable is set to UTF-8 but the terminal app is configured for Windows Latin1. In this third example, all the characters are from the Latin1 inventory, but only the ASCII lowercase *a* is rendered correctly. Note that the lowercase *a* with grave accent is garbled. Although this character in the Latin1 character set, its byte-level representation is not the same in UTF-8 and Latin1. Because communication between Ant and the terminal app is at the byte level, this difference is problematic. The byte-level encoding of characters is covered in detail in chapter 2.

1.4 Introduction to Ant Build Files

Although we will typically skip discussing the Ant build files, as they're almost all the same, we will go over the one for the "hello world" program in some detail. The build file for this chapter is located at `javabook/src/intro/build.xml`.

```
test:
    [java] small a: a
    [java] small a with grave accent: à
    [java] Cyrillic capital eN: H
    [java] Hangul syllable geon: 건
```

Fig. **1.1:** *Results from* ConfigTest, *Ant configured for UTF-8, terminal configured for UTF-8.*

```
test:
    [java] small a: a
    [java] small a with grave accent: ??
    [java] Cyrillic capital eN: ??
    [java] Hangul syllable geon: ???
```

Fig. **1.2:** *Results from* ConfigTest, *Ant configured for ASCII, terminal configured for UTF-8.*

```
test:
    [java] small a: a
    [java] small a with grave accent: Ã
    [java] Cyrillic capital eN: Ð
    [java] Hangul syllable geon: ê±´
```

Fig. **1.3:** *Results from* ConfigTest, *Ant configured for UTF-8, terminal configured for Latin1.*

1.4.1 XML Declaration

The first thing in any Ant build file is the XML declaration, here:

```
<?xml version="1.0" encoding="ASCII"?>
```

This just tells Ant's XML parser that what it's looking at is an XML file and that the ASCII character encoding is being used for subsequent data. We chose ASCII because we didn't anticipate using any non-ASCII characters; we could have chosen Latin1 or UTF-8 or even Big5 and written the build file in Chinese. Most XML parsers are robust enough to infer the character encoding, but it's always good practice to make it explicit.

The ellipses (...) indicate elided material that will be filled in (or not) in continuing discussion.

1.4.2 Top-Level Project Element

The top-level element in the XML file is the project declaration. The project element's tag is project, and there are no required attributes. The project declaration may optionally be given a name as the value of attribute name, a default target to invoke as the value of attribute default, and a base directory from which to run as the value of `basedir`. The base directory defaults to the directory containing the build file, which is where we set everything up to run from. We will not need a default target as we will specify all targets explicitly for clarity. The name doesn't really have a function.

1.4.3 Ant Properties

We organize Ant build files in the conventional way starting with properties, which are declared first in the project element's content. The properties define constant values for reuse. Here, we have

```
<property name="version"
          value="1.0"/>

<property name="jar"
          value="build/tj-intro-${version}.jar"/>
```

The first property definition defines a property `version` with value `1.0` (all values are strings). The second property is named `jar`, with a value, defined in terms of the first property, of `build/tj-intro-1.0.jar`. Note that the value of the property `version` has been substituted for the substring `${version}`. In general, properties are accessed by `${...}` with the property filled in for the ellipses.

Properties may be overridden from the command line by declaring an environment variable for the command. For example,

```
> ant -Djar=foo.jar jar
```

calls the build file, setting the value of the `jar` property to be the string `foo.jar` (which would create a library archive called `foo.jar`). The value of a property in Ant is always the first value to which it is set; further attempts to set it will be ignored. Because the command line properties are evaluated first, the properties in the `build.xml` are ignored.

1.4.4 Ant Targets

Next, we have a sequence of targets, each of which groups together a sequence of tasks. The order of targets is not important.

Clean Target

The first target we have performs cleanup.

```
<target name="clean">
  <delete dir="build"/>
</target>
```

This is a conventional cleanup target, given the obvious name of `clean`. Each target has a sequence of tasks that will be executed whenever the target is invoked. Here, the task is a delete task, which deletes the directory named `build`.

It is conventional to have a clean task that cleans up all of the automatically generated content in a project. In this case, this includes the `.class` files generated by the compiler in the deletable subdirectory `build`) and the `.jar` file produced by the Java archiver in the top-level directory.

Compilation/Archive Target

The next target is the compilation target, named `jar`:

```
<target name="jar">
  <mkdir dir="build/classes"/>
  <javac debug="yes"
         debuglevel="source,lines,vars"
         destdir="build/classes"
         includeantruntime="false">
    <compilerarg value="-Xlint:all"/>
    <src path="src/"/>
  </javac>
  <jar destfile="${jar}">
    <fileset dir="build/classes"
             includes="**/*.class"/>
  </jar>
</target>
```

Invoking the `jar` target executes three tasks, a make-directory (`mkdir`), java compilation (`javac`), and Java archive creation (`jar`). Note that, as we exploit here, it is allowable to have a target with the same name as a task, because Ant keeps the namespaces separate.

The first task is the make-directory task, `mkdir`; it takes the path for a directory and creates that directory and all of its necessary parent directories. Here, it builds the directory `build/classes`. All files are relative to the base directory, which is by default the directory containing the `build.xml` file, here `javabook/src/intro`.

The second task is the Java compilation task, `javac`; it does the actual compilation. Here we have supplied the task element with four attributes. The first two, **debug** and **debuglevel**, are required to insert debugging information into the compiled code so that we can get stack traces with line numbers when processes crash. These can be removed to save space, but they can be very helpful for deployed systems, so we don't recommend it. The **debug** element says to turn debugging on, and the **debuglevel** says to debug the source down to lines and variable names, which is the maximal amount of debugging information available. The javac task may specify the character encoding used for the Java program using the attribute encoding.

The destination directory attribute, destdir, indicates where the compiled classes will be stored. Here, the path is build/classes. Note that this is in the directory we first created with the make-directory task. Further recall that the build directory will be removed by the clean target.

Finally, we have a flag with attribute includeantruntime that says the Ant runtime libraries should not be included in the classpath for the compilation. In our opinion, this should have defaulted to false rather than true and saved us a line in all the build files. If you don't specify this attribute, Ant gripes and tells you what it's defaulting to.

The javac element has content, starting with a compiler argument. The element compilerarg passes the value of the attribute value to the underlying call to the javac executable in the JDK. Here, we specified a value of -Xlint:all. The -X options to javac are documented by running the command javac -X. This -X option specifies lint:all, which says to turn all lint detection on. This provides extended warnings for form, including deprecation, unchecked casts, lack of serial version IDs, lack or extra override specifications, and so on. These can be turned on and off one by one, but we prefer to leave them all on and produce lint-free programs. This often involves suppressing warnings that would otherwise be unavoidable, such as casts after object I/O or internal uses of deprecated public methods.

When compilation requires external libraries, we may add the classpath specifications either as attributes or as elements in the javac task. For instance, we can have a classpath specification, which is much like a property definition:

```
<path id="classpath">
  <pathelement location="${jar}"/>
  <pathelement location="lib/icu4j-4_4_1.jar"/>
</path>
```

In the java target, we'd use the id attribute of the named path element to specify the classpath:

```
<classpath refid="classpath"/>
```

The javac task's content continues a source element with tag src. This says where to find the source code to compile. Here we specify the value of attribute for the path to the source, path, as src/. As usual, this path is interpreted relative to the base directory, which by default is the one holding the build.xml file, even if it's executed from elsewhere.

The third task is the Java archive task, jar, which packages up the compiled code into a single compressed file, conventionally suffixed with the string

`.jar`. The file created is specified as the value of the `destfile` attribute, here given as `${jar}`, meaning the value of the `jar` property will be substituted, here `build/lpb-intro-4.0.jar`. As ever, this is interpreted relative to the base project directory. Note that the jar is being created in the `build` directory, which will be cleaned by the clean target.

Java Execution Task

The final target is the one that'll run Java:

```
<target name="hello"
        depends="jar">
  <java classname="com.colloquial.intro.HelloWorld"
        classpath="${jar}"
        fork="true">
  </java>
</target>
```

Unlike the previous targets, this target has a dependency, as indicated by the `depends` attribute on the target element. Here, the value is `jar`, meaning that the `jar` target is invoked before the tasks in the `hello` target are executed. This means that the compilation and archive tasks are always executed before the `hello` target's task.

It may seem at this point that Ant is using some notion of targets being up-to-date. In fact, it's Java's compiler, `javac`, and Java's `jar` command that are doing the checking. In particular, if there is a compiled class in the compilation location that has a later date than the source file, it is not recompiled.[3] Similarly, the `jar` command will not rebuild the archive if all the files from which it was built are older than the archive itself.

In general, there can be multiple dependencies specified as target names separated by commas, which will be invoked in order before the target declaring the dependencies. Furthermore, if the targets invoked through `depends` themselves have dependencies, these will be invoked recursively.

The `hello` target specifies a single task as content. The task is a run-Java task, with element tag `java`. The attribute `classname` has a value indicating which class is executed. This must be a fully specified class with all of its package qualifiers separated by periods (`.`).

To invoke a Java program, we must also have a classpath indicating where to find the compiled code to run. In Ant, this is specified with the `classpath` attribute on the `java` task. The value here is `${jar}`, for which the value of the

---

[3]This leads to a confusing situation for statics. Static constants are compiled by value, rather than by reference if the value can be computed at compile time. These values are recomputed only when a file containing the static constant is recompiled. If you're changing the definition of classes on which static constants depend, you need to recompile the file with the constants. Just clean first.

Java archive for the project will be substituted. In general, there can be multiple archives or directories containing compiled classes on the classpath, and the classpath may be specified with a nested element as well as an attribute. Ant contains an entire syntax for specifying path-like structures.

Finally, there is a flag indicated by the attribute `fork` being set to value `true`, which tells Ant to fork a new process with a new JVM in which to run the indicated class.

The target `hello-name` that we used for the "hello world" program with two arguments consists of the following Java task:

```
<java classname="com.colloquial.intro.HelloName"
      classpath="${jar}"
      fork="true">
  <arg value="${first}"/>
  <arg value="${last}"/>
</java>
```

This time, the element tagged `java` for the Java task has content, specifically two argument elements. Each argument element is tagged `arg` and has a single attribute `value`, the value of which is passed to the `main()` of the named Java program as arguments. As a convention, our programs start by creating string variables of the same name as the named arguments, just as in our "hello world" program with arguments, which we repeat here:

```
public class HelloName {

    public static void main(String[] args) {
        String first = args[0];
        String last = args[1];
        System.out.printf("Hello, %s %s!\n",first,last);
```

In more elaborate uses of the `java` task, we can also specify arguments to the Java virtual machine such as the maximum amount of memory to use or to use ordinary object pointer compression, set Java system properties, and so on.

The attributes and elements of the Ant `java` task code up the command-line arguments to the Java executable. The command-line equivalent of the `hello` task would be:

```
java -cp build/tj-intro-1.0.jar com.colloquial.intro.HelloWorld
```

1.4.5 Property Files

Properties accessed in an Ant build file may also be specified in an external Java properties file. This is particularly useful in a setting where many users access the same build file in different environments. Typically, the build file itself is checked into version control. If the build file specifies a properties file, each user may have his or her own version of the properties file.

Properties may be loaded directly from the build file, or they may be specified on the command line. From within an Ant build file, the `file` attribute in the `property` element may be used to load properties. For example,

```
<property file="build.properties"/>
```

From the command line, a properties file may be specified with

```
> ant -propertyfile build.properties ...
```

The properties file is interpreted as a Java properties file. For instance, we have supplied a demo properties file `demo.properties` in this chapter's directory that we can use with the target `hello-name`. The contents of this file are:

```
first: Jacky
last: R
```

We invoke the Ant target `hello-name` to run the demo, specifying that the properties from the file `demo.properties` be read in.

```
> ant -propertyfile demo.properties hello-name
Hello, Jacky R!
```

Any command-line specifications using -D override properties. For example, we can override the value of `first`:

```
> ant -Dfirst=Brooks -propertyfile demo.properties hello-name
Hello, Brooks R!
```

Parsing Properties Files

The parser for properties file is line oriented, allowing the Unix (\n), Macintosh (\r\n), and Windows (\r) line-termination sequences. Lines may be continued with a backslash character. Lines beginning with the hash sign (#) or exclamation point (!) are taken to be comments and ignored. Blank lines are also ignored.

Each line is interpreted as a key followed by a value. The separation between key and value can be either an equal sign (=), colon (:) or a whitespace character. Character escapes, including Unicode escapes, are parsed pretty much as in Java string literals with a bit more liberal syntax, a few additional escapes (notably for the colon and equals sign) and some excluded characters (notably backspace).

1.4.6 Precedence of Properties

In Ant, whichever property is read first survives. The command-line properties precede any other properties, followed by properties read in from a command-line properties file, followed by the properties read in from Ant build files in the order they appear.

1.4.7 Troubleshooting Ant

Invoking Ant with the -v flag causes Ant to be extra verbose and can be very useful when trying to understand unexpected behaviors.

Chapter 2

Characters and Strings

Java uses Unicode character representations. In this chapter, we describe the Unicode character set, discuss character encodings, and show how strings and other character sequences are created and used in Java. The programs for this chapter are in the example source code distribution subdirectory:

```
javabook/src/chars
```

This directory contains an Ant `build.xml` file that has targets to compile and run the examples. The programs belong to package `com.colloquial.chars`. The subdirectory `javabook/src/chars/src` contains the Java source files.

2.1 Character Encodings

For processing natural language text, we are primarily concerned with the representation of characters in natural languages. A set of (abstract) characters is known as a *character set*. These range from the relatively limited set of 26 characters (52 if you count upper- and lowercase characters) used in English to the tens of thousands of characters used in Chinese.

What Is a Character?

Giving precise definitions of characters in human writing systems is a notoriously tricky business.

Types of Character Sets

Characters are used in language to represent sounds at the level of phonemic segments (e.g., Latin), syllables (e.g., Japanese Hiragana and Katakana scripts,

Linear B, and Cherokee), or words or morphemes, also known as logograms (e.g., Chinese Han characters, Egyptian hieroglyphics).

These distinctions are blurry. For instance, both Chinese characters and Egyptian hieroglyphs are typically pronounced as single syllables, and words may require multiple characters.

Abstraction over Visualization

One problem with dealing with characters is the issue of visual representation versus the abstraction. Character sets abstract away from the visual representations of characters.

A sequence of characters is also an abstract concept. When visualizing a sequence of characters, different writing systems lay them out differently on the page. When visualizing a sequence of characters, we must make a choice in how to lay them out on a page. English, for instance, traditionally lays out a sequence of characters in left to right order horizontally across a page. Arabic, on the other hand, lays out a sequence of characters on a page horizontally from right to left. In contrast, Japanese was traditionally set from top to bottom with the following character being under the preceding characters.

English stacks lines of text from top to bottom, whereas traditional Japanese orders its columns of text from right to left.

When combining multiple pages, English has pages that "turn" from right to left, whereas Arabic and traditional Japanese conventionally order their pages in the opposite direction. Obviously, page order isn't relevant for digital documents rendered a page at a time, such as on e-book readers.

Even with conventional layouts, it is not uncommon to see calligraphic writing or signage laid out in different directions. It's not uncommon to see English written from top to bottom or diagonally from upper left to lower right.

Compound Characters

Compound characters can be decomposed into combinations of other characters or of characters and diacritics. Diacritics are visual representations added to other characters, but they are not characters in and of themselves. Only some diacritic-character pairs are valid.

Hebrew and Arabic are typically written without vowels. In very formal writing, vowels may be indicated in these languages with diacritics on the consonants. Devanagari, a script used to write languages including Hindi and Nepali, includes pitch accent marks.

The Hangul script used for Korean is a compound phonemic system often involving multiple glyphs overlaid to form syllabic units.

A diacritic mark can have different functions in different languages. For example, the diacritic consisting of two dots over a letter (¨) goes by the general name *trema*. In some Germanic languages it is called the *umlaut*. An umlaut mark over a vowel indicates that the vowel sound is shifted. In other languages, including Dutch, English, Catalan, French, and Spanish, it is called the *diaeresis*. The diaeresis mark on a letter indicates that it should be pronounced separately from the letter that precedes it. For example, in the French word *Noël* the diaeresis on the *e* indicates that it is pronounced distinct from the preceding *o*. In English the diaeresis mark has fallen out of use but was formerly used in words such as *coöperate*. Nowadays the trema is popularly used to give words a foreign feel, as in the brand name *Häagen-Dazs*. It is often used in the names of heavy metal bands such as *Mötley Crüe*, hence the term *metal umlaut*.

In some languages a diacritic-character pair is considered to be a distinct letter of the alphabet. For example, in German and the Scandinavian languages the letter *o* with umlaut is a different letter of the alphabet from the letter *o* without umlaut. In French, however, *e, è, é, ê, ë* are all the same letter but with a different accent mark.

Different languages use different orderings on these letters. In the German alphabet the letter *o* with umlaut is ordered between the letters *o* without umlaut and *p*, but in the Scandinavian languages the letter *o* with umlaut is the very last letter in the alphabet.

2.2 Coded Sets and Encoding Schemes

Eventually, we need to represent sequences of characters as sequences of bytes. There are two components to a full character encoding.

The first step is to define a coded character set, which assigns each character in a character set a unique non-negative integer code point. For instance, the English character 'A' (capital A) might be assigned the code point 65 and 'B' to code point 66, and so on. Code points are conventionally written using hexadecimal notation, so we would typically use the hexadecimal notation 0x41 instead of the decimal notation 65 for capital A.

The second step is to define a character encoding scheme that maps each code point to a sequence of bytes (bytes are often called octets in this context).

Translating a sequence of characters in the character set to a sequence of bytes thus consists of first translating characters to their corresponding code points, then encoding these code points into a sequence of bytes.

2.3 Unicode

Unicode is the de facto standard for character sets of all kinds. It contains more than 1,000,000 distinct characters drawn from hundreds of languages.

Technically, it assigns characters to code points in the range 0x0 to 0x10FFFF (0 to 1,114,111 in decimal notation).

One reason Unicode has been so widely adopted is that it contains almost all of the characters in almost all of the widely used character sets in the world. It also happens to have done so in a thoughtful and well-defined manner. Unicode's first 256 code points (0–255) exactly match those of Latin1, hence Unicode's first 128 code points (0–127) exactly match those of ASCII. However, *not all ASCII characters are legal Unicode characters.* This is because the first 32 ASCII codes (0x00 through 0x1F) were originally intended not to represent printable information but rather to control devices such as printers or magnetic tapes, whereas Unicode is designed to represent characters. Of the ASCII control characters only tab (0x09), carriage return (0x0A), and line feed (0x0D) are valid Unicode characters.

Unicode code points are conventionally displayed in text using a hexadecimal representation of their code point padded to at least four digits with initial zeros, prefixed by U+. For instance, code point 65 (0x41), which represents capital A in ASCII, Latin1, and Unicode, is conventionally written U+0041 for Unicode.

2.3.1 Unicode Planes: The Basic Multilingual Plane and Supplementary Planes

All Unicode code points are in the range 0x0 to 0x10FFFF. These are logically divided into 17 *planes* where each plane contains 65,536 characters ($2^{16} = 16^4$). If we express all Unicode code points as a 6-digit hex value, then the first two digits give us the Unicode plane. For example, if we write capital A as U+000041, we see that it is in code plane 0 (0x00). The highest Unicode code point (0x10FFFF) is in code plane 16 (0x10); thus, we have a total of 17 code planes altogether.

Plane 0 is known as the *Basic Multilingual Plane* (BMP). It consists of code-points in the range 0x0 to 0xFFFF, although not all values in this range are legal code points. The BMP contains characters for almost all modern languages and a large number of symbols and special characters. The code points in the BMP can be represented in 16 bits or fewer.

Planes 1 through 17 are known at *Supplementary Planes.* Plane 1 is known at the *Supplementary Multilingual Plane* (SMP). It is used for historical scripts such as Linear B and symbols including mathematical symbols and game symbols such as domino and Mahjong tiles. Plane 2 is known as the *Supplementary Idiographic Plane* (SIP). It is used for Chinese, Japanese, and Korean (CJK) ideographs that weren't included in the BMP. The planes above code plane 2 are not currently in use.

2.3.2 UTF: Unicode Transformation Formats

Unicode is a coded character set; it assigns characters to code points. A Unicode Transformation Format (UTF) is an encoding scheme; it maps Unicode code points to a sequence of bytes.

The problem with having more than a million characters is that it would require 3 bytes to store each character ($2^{24} = 16,777,216$). This is very wasteful for encoding languages based on Latin characters such as Spanish or English, which have code points below 256 and therefore can fit into a single byte. They are also problematic in that a 3-byte sequence takes up 1.5 words on 32-bit machines but less than a word on 64-bit machines.

There are three standard encodings for Unicode code points that are specified in the Unicode standard: UTF-8, UTF-16, and UTF-32.[1] The numbers represent the coding size; UTF-8 uses single bytes, UTF-16 pairs of bytes, and UTF-32 quadruples of bytes.

2.3.3 UTF-32

The UTF-32 encoding is fixed width, meaning each character occupies the same number of bytes (in this case, 4). As with ASCII and Latin1, the code points are encoded directly as bits in base 2.

There are actually two UTF-32 encodings, UTF-32BE and UTF-32LE, depending on the order of the 4 bytes making up the 32-bit blocks. In the big-endian (BE) scheme, bytes are ordered from left to right from most significant to least significant digits (as for bits in a byte).

In the little-endian (LE) scheme, they are ordered in the opposite direction. For instance, in UTF-32BE, U+0041 (capital A) is encoded as 0x00000041, indicating the 4-byte sequence 0x00, 0x00, 0x00, 0x41. In UTF32-LE, it's encoded as 0x41000000, corresponding to the byte sequence 0x41, 0x00, 0x00, 0x00.

There is also an unmarked encoding scheme, UTF-32, which tries to infer which order the bytes come in. Due to restrictions on the coding scheme, this is usually possible. In the simplest case, 0x41000000 is legal only in little-endian, because it'd be out of range in big-endian notation.

Different computer processors use different endianness internally. For example, Intel and AMD x86 architecture is little-endian, and Motorola's PowerPC is big-endian. Some hardware, such as Sun Sparc, Intel Titanium, and the ARM, is called bi-endian, because endianness may be switched.

---

[1] There are also non-standard encodings of (subsets of) Unicode, such as Apache Lucene's and the one in Java's `DataOutput.writeUTF()` method.

2.3.4   UTF-16

The UTF-16 encoding is variable length, meaning that different code points use different numbers of bytes. For UTF-16, each character is represented using either 2 bytes (16 bits) or 4 bytes (32 bits).

Because there are pairs of bytes involved, their order must be defined. As with UTF-32, UTF-16BE is the big-endian order and UTF-16LE the little-endian order.

In UTF-16, code points below U+10000, i.e., code points in the Basic Multilingual Plane (BMP, see section 2.3.1), are represented using a pair of bytes using the natural unsigned encodings. For instance, our old friend U+0041 (capital A) is represented in big endian as the sequence of bytes 0x00, 0x41.

Code points from the Supplementary Planes are represented using 4 bytes arranged in two pairs called *surrogate pairs*. The constants 110110 and 110111 are used to indicate the two halves of the pair. The hex value of the leading half of a surrogate pair will range from 0xD800 to 0xDBFF, and the hex value of the trailing half of a surrogate pair will range from 0xDC00 to 0xDFFF. In order to distinguish pairs of bytes that are members of surrogate pairs and other pairs of bytes, the values 0xD800 through 0xDFFF are excluded from the BMP. Given this, any 16-bit sequence starting with 110110 is the leading half of a surrogate pair, and any sequence starting with 110111 is the trailing half of a surrogate pair. Any other sequence of initial bits means a 16-bit encoding of the code point. Since the ranges for the lead surrogates, trail surrogates, and valid BMP characters are disjoint, searches are simplified: it is not possible for part of one character to match a different part of another character. Furthermore, it is possible to determine by looking at a pair of bytes whether we have a whole character, the first half of a character represented as a surrogate pair, or the second half of a character represented as a pair.

Code points from the Supplementary Planes are in the range 0x10000 to 0x10FFFF. The binary representation of code point 0x10FFFF is 10000111111111111111, which is 21 bits long. All values less than this require at most 20 bits. The UTF-16 encoding scheme is designed so that all code points in the Supplementary Planes can be represented using 20 bits that are split between the two pairs of bytes such that of the 16 bits in each pair of bytes the first 6 bits encode information about which member of the surrogate pair it is, and the remaining 10 bits encode the code point information.

We use the following table to visualize the encoding of code points from the BMP and Supplementary Planes.[2]

Code Point Bits	UTF-16 Bytes
xxxxxxx xxxxxxx	xxxxxxx xxxxxxx
000*uuuuu* xxxxxxx xxxxxxx   110110*ww ww*xxxxxx 110111xx xxxxxxx

---

[2] Adapted from *Unicode Standard Version 5.2*, table 3-5.

Here wwww = uuuuu - 1 (interpreted as numbers then recoded as bits). The first line indicates is that if the value fits in 16 bits, those 16 bits are used as is. Note that this representation is possible only because not all code points between 0 and $2^{16} - 1$ are legal. The second line indicates that if we have a code point above U+10000, we strip off the high-order 5 bits uuuuu and subtract one from it to get 4 bits wwww; again, this is possible only because of the size restriction on uuuuu. Then, distribute these bits in order across the 4 bytes shown on the right.

Calculating the two pairs of bytes involves bit twiddling. For instance, given an integer code point codepoint, the following code calculates the 4 bytes. [3]

```
int LEAD_OFFSET = 0xD800 - (0x10000 >> 10);
int SURROGATE_OFFSET = 0x10000 - (0xD800 << 10) - 0xDC00;

int lead = LEAD_OFFSET + (codepoint >> 10);
int trail = 0xDC00 + (codepoint & 0x3FF);

int byte1 = lead >>> 8;
int byte2 = lead & 0xFF;
int byte3 = trail >>> 8;
int byte4 = trail & 0xFF;
```

Happily, the Java Character class provides static methods that do this bit twiddling for us. The static method isSupplementaryCodePoint(int) can be used to identify supplemental code points. The static methods highSurrogate(int) and lowSurrogate(int) return the specified byte pairs.

2.3.5 UTF-8

UTF-8 works in much the same way as UTF-16 (see the previous section), only using single bytes as the minimum code size. We use the table-based visualization of the encoding scheme.[4]

Code Point Bits	*UTF-8 Bytes*			
0xxxxxxx				0xxxxxxx
00000yyyyyxxxxxx			110yyyyy	10xxxxxx
zzzzyyyyyyxxxxxx		1110zzzz	10yyyyyy	10xxxxxx
000uuuuuzzzzyyyyyyxxxxxx	11110uuu	10uuzzzz	10yyyyyy	10xxxxxx

Thus, 7-bit ASCII values, which have values from U+0000 to U+007F, are encoded directly in a single byte. Values from U+0080 to U+07FF are represented

---

[3]This code example and the following one for decoding were adapted from the example code supplied by the Unicode Consortium in their FAQ at

```
http://unicode.org/faq/utf_bom.html
```

[4]Adapted from *Unicode Standard Version 5.2*, Table 3-6.

with 2 bytes, values between U+0800 and U+FFFF with 3 bytes, and values between U+10000 and U+10FFFF with 4 bytes.

2.3.6   Non-Overlap Principle

The UTF-8 and UTF-16 encoding schemes obey what the Unicode Consortium calls the "non-overlap principle." Technically, the leading, continuing, and trailing code units (bytes in UTF-8, pairs of bytes in UTF-16) overlap. Take UTF-8, for example. Bytes starting with 0 are singletons, encoding a single character in the range U+0000 to U+007F, which is the range of the ASCII character encoding. Therefore, the ASCII characters are represented by a single byte in UTF-8, which is why UTF-8 is the recommended encoding for applications where the data are mostly or only ASCII.

Bytes starting with 110 are the leading byte in a 2-byte sequence representing a character in the range U+0080 to U+07FF. Similarly, bytes starting with 1110 represent the leading byte in a 3-byte sequence, and 11110 the leading byte in a 4-byte sequence. Any bytes starting with 10 are continuation bytes.

If we look at the total number of bits that contain code point information, we see that for a singleton byte this is 7 because the first bit is 0, identifying the sequence type, and the remaining 7 bits contain code point information. For a 2-byte UTF-8 sequence, the first byte contains 5 bits of code point information and the second byte contains 6 bits since the first two bits must be 10, for a total of 11 bits' worth of information. For a 3-byte UTF-8 sequence, the first byte contains 4 bits, and the next two contain 6 bits apiece, for a total of 16 bits of information. For a 4-byte UTF-8 sequence, the first byte contains 3 bits and the next three contain 6 bits, for a total of 21 bits of information.[5]

The non-overlap principle means that it is possible to reconstruct characters locally, without going back to the beginning of a file. At most, if a byte starts with 10, you have to look back up to 3 bytes to find the first byte in the sequence. Furthermore, the corruption of a byte is localized so that the rest of the stream doesn't get corrupted if one byte is corrupted.

Another advantage is that the sequence of bytes encoding one character is never a subsequence of the bytes making up another character. This makes applications such as search more robust.

2.3.7   Byte-Order Marks

In the encoding schemes that are not explicitly marked as being little- or big-endian, namely, UTF-32, UTF-16 and UTF-8, it is also legal, according to the Unicode standard, to prefix the sequence of bytes with a byte-order mark (BOM).

---

[5]In theory, UTF-8 can represent twice as many code points as UTF-16. In practice, the Unicode standard limits the maximum code point to 0x10FFFF.

It is not legal to have byte-order marks preceding the explicitly marked encodings, UTF-32BE, UTF-32LE, UTF-16BE, UTF-16LE.

For UTF-32, the byte-order mark is a sequence of 4 bytes indicating whether the following encoding is little-endian or big-endian. The sequence 0x00, 0x00, 0xFE, 0xFF indicates a big-endian encoding, and the reverse, 0xFF, 0xFE, 0x00, 0x00, indicates little-endian.

For UTF-16, 2 bytes are used, 0xFE, 0xFF for big endian, and the reverse, 0xFF, 0xFE for little endian.

Although superfluous in UTF-8, the 3-byte sequence 0xEF, 0xBB, 0xBF is a byte-order mark, though there is no byte order to mark. As a result, all three UTF schemes may be distinguished by inspecting their initial bytes.

Any text processor dealing with Unicode needs to handle the byte-order marks. Some text editing packages automatically insert byte-order marks for UTF encodings and some don't.

2.3.8 Non-characters

Unicode specifies 66 codes points as non-characters, including the last two code points in each plane, U+FFFE, U+FFFF, U+1FFFE, U+1FFFF, and so forth. Note that the code point U+FFFE has the reverse binary sequence of the byte-order mark (U+FEFF). If this is found in some text, it is an indication that it was processed using the wrong byte order.

Software implementations are therefore free to use these code points for internal use. In Java, the interface `java.text.CharacterIterator` defines the constant DONE

```
public static final char DONE = '\uFFFF';
```

Because this value should not occur in any valid Unicode string, it is used as the value returned when the iterator has reached either the end or the beginning of the text.

2.3.9 Character Types and Categories

The Unicode specification defines a number of character types and general categories of character. These are useful in Java applications because characters may be examined programmatically for their class membership and the classes may be used in regular expressions.

For example, category "Me" is the general category for enclosing marks and "Pf" the general category for final quote punctuation, whereas "Pd" is the general category for dash-like punctuation and "Sc" the category of currency symbols. Unicode supplies a notion of case, with the category "Lu" used for uppercase characters and "Ll" for lowercase.

Unicode marks the directionality in which characters are typically written using character types like "R" for right to left and "L" for left to right.

We provide a sample program in section 2.7.3 for exploring the types of properties in Java.

2.3.10   Unicode Normalization Forms

In section 2.1 we saw how different languages treat compound characters differently. In section 2.4.2 we mentioned that Latin1 introduced ambiguity in coding because compound characters can have more than one possible encoding in Latin1. For example, Latin1 contains all of *a*, ¨, and *ä*. This ambiguity carries over into Unicode and increases since Unicode contains many other characters and combining characters whose composed form is confusable with a lowercase *a* with umlaut.

In order to aid text processing efforts, such as sorting and search, Unicode defines several notions of normalization. These are defined in great detail in Unicode Standard Annex #15, *The Unicode Normalization Forms*.

First, we consider decomposition of precomposed characters. For example, consider the three Unicode characters: U+00E0, LATIN SMALL LETTER A WITH GRAVE, rendered *à*; U+0061, LATIN SMALL LETTER A, rendered as *a*; and U+0300, COMBINING GRAVE ACCENT, which is typically rendered by combining it as an accent over the previous character. For most purposes, the combination U+00E0 means the same thing in text as U+0061 followed by U+0300.

There are four basic normalization forms, reproduced here from table 1 in the normalization annex document.

Normalization Form	Description
NFD	canonical decomposition
NFC	canonical decomposition, followed by canonical composition
NFKD	compatibility decomposition
NFKC	compatibility decomposition, followed by canonical composition

The first two forms, NFD and NFC, first perform a canonical decomposition of character sequences. This breaks compound characters into a base character plus accent marks, sorting multiple accent marks into a canonical order. For instance, the canonical decomposition of the sequence U+0061, U+0300 (small a followed by grave accent) is the same as that of the single character U+00E0 (small a with grave accent), namely, the sequence U+0061, U+0300. In general, a full canonical decomposition continues to decompose characters into their components until a sequence of non-decomposable characters is produced.

NFC differs from NFD in that it further puts the characters back together into their canonical composed forms, whereas NFD leaves them as a sequence.

Applying NFC normalization to either the sequence U+0061, U+0300 or the precomposed character U+00E0 results in the canonical composed character U+00E0.

The second two forms, NFKD and NFKC, replace the canonical decomposition with a compatibility decomposition. This reduces different Unicode code points that are in some sense the same character to a common representation. As an example, the character U+2075, SUPERSCRIPT FIVE, is typically written as a superscripted version of U+0035, DIGIT FIVE, namely, as ^{5}. Both involve the underlying character 5. With canonical decomposition, U+2075 is normalized to U+0035. Similarly, the so-called "full width" forms of ASCII characters, U+FF00 to U+FF5E, are often used in Chinese; each has a corresponding ASCII character in U+0021 to U+007E to which it is compatibility normalized.

There are special behaviors for multiple combining marks. When recombining, only one mark may wind up being combined, as the character with multiple marks may not have its own precomposed code point.

There is also special behavior for composites such as the ligature character fi, which in Unicode gets its own precomposed code point, U+FB01, LATIN SMALL LIGATURE FI. Only the compatibility version decomposes the ligature into U+0066, LATIN SMALL F, followed by U+0069, LATIN SMALL I.

Two strings are said to be canonical equivalent if they have the same canonical decomposition and compatibility equivalent if they have the same compatibility decomposition.

The normalizations are nice in that if strings are canonical equivalents, then their NFC normalizations are the same. If two strings are canonical equivalents, their NFD normalizations are also the same. The NFD normalization and NFC normalization of a single string are not necessarily the same. The same properties hold for compatibility equivalents and NFKC and NFKD normalizations. Another nice property is that the transformations are stable in that applying a normalization twice (in the sense of applying it once, then applying it again to the output) produces the same result as applying it once (i.e., it's an idempotent transformation).

We show how to convert character sequences to their canonical forms programmatically using the ICU package in section 2.13.1.

2.4 Legacy Character Encodings

We consider in this section some widely used character encodings, but because there are literally hundreds of them in use, we can't be exhaustive. The characters in these and many other character sets are part of Unicode. In Java the only thing you need to know about a character encoding in order to convert data in that encoding to Unicode is its name.

2.4.1 ASCII

ASCII is a character encoding consisting of a small character set of 128 code points. Being designed by computer scientists, the numbering starts at 0, so the code points are in the range 0–127 (inclusive). Each code point is then encoded as the corresponding single unsigned byte with the same value. It includes characters for the standard keys of an American typewriter.

The ASCII codes 0-31 are the control characters. These are not characters, per se, but rather control signals sent to attached devices such as printers and tape drives. The control characters include line feed, backspace, ring margin bell, and data transmission controls.

The term "ASCII" is sometimes used informally to refer to character data in general, rather than the specific ASCII character encoding.

2.4.2 Latin1 and the Other Latins

Given that ASCII uses only 7 bits and bytes are 8 bits, the natural extension is to add another 128 characters to ASCII. Latin1 (officially named ISO-8859-1) did just this, adding common accented European characters to ASCII, as well as punctuation such as upside down exclamation points and question marks, French quote symbols, section symbols, a copyright symbol, and so on.

There are 256 code points in Latin1, and the encoding just uses the corresponding unsigned byte to encode each of the 256 characters numbered 0–255.

The Latin1 character set includes the entire ASCII character set. Conveniently, Latin1 uses the same code points as ASCII for the ASCII characters (code points 0–127). This means that every ASCII encoding is also a Latin1 encoding of exactly the same characters.

Latin1 also introduced ambiguity in coding, containing both an a character, the ¨ umlaut character, and their combination $ä$. It also includes all of a, e, and the compound $æ$, as well as both the symbols 1, $/$, 2 and the compound $\frac{1}{2}$.

With only 256 characters, Latin1 couldn't render all of the characters in use in Indo-European languages, so a slew of similar standards were defined, such as Latin2 (ISO-8859-2) for (some) Eastern European languages, Latin3 (ISO-8859-1) for Turkish, Maltese, and Esperanto, up through Latin16 (ISO-8859-16) for other Eastern European languages, new styles of Western European languages, and Irish Gaelic.

2.4.3 ASCII and Latin1 vs. UTF-8 and UTF-16

Unicode's first 256 code points (0–255) exactly match those of Latin1, hence Unicode's first 128 code points (0–127) exactly match those of ASCII. The Latin1 encoding uses a single byte per character. In UTF-8, ASCII values are encoded directly in a single byte. Unicode code points between U+0080 to U+07FF are represented with 2 bytes. The table below illustrates the difference between the Latin1 and UTF-8 encodings of the Unicode code points for a character from the Unicode ASCII code block and one from the Unicode Latin-1 Supplement block.

Character	Code Point	Latin1 Byte	UTF-8 Byte(s)	
A	U+0041	01000001		01000001
À (A grave)	U+00C0	11000000	11000011	10000000

In UTF-16, both of the above code points are represented as a pair of bytes using the natural unsigned encodings. Capital A is represented in big endian as the sequence of bytes 0x00, 0x41, and capital A with grave is 0x00, 0xC0.

2.4.4 Windows-1252

Microsoft Windows, insisting on doing things its own way, uses a character set known as Windows-1252, which is almost identical to Latin1 but uses code points 128–159 (0x80-0x9F). Latin1 assigns some control codes in this range. Windows-1252 has several characters, punctuation, arithmetic, and business symbols assigned to these code points such as curly quotes, the en and em dash, and the euro and yen symbols.

2.4.5 Big5 and GB(K)

The Big5 character encoding is used for traditional Chinese scripts and the GB (more recently GBK) for simplified Chinese script. Because there are so many characters in Chinese, both were designed to use a fixed-width 2-byte encoding of each character. Using 2 bytes allows up to $2^{16} = 65,536$ characters, which is enough for most of the commonly used Chinese characters.

2.5   Encoding Java Programs

Java has native support for many encodings, as well as the ability to plug in additional encodings as the need arises (see section 2.12.3). Java programs themselves may be written in any supported character encoding.

If you use characters other than ASCII characters in your Java programs, you should provide the `javac` command with a specification of which character set you used. If it's not specified, the platform default is used, which is typically Windows-1252 on Windows systems and Latin1 on other systems, but can be modified as part of the install.

The command line to write your programs in Chinese using Big5 encoding is

```
>javac -encoding Big5 ...
```

For Ant, you want to use the `encoding` attribute on the `javac` task, as in

```
>javac encoding="Big5" ...
```

2.5.1   Unicode Characters in Java Programs

Even if a Java program is encoded in a small character set encoding such as
ASCII, it has the ability to express arbitrary Unicode characters by using escapes. In a Java program, the sequence \u*xxxx* behaves like the character
U+*xxxx*, where *xxxx* is a hexadecimal-encoded value padded to four characters with leading zeros. For example, instead of writing

```
int n = 1;
```

we could write

```
\u0069\u006E\u0074\u0020\u006E\u0020\u003D\u0020\u0031\u003B
```

and it would behave exactly the same way, because *i* is U+0069, *n* is U+006E, *t*
is U+0074, the space character is U+0020, and so on, up through the semicolon
character (*;*), which is U+003B.

   As popular as Unicode is, it's not widely enough supported in components
like text editors and not widely enough understood among engineers. Writing
your programs in any character encoding other than ASCII is thus highly error
prone. Our recommendation is to write your Java programs in ASCII, using the
full \u*xxxx* form of non-ASCII characters.

2.6   char Primitive Type

Java's primitive `char` data type stores Unicode characters in UTF-16. A `char` is
16 bits. For Unicode code points below U+FFFF, a `char` transparently contains
the value of that code point. Unicode code points above U+FFFF are encoded
as a sequence of two `char`s using the UTF-16 encoding (see section 2.3.4).

   A `char` is essentially a 16-bit (2-byte) unsigned integer. Thus, a `char` can
hold values between 0 and $2^16 - 1 = 65,535$. Furthermore, arithmetic over `char`
types works like an unsigned 16-bit representation, including casting a `char`
to a numerical primitive type (i.e., `byte`, `short`, `int`, or `long`).

Character Literals

In typical uses, instances of `char` will be used to model text characters. For this
reason, there is a special syntax for character literals. Any character wrapped
in single quotes is treated as a character in a program. For instance, we can
assign a character to a variable with

```
char c = '\u00E0';
```

Given the availability of arbitrary Unicode characters in Java programs using the syntax \uxxxx, it's easy to assign arbitrary Unicode characters. For instance, to assign the variable c to the character *à*, U+00E0 small Latin a with grave, use

```
char c = '\u00E0';
```

Equivalently, because values of type char act like unsigned short integers, it's possible to directly assign integer values to them, as in

```
char c = 0x00E0;
```

The expression 0x00E0 is an integer literal in hexadecimal notation. In general, the compiler will infer which kind of integer is intended.

Because the Java char data type is only 16 bits, the Unicode escape notation goes up to only U+FFFF.

Several characters may not be used directly within character (or string) literals: newlines, returns, form feeds, backslash, or a single quote character. We can't just drop in a Unicode escape such as \u000A for a newline, because that behaves just like a newline itself. To get around this problem, Java provides some special escape sequences that may be used in character and string literals.

Escape	*Code Point*	*Description*
\n	U+000A	LINE FEED
\t	U+0009	CHARACTER TABULATION
\b	U+0008	BACKSPACE
\r	U+000D	CARRIAGE RETURN
\f	U+000C	FORM FEED
\\	U+005C	REVERSE SOLIDUS
\'	U+0027	APOSTROPHE
\"	U+0022	QUOTATION MARK

For instance, we'd write

```
char c = '\n';
```

to assign the newline character to the variable c.

Character Arithmetic

A character expression may be assigned to an integer result, as in

```
int n = 'a';
```

After this statement is executed, the value of the variable n will be 97. This is often helpful for debugging, because it allows the code points for characters to be printed or otherwise examined.

It's also possible, though not recommended, to do arithmetic with Java character types. For instance, the expression 'a'+1 is equal to the expression 'b'.

Character data types behave differently from integers in the context of string concatenation. The expressions 'a' + "bc" and \u0061 + "bc" are identical because the compiler treats \u0061 and 'a' identically, because the Unicode code point for *a* is U+0061. Both expressions evaluate to a string equal to "abc".

The expression 0x0061 + "bc" evaluates to "97bc", because 0x0061 is taken as a hexadecimal integer literal, which when concatenated to a string first gets converted to its string-based decimal representation, "97". There are static methods in java.lang.Integer to convert integers to string-based representations. The method Integer.toString(int) may be used to convert an integer to a string-based decimal notation; Integer.toHexString(int) does the same for hex.

Characters Interpreted as UTF-16

Java made the questionable decision to use 2-byte representations for characters. This is both too wide and too narrow. It's wasteful for representing text in Western European languages, where most characters have single-byte representations. It's also too narrow, in that any code point above U+FFFF requires two characters to represent in Java; to represent code points would require an integer (primitive int type, which is 4 bytes).[6]

When char primitives are used in strings, they are interpreted as UTF-16. For any code point that uses only 2 bytes in UTF-16, this is just the unsigned integer representation of that code point. This is why UTF-16 seemed so natural for representing characters in the original Java language design. Unfortunately, for code points requiring 4 bytes in UTF-16, Java requires two characters, so now we have all the waste of 2 bytes per character and all the disadvantages of having Unicode code points that require multiple characters.

2.7 Character Class

Just as for the numerical types, there is a class, Character, used to box an underlying primitive of type char with an immutable reference. As for numbers, the preferred way to acquire an instance of Character is with the static

---

[6]The designers' choice is more understandable given that there were no code points that used more than a single pair of bytes for UTF-16 when Java was designed, though Unicode all along advertised that it would continue to add characters and was not imposing a 16-bit upper limit.

factory method `Character.valueOf(char)`. Autoboxing and unboxing work the same way as for numerical values.

Like the numerical classes, the `Character` class is also serializable and comparable, with comparison being carried out based on interpreting the underlying `char` as an unsigned integer. There are also utilities in Java to sort sequences of `char` values (such as strings) in a locale-specific way, because not every dialect of a language uses the same lexicographic sorting.

Equality and hash codes are also defined similarly, so that two character objects are equal if and only if they reference the same underlying character.

2.7.1 Static Utilities

The `Character` class supports a wide range of Unicode-sensitive static utility constants and methods in addition to the factory method `valueOf()`.

There are a number of utility methods for detecting and encoding supplemental code points (see section 2.3.1 and section 2.3.4). In Java, code points about 0xFFFF are encoded as a pair of `chars`. Given an array of `char`, there is not necessarily a one-to-one correspondence between the encoded characters in the text and the `char` elements of the array. The method `codePointCount(char[],int,int)` returns the number of code points encoded by the specified `char` array slice. The method `codePointAt(char[],int)` determines the code point that starts at the specified index in the array of `char`.

The static method `charCount(int)` returns the number of `char` values required to represent the code point (so the value will be 1 or 2, reflecting 2 or 4 bytes in UTF-16). The static method `Character.toChars(int)` does the conversion. The methods `isLowSurrogate(char)` and `isHighSurrogate(char)` determine whether the `char` represents the first or second half of the UTF-16 representation of a code point above U+FFFF. For a code point with `int` value x, if

```
isSupplementaryCodePoint(x)
```

is true, then the following expressions are also true:

```
isHighSurrogate(highSurrogate(x))
isLowSurrogate(lowSurrogate(x))
toCodePoint(highSurrogate(x), lowSurrogate(x)) == x
```

2.7.2 Unicode Character Categories and Properties

Every Unicode character is assigned a general category and subcategory. The general categories are: letter, mark, number, punctuation, symbol, or control (for formatting or non-graphical characters). For each of the Unicode categories, there is a constant, represented using a byte, because the class predates enums. For instance, the general category "Pe" in the Unicode specification is represented by the constant END_PUNCTUATION and the general category of mathematical symbols, "Sm" in Unicode, is represented by the constant MATH_SYMBOL.

Unicode also assigns character properties to each code point. They are used by processes such as finding line breaks, laying out script direction, or applying controls. For many of these constants, there are corresponding methods. For instance, the method getDirectionality(char) returns the directionality of a character as a byte value, which can then be tested against the possible values represented as static constants. There are also useful methods for determining the category of a character, such as isLetter(char) and isWhitespace(char).

Because a code point may require a pair of char instances, there are also methods operating on code points directly using integer (primitive int) arguments. For instance, isLetter(int) is the same as isLetter(char) but generalized to arbitrary code points.

2.7.3 Demo: Exploring Unicode Types

The full set of character categories recognized by Java is detailed in the constant documentation for java.lang.Character. There's a missing component to the implementation, which makes it hard to take a given char value (or code point) and find its Unicode properties. To that end, we've written a utility class UnicodeProperties that displays properties of Unicode. The code just enumerates the constants in Character, indexes them by name, and writes out a key to the values produced by Character.getType(char) along with their standard abbreviations (as used in regular expressions) and names.

The Ant target unicode-properties runs this program. This target will print the key to the types, then the type of each character in a range specified by the properties low.hex and high.hex (both inclusive).

```
> cd javabook/src/chars
> ant -Dlow.hex=0 -Dhigh.hex=FF unicode-properties
ID CD TYPE                      ID CD TYPE
-- -- ----                      -- -- ----
 0 Cn UNASSIGNED                15 Cc CONTROL
                                16 Cf FORMAT
 1 Lu UPPERCASE_LETTER          18 Co PRIVATE_USE
 2 Ll LOWERCASE_LETTER          19 Cs SURROGATE
 3 Lt TITLECASE_LETTER
 4 Lm MODIFIER_LETTER           20 Pd DASH_PUNCTUATION
```

5	Lo	OTHER_LETTER	21	Ps	START_PUNCTUATION
			22	Pe	END_PUNCTUATION
6	Mn	NON_SPACING_MARK	23	Pc	CONNECTOR_PUNCTUATION
7	Me	ENCLOSING_MARK	24	Po	OTHER_PUNCTUATION
8	Mc	COMBINING_SPACING_MARK	29	Pi	INITIAL_QUOTE_PUNCTUATION
			30	Pf	FINAL_QUOTE_PUNCTUATION
9	Nd	DECIMAL_DIGIT_NUMBER			
10	Nl	LETTER_NUMBER	25	Sm	MATH_SYMBOL
11	No	OTHER_NUMBER	26	Sc	CURRENCY_SYMBOL
			27	Sk	MODIFIER_SYMBOL
12	Zs	SPACE_SEPARATOR	28	So	OTHER_SYMBOL
13	Zl	LINE_SEPARATOR			
14	Zp	PARAGRAPH_SEPARATOR			

For display, we have organized the results based on primary type. The initial character of a type, which is capitalized, indicates the main category, and the second character, which is lowercase, indicates the subtype. We've added extra space in the output to pick out the groupings. For instance, there are five letter types, all of which begin with L, and three number types, which begin with N.

After displaying all types, the program prints out all of the characters in range (in hex) followed by their type. We specified the entire Latin1 range in the Ant invocation but display only the first instance of each type rather all 256 characters.

CH	CD	TYPE	CH	CD	TYPE
--	--	----	--	--	----
0	Cc	CONTROL	41	Lu	UPPERCASE_LETTER
20	Zs	SPACE_SEPARATOR	5E	Sk	MODIFIER_SYMBOL
21	Po	OTHER_PUNCTUATION	5F	Pc	CONNECTOR_PUNCTUATION
24	Sc	CURRENCY_SYMBOL	61	Ll	LOWERCASE_LETTER
28	Ps	START_PUNCTUATION	A6	So	OTHER_SYMBOL
29	Pe	END_PUNCTUATION	AB	Pi	INITIAL_QUOTE_PUNCTUATION
2B	Sm	MATH_SYMBOL	AD	Cf	FORMAT
2D	Pd	DASH_PUNCTUATION	B2	No	OTHER_NUMBER
30	Nd	DECIMAL_DIGIT_NUMBER	BB	Pf	FINAL_QUOTE_PUNCTUATION

Letter Characters

U+0041, LATIN CAPITAL LETTER A (*A*), and U+0061, LATIN SMALL LETTER A (*a*), are typed as uppercase and lowercase letters (Lu and Ll), respectively. All the other Latin1 letters, even the ones with accents, are typed as letters.

Number Characters

U+0030, DIGIT ZERO (*0*), is marked as a decimal digit number (Nd), as are the other digits.

U+00B2, SUPERSCRIPT TWO (²), is assigned to the other number type (No).

Separator Characters

U+0020, SPACE, the ordinary (ASCII) space character, is typed as a space separator (Zs). There are also types for line separators (Zl) and paragraph separators (Zp), but there are no characters of these types in Latin1.

Punctuation Characters

U+0021, EXCLAMATION MARK (*!*) is classified as other punctuation (Po), as is the question mark (*?*) and period (*.*), as well as the pound sign (*#*), asterisk (***), percentage sign (*%*), and at-sign (*@*).

Characters U+0028 and U+0029, LEFT PARENTHESIS (*(*) and RIGHT PARENTHESIS (*)*), the round parentheses, are assigned start and end punctuation types (Ps and Pe), respectively. Other brackets, such as the ASCII curly and square varieties, are also assigned start and end punctuation types.

U+002D, HYPHEN-MINUS (-), used for hyphenation and for arithmetical subtraction, is typed as a dash punctuation (Pd). It can also be used as an arithmetic operation, presenting a problem for a typology based on unique types for characters. The problem with whitespace (typed as a separator) and newline (typed as a control character) is similar.

U+005F, LOW LINE (_), the ASCII underscore character, is typed as connector punctuation (Pc).

U+00AB, LEFT-POINTING DOUBLE ANGLE QUOTATION MARK («), and U+00BB, RIGHT-POINTING DOUBLE ANGLE QUOTATION MARK (»), traditionally known as the left and right guillemet and used in French like open and close quotation marks in English, are initial quote and final quote punctuation categories (Pi and Pf), respectively. The "curly" quotes, U+201C ("), and U+201D ("), are also divided into open and initial and final quote punctuation.

In contrast, U+0022, QUOTATION MARK ("), and U+0027, APOSTROPHE ('), the standard ASCII undirected quotation mark and apostrophe, are marked as other punctuation (Po). This is problematic because they are also used for quotations in ASCII-formatted text, which is particularly prevalent on the web.

Symbol Characters

U+0024, DOLLAR SIGN (*$*), is marked as a currency symbol (Sc), as are the signs for the euro, the yen, and other currencies.

U+002B, PLUS SIGN (+), the symbol for arithmetic addition, is characterized as a math symbol (Sm).

U+005E, CIRCUMFLEX ACCENT (̂), is typed as a modifier symbol (Sm). This is a modifier in the sense that it is typically rendered as a circumflex on the following character.

U+00A6, the Latin1 BROKEN BAR, which is usually displayed as a broken horizontal bar, is typed as an other symbol (So).

Control Characters

U+0000, <CONTROL> NULL, is the null control character and is typed as a control character (Cc). Backspaces, carriage returns, line feeds, and other control characters get the same type. This can be confusing for newlines and their ilk, which aren't treated as space characters in the Unicode typology but are in contexts such as regular expressions.

Although it is usually rendered visually, U+00AD, SOFT HYPHEN, is typed as a format character (Cf). It's used in typesetting for continuation hyphens used to split words across lines. This allows a word split with a hyphen across lines to be put back together. This character shows up in conversions from PDF documents generated by LaTeX, such as the one for this book.

2.8 CharSequence Interface

Java provides an interface for dealing with sequences of characters aptly named CharSequence. It resides in the package java.lang, so it's automatically imported. Implementations include strings and string builders, which we describe in the next sections.

The character sequence interface specifies a method length() that returns the number of 16-bit characters in the sequence. Because lengths are instances of int, they are allowed to be only as long as the longest positive int value, $2^{32-1} - 1$, which is approximately 2 billion. Any longer sequence of characters needs to be streamed (e.g., with a Reader or Writer) or scanned (e.g., with a RandomAccessFile).

The method charAt(int) may be used to return the character at a specified position. Like arrays, positions are numbered starting from zero. Thus, integer argument must be in the range from zero (inclusive) to the length of the sequence (exclusive). An argument that's out of range raises an IndexOutOfBoundsException, which is also in the java.lang package.

Indexing from position zero (inclusive) to length (exclusive) supports the conventional for loop for iterating over items in a sequence. For instance, if cs is a variable of type CharSequence, we can loop

```
for (int i = 0; i < cs.length(); ++i) {
    char c = cs.charAt(i);
    // do something
```

Creating Subsequences

Given a character sequence, a subsequence may be generated using subSequence(int,int), where the two indexes are start position (inclusive) and end position (exclusive). As for charAt, the indexes must be in range. The start index must be greater than or equal to zero and less than or equal to the end index, and the end index must be less than or equal to the sequence length. One nice feature of this inclusive-start/exclusive-end encoding is that the length of the subsequence is the end minus the start.

The mutable implementations of CharSequence approach subsequencing differently. The StringBuffer and StringBuilder classes return instances of String, which are immutable. Thus, changes to the buffer or builder won't affect any subsequences generated. The CharBuffer abstract class in java.nio returns a view into itself rather than an independent copy. Thus, when the underlying buffer changes, so does the subsequence.

Converting Character Sequences to Strings

The last method in CharSequence is toString(), which is specified to return a string that has the same sequence of characters as the character sequence.

Equality and Hashing

The CharSequence interface does not place any constraints on the behavior of equality or hash codes. Thus two character sequences may contain the same sequence of characters while not being equal and having different hash codes. We'll discuss equality and hash codes for particular implementations of CharSequence in the next few sections.

2.9 String Class

Strings are so fundamental to Java that they have special literals and operators built into the Java language. Functionally, the class String, in the package java.lang, provides an immutable implementation of CharSequence. Sequence immutability, along with a careful lazy initialization of the hash code, makes strings thread safe.

Because String is declared to be final, there can be no subclasses defined that might potentially override useful invariants such as equality, comparability, and serializability. This is particularly useful because strings are so widely used as constants and method inputs and outputs.

2.9.1 Constructing a String

Strings may be constructed from arrays of integer Unicode code points, arrays of characters, or arrays of bytes. In all cases, a new array of characters is allocated to hold the underlying `char` values in the string. Thus, the string becomes immutable, and subsequent changes to the array from which it was constructed will not affect it.

From Unicode Code Points

When constructing a string from an array of Unicode code points, the code points are encoded using UTF-16 and the resulting sequence is converted to a sequence of `char` values. Not all integers are valid Unicode code points. This constructor will throw an `IllegalArgumentException` if there are illegal code points in the sequence.

From char Values

When constructing a string from an array of characters or another string or character sequence, the characters are just copied into the new array. There is no checking to ensure that the sequence of `char` values is a legal UTF-16 sequence. Thus, we don't know whether the newly constructed string is well-formed Unicode.

A string may also be constructed from another string. In this case, a deep copy is created with its own fresh underlying array. This may seem useless, but consider the behavior of `substring()`, as defined below; in this case, constructing a new copy may actually save space. Strings may also be constructed by copying the current contents of a string builder or string buffer (see the next section for more about these classes, which implement the builder pattern for strings).

From Bytes

When constructing a string from bytes, a character encoding is used to convert the bytes into `char` values. Typically, character encodings are specified by name. Any supported encoding or one of its aliases may be named; the list of available encodings may be accessed programmatically and listed as shown in section 2.12.3. If a character encoding is not specified, the platform's default is used, resulting in highly non-portable behavior.[7]

---

[7]This default encoding is specified by the system property *file.encoding*.

A character encoding is represented as an instance of `CharSet`, which is in the `java.nio.charset` package. A `CharSet` may be provided directly to the constructor for `String`, or it may be specified by name. Instances of `CharSet` may be retrieved by name using the static method `CharSet.forName(String)`.

If a byte sequence can't be converted to Unicode code points, its behavior is determined by the underlying `CharSetDecoder` referenced by the `CharSet` instance. This decoder will typically replace illegal sequences of bytes with a replacement string determined by `CharSetDecoder.replacement()`, typically a question mark character.

If you need more control over the behavior in the face of illegal byte sequences, you may retrieve the `CharSet` by name and then use its `newDecoder()` method to get a `CharSetDecoder`.

2.9.2   String Literals

In Java code, strings may be represented as characters surrounded by double quotes. For instance,

```
String name = "Fred";
```

The characters between the quotes can be any characters in the Java program. Specifically, they can be Unicode escapes, so we could've written the above replacing F and e with Unicode escapes, as in

```
String name = "\u0046r\u0065d";
```

In practice, string literals essentially create static constants for the strings. Because strings are immutable, the value of string constants, including literals, will be shared. Thus, `"abc" == "abc"` will evaluate to true because the two literals will denote reference identical strings. This is carried out as if `intern()` had been called on constructed strings, as described in section 2.9.12.

String literals may contain the same character escape sequences as character literals (see section 2.6).

2.9.3   Contents of a String

Strings are very heavy objects in Java. First, they are full-fledged objects, as opposed to the C-style strings consisting only of a pointer into an array. Second, they contain references to an array of characters, `char[]`, holding the actual characters, as well as an integer start index into that array and an integer length. They also store their hash code as an integer. Thus, an empty string will be 36 bytes in the 32-bit Sun/Oracle JVM and 60 bytes in the 64-bit JVM.[8]

---

[8]The JVM option `-XX:+UseCompressedOops` will reduce the memory footprint of 64-bit objects to the same size as 32-bit objects in many cases.

2.9.4 String Equality and Comparison

Two strings are equal if they have the same length and the same character at each position. Strings are not equal to objects of any other runtime class, even other implementations of CharSequence.

Strings implement Comparable<String> in a way that is consistent with equality. The order they use is lexicographic sort over the underlying char values. This is exactly the way words are sorted in dictionaries. The easiest way to define lexicographic sort is with code, here comparing strings s and t.

```
for (int i = 0; i < Math.min(s.length(),t.length()); ++i)
    if (s.charAt(i) != t.charAt(i))
        return s.charAt(i) - t.charAt(i);
return s.length() - t.length();
```

We walk over both strings from the beginning until we find a position where the characters are different, at which point we return the difference.[9] For instance, "abc" is less than "abde", "ae", and "e". If we finish either string, we return the difference in lengths. Thus, "a" is less than "ab". If we finish one of the strings and the strings are the same length, we return zero, because they are equal.

2.9.5 Hash Codes

The hash code for a string s is computed as if by

```
int hashCode = 0;
for (int i = 0; i < s.length(); ++i)
    hashCode = 31 * hashCode + s.charAt(i);
```

This definition is consistent with equals in that two equal strings have the same character sequence and hence the same hash code.

Because the hash code is expensive to compute, requiring an assignment, add, and multiply for each character, it is lazily initialized. What this means is that when hash code is called, if there is not a value already, it will be computed and stored. This operation is thread safe without synchronization because integer assignment is atomic and the sequence of characters is immutable.

2.9.6 Substrings and Subsequences

The substring(int,int) and method return subsequences of a string specified by a start position (inclusive) and an end position (exclusive). The subSequence(int,int) method just delegates to the substring method.

---

[9]Conveniently, char values are converted to integers for arithmetic, allowing negative results for the difference of two values. Also, because string lengths are non-negative, there can't be underflow or overflow in the difference.

When a substring is generated from a string, it shares the same array as the string from which it was generated. Thus, if a large string is created and a substring generated, the substring will actually hold a reference to a large array, potentially wasting a great deal of memory. Alternatively, if a large string is created and a large number of substrings are created, this implementation potentially saves space.

A copy of the character array underlying the string is returned by toCharArray().

2.9.7   Simple Pattern Matching

Simple text processing may be carried out using methods supplied by String. For instance, endsWith(String) and startsWith(String) return boolean values based on whether the string has the specified exact suffix or prefix. These comparisons are carried out based on the underlying char[] array. There is also a multiple argument regionMatches() method that compares a fixed number the characters starting at a given position to be matched against the characters starting at a different position in a second string.

There is also a method contains(CharSequence), which returns true if the string contains the characters specified by the character sequence argument as a substring. And there is a method contentEquals(CharSequence) that compares the character content of the string with a character sequence.

The indexOf(char,int) method returns the index of the first appearance of a character after the specified position, and lastIndexOf(char,int) does the same thing in reverse, returning the last instance of the character before the specified position. There are also string-based methods, indexOf(String,int) and lastIndexOf(String,int).

2.9.8   Manipulating Strings

Several useful string manipulation methods are provided, such as trim(), which returns a copy of the string with no whitespace at the front or end of the string. The methods toLowerCase(Locale) and toUpperCase(Locale) return a copy of the string in the specified locale.

2.9.9   Unicode Code Points

The String class also defines methods for manipulating Unicode code points, which may be coded by either one or two underlying char values. The method codePointAt(int) returns the integer code point starting at the specified index. To find out the length of a string in Unicode code points, there is the method codePointCount(int,int), which returns the number of Unicode

code points coded by the specified range of underlying characters. It is up to the user to get the boundaries correct.

2.9.10 Testing String Validity

As observed in section 2.9.1, it is possible to create strings from sequences of chars that themselves aren't a legal UTF-16 sequence, in which case the string will not be well-formed Unicode. To do this validation, we have written the utility class `ValidateUtf16`.

```
public static boolean isValidUtf16(CharSequence cs) {
    for (int i = 0; i < cs.length(); ++i) {
        char c = cs.charAt(i);
        if (Character.isLowSurrogate(c))
            return false;
        if (!Character.isHighSurrogate(c)) {
            int codePoint = Character.codePointAt(cs,i);
            if (!Character.isValidCodePoint(codePoint))
                return false;
            continue;
        }
        ++i;
        if (i >= cs.length()) return false;
        char c2 = cs.charAt(i);
        if (!Character.isLowSurrogate(c2))
            return false;
        int codePoint = Character.toCodePoint(c,c2);
        if (!Character.isValidCodePoint(codePoint))
            return false;
    }
    return true;
}
```

The static utility method `isValidUTF16(CharSequence)` checks that every high surrogate UTF-16 char value is followed by a low surrogate UTF-16 value and that every low surrogate is preceded by a high surrogate. Surrogacy is defined as by Java's `Character.isHighSurrogate()` and `Character.isLowSurrogate()` methods (see section 2.7.1). It uses the method `Character.isValidCodePoint(int)` to check the code point values.

We test this method on a `String` object constructed from a pair of chars that correspond to a Unicode code point in the supplemental plane.

```
int codepoint = 0x2070E;
char[] chars = Character.toChars(codepoint);
```

```
String s1 = new String(chars);
validate(s1);
```

We expect this test to succeed. Then we swap the order of the chars and run this test again.

```
char tmp = chars[0];
chars[0] = chars[1];
chars[1] = tmp;
String s2 = new String(chars);
validate(s2);
```

We expect this test to fail. We run this code using the Ant target validate-utf16 and see that this is indeed what happens.

```
> ant validate-utf16
UTF-16 chars in s: [ d841 df0e ], s is valid string: true
UTF-16 chars in s: [ df0e d841 ], s is valid string: false
```

2.9.11   Iterating over Code Points

The conventional for loop can be used to iterate over the chars in a String or CharSequence.

```
for (int i = 0; i < cs.length(); ++i) {
    char c = cs.charAt(i);
    // do something
```

To iterate through the code points in a String, we use the method codePointAt(int).

```
String s = "abc";
for (int i = 0; i < s.length(); ) {
    int codepoint = s.codePointAt(i);
    // Do something with codepoint.
    i += Character.charCount(codepoint);
}
```

This variant uses the static utility method Character.charCount(int) to increment the index into the String's underlying char array instead of the simple increment operator.

2.9.12   Interning Canonical Representations

The JVM keeps an underlying pool of string constants. A call to intern() on a string returns a string in the constant pool. The method intern() returns a string that is equal to the string on which it is called and is furthermore reference identical to any other equal string that has also been interned. For example, suppose we call

```
String s = new String("abc");
String t = new String("abc");
```

The expression s.equals(t) will be true, but s == t will be false. The constructor new always constructs new objects. Next, consider calling

```
String sIn = s.intern();
String tIn = t.intern();
```

Afterward, sIn == tIn will evaluate to true, as will sIn.equals(tIn). The interned strings are equal to their originals, so that sIn.equals(s) and tIn.equals(t) also return true.

2.9.13 Utility Methods

There are a number of convenience methods in the String class that reproduce behavior available elsewhere.

Regular Expression Utilities

The String class contains various split and replace methods based on regular expressions. For instance, split(String) interprets its argument as a regular expression and returns an array of strings containing the sequences of text between matches of the specified pattern. The method replaceFirst(String,String) replaces the first match of a regular expression (the first argument) with a given string (the second argument). In both cases, matching is defined as in the regular expression method Matcher.find().

String Representations of Primitives

The String class contains a range of static valueOf() methods for converting primitives, objects, and arrays of characters to strings. For instance, valueOf(double) converts a double-precision floating point value to a string using the same method as Double.toString(double).

2.9.14 String to Byte and Byte to String Conversions

The class ByteToString shows how to encode a string as an array of bytes and how to decode an array of bytes to a string.

```
public static void main(String[] args)
    throws UnsupportedEncodingException {
```

```
String s = "D\u00E9j\u00E0 vu";
String toBytes = args[0];
String toString = args[1];
byte[] bs = s.getBytes(toBytes);
String t = new String(bs,toString);
```

First, the string *Déjà vu* is assigned to variable s. The string literal uses two Unicode escapes, \u00E9 for *é* and \u00E0 for *à*. The names of the character encodings are read from the command line.

We convert the string s to an array of bytes bs using the character encoding specified by toBytes. Then we reconstitute a string from this array of bytes using the character encoding name specified by toString. Both of these methods might raise an exception if the specified encoding is not supported, so the main() method is declared to throw an UnsupportedEncodingException, imported from java.io. The rest of the code prints the characters and bytes.

There is an Ant target byte-to-string that's configured to take the two character encoding names as its arguments. When we specify UTF-8 and Latin1 (ISO-8859-1) as the encodings, the program prints

```
> ant -DtoBytes=UTF-8 -DtoString=Latin1 byte-to-string
char[] from string s
   44     e9     6a     e0     20     76     75

byte[] from string s using encoding: UTF-8
   44     c3     a9     6a     c3     a0     20     76     75

convert bytes to string t using encoding: Latin1
char[] from string t
   44     c3     a9     6a     c3     a0     20     76     75
```

The characters are printed using hexadecimal notation. The initial printout of the character values in hex is just what we'd expect; the first char value 0x44 is the code point and UTF-16 representation of U+0044, LATIN CAPITAL LETTER D, the second char value 0xe9 matches U+00E9, LATIN SMALL LETTER E WITH ACUTE, and so on.

We print out the values of the bytes using unsigned hexadecimal notation (see section A.1.5 for more information about signs and bytes). Note that there are more bytes than char values. This is because characters above U+0080 require 2 bytes or more in the UTF-8 encoding (see section 2.3.5). For instance, the second and third bytes in this sequence are 0xC3, 0xA9, which comprises the UTF-8 encoding of U+00E9, LATIN SMALL LETTER E WITH ACUTE.

Next we create a new string t from this array of bytes where the value of toBytes specifies the encoding. In this example this value is Latin1, which simply translates the bytes one-for-one into unsigned characters. Finally, we print values of the characters in t. The first char value is the same as the first byte value, which is the same as the first character of string s because 0x44 corresponds to U+0044. Things go wrong for the second character. Rather than recover the single char value U+00E9, we have 0xC3 and 0xA9, which are U+00C3, LATIN CAPITAL LETTER A WITH TILDE, and U+00A9, COPYRIGHT SIGN. Further down, we see 0xA0, which represents U+00A0, NO-BREAK SPACE. Thus, instead of getting *Déjà vu* back, we get *D©Ãj© vu.*

If we use -DtoBytes=UTF-16 when invoking the Ant target byte-to-string, we get the bytes

```
convert bytes to string t using encoding: Latin1
char[] from string t
  fe   ff    0   44    0   e9    0   6a    0   ...
```

The first two bytes are the byte-order marks U+00FE and U+00FF; in this order, they indicate big-endian (see section 2.3.7). The two bytes following the byte-order marks are 0x0 and 0x44, which is the UTF-16 big-endian representation of the character U+0044, LATIN CAPITAL LETTER D. Similarly, 0x0 and 0xE9 are the UTF-16 big-endian representation of U+00E9, LATIN SMALL LETTER E WITH ACUTE. The UTF-16 encoding is twice as long as the Latin1 encoding, plus an additional two bytes for the byte-order marks.

In the above examples we have seen that when we convert an array of bytes to a String by specifying Latin1 as the encoding, there is a one-to-one correspondence between the byte values and the char values of the new String object. Latin1 is the only encoding with this property. We encourage you to play with the example class ByteToString to convince yourself of this fact.

2.10 StringBuilder Class

The StringBuilder class is essentially a mutable implementation of the CharSequence interface. It contains an underlying array of char values, which it resizes as necessary to support a range of append() methods. It implements a standard builder pattern for strings, where after adding content, toString() is used to construct a string based on the buffered values.

A typical use would be to create a string by concatenating the members of an array, as in the following, where xs is an array of strings of type String[],

```
StringBuilder sb = new StringBuilder();
for (String x : xs)
    sb.append(x);
String s = sb.toString();
```

First, a StringBuilder object is created, then values are appended to it, then it is converted to a String object. When a StringBuilder is converted to a

String, a new array is constructed and the buffered contents of the builder are copied into it.

The StringBuilder class lets you append any type of argument, with the effect being the same as if appending the string resulting from the matching String.valueOf() method. For instance, non-null objects get converted using their toString() methods, and null objects are converted to the string *null*. Primitive numbers are converted to their decimal notation, using scientific notation if necessary, and booleans to either *true* or *false*.

The underlying array for buffering characters starts at length 16 by default, though the length may be set explicitly in the constructor. Resizing the array adds one to the length and then doubles it, leading to roughly log (base 2) resizings in the length of the buffer (e.g., 16, 34, 70, 142, 286, 574, ...). Because StringBuilder objects are rarely used in locations that pose a computational bottleneck, this is usually an acceptable behavior.

In cases where character sequence arguments suffice, this allows us to bypass the construction of a string altogether.

2.10.1 Unicode Support

The append method appendCodePoint(int) appends the characters representing the UTF-16 encoding of the specified Unicode code point. The builder also supports a codePointAt(), codePointBefore(), and codePointCount() methods with behavior such as those for strings.

2.10.2 Modifying the Contents

StringBuilder objects are mutable and hence support operations like setCharAt(int,char), which replaces a single character, and insert(int,String) and the longer form replace(int,int,String), which splice the characters of a string into the buffer in place of the specified character slice. There is also a setLength(int) method that changes the length of the character sequence, either shrinking or extending the underlying buffer as necessary. Calling setLength(0) resets the underlying buffer to a zero-length (empty) array.

2.10.3 Reversing Strings

The method reverse() method in StringBuilder reverses the char values in a string, except valid high-low surrogate pairs, which maintain the same ordering. Thus, if the string builder holds a well-formed UTF-16 sequence representing a sequence of code points, the output will be the well-formed UTF-16 sequence representing the reversed sequence of code points. For instance, the string literal "\uDC00\uD800" constructs a string whose length() returns 2.

Because \uDC00 is a high-surrogate UTF-16 char value and \uD800 is a low-surrogate, together they pick out the single code point U+10000, the first code point beyond the basic multilingual plane. We can verify this by evaluating the expression "\uDC00\uD800".codePointAt(0) and verifying the result is 0x10000.

2.10.4 Chaining and String Concatenation

Like many builder implementations, string builders let you chain arguments. Thus, it's legal to write

```
int n = 7;    String s = "ABC";    boolean b = true;
char c = 'C';    Object z = null;
String t = new StringBuilder().append(n).append(s).append(b)
    .append(c).append(z).toString();
```

with the result that string t has a value equal to the literal "7ABCtrueCnull".

In fact, this is exactly the behavior underlying Java's heavily overloaded addition (+) operator. When one of the arguments to addition is a string, the other argument is converted to a string as if by the appropriate String.valueOf() method. For example, the variables u and v will have equivalent values after executing the following pair of statements.

```
String u = 7 + "ABC";
String v = String.valueOf(7) + "ABC";
```

2.10.5 Equality and Hash Codes

The StringBuilder class does not override the definitions of equality or hash codes in Object. Thus, two string builders are equal only if they are reference equal. In particular, string builders are never equal to strings. There is a utility method on strings, String.contentEquals(CharSequence) method, which returns true if the char sequence is the same length as the string and contains the same character as the string at each position.

2.10.6 String Buffers

The class StringBuffer, which predates StringBuilder, is essentially a string builder with synchronization. Because it is rarely desirable to write to a string buffer concurrently, StringBuffer has all but disappeared from contemporary Java programs.

2.11 CharBuffer Class

The CharBuffer class resides in the java.nio package along with corresponding classes for other primitive types, such as ByteBuffer and IntBuffer.
These buffers all hold sequences of their corresponding primitive types and
provide efficient means to bulk load or bulk dump sequences of the primitive
values they hold.

2.11.1 Basics of Buffer Positions

The buffers all extend the Buffer class, also from java.nio. Buffers may be
created backed by an array that holds the appropriate primitive values, though
array backing is not required.

Every buffer has four important integer values that determine how it behaves, its capacity, position, mark and limit. Buffers may thus have a capacity
of only up to Integer.MAX_VALUE (about 2 billion) primitive values.

The capacity of a buffer is available through the capacity() method. This
is the maximum number of items the buffer can hold.

The position of a buffer is available through the position() method and
settable with setPosition(int). The position is the index of the next value
to be accessed. The position must always be between zero (inclusive) and the
buffer's capacity (inclusive).

Relative read and write operations start at the current position and increment the position by the number of primitive values read or written. Underflow
or overflow exceptions will be thrown if there are not enough values to read
or write, respectively. There are also absolute read and write operations that
require an explicit index.

The limit for a buffer indicates the first element that should not be read or
written to. The limit is always between the position (inclusive) and the capacity
(inclusive).

Three general methods are used for resetting these values. The clear()
method sets the limit to the capacity and the position to zero. The flip()
method sets the limit to the current position and the position to zero. The
rewind() method just sets the position to zero.

All of the buffers in java.nio also implement the compact() operation,
which moves the characters from between the current position and the limit
to the start of the buffer, resetting the position to be just past the moved
characters (limit minus original position plus one).

Finally, the mark for a buffer indicates the position the buffer will have
after a call to reset(). It may be set to the current position using mark(). The
mark must always be between the zero (inclusive) and the position (inclusive).

2.11.2 Equality and Comparison

Equality and comparison work on the remaining characters, which is the sequence of characters between the current position and the limit. Two CharBuffer instances are equal if they have the same number of (remaining) elements and all these elements are the same. Thus, the value of hashCode() depends only on the remaining characters. Similarly, comparison is done lexicographically using the remaining characters.

Because hash codes for buffers may change as their elements change, they should not be put into collections based on their hash code (i.e., HashSet or HashMap) or their natural order (i.e., TreeSet or TreeMap).

The length() and charAt(int) methods from CharSequence are also defined relative to the remaining characters.

2.11.3 Creating a **CharBuffer**

A CharBuffer of a given capacity may be created along with a new backing array using CharBuffer.allocate(int); a buffer may also be created from an existing array using CharBuffer.wrap(char[]) or from a slice of an existing array. Wrapped buffers are backed by the specified arrays, so changes to them affect the buffer and vice versa.

2.11.4 Absolute Sets and Gets

Values may be added or retrieved as if it were an array, using get(int), which returns a char, and set(int,char), which sets the specified index to the specified char value.

2.11.5 Relative Sets and Gets

There are also relative set and get operations, whose behavior is based on the position of the buffer. The get() method returns the character at the current position and increments the position. The put(char) method sets the character at the current position to the specified value and increments the position.

In addition to single characters, entire CharSequence or char[] values or slices thereof may be put into the array, with overflow exceptions raised if not all values fit in the buffer. Similarly, get(char[]) fills the specified character array starting from the current position and increments the position, throwing an exception if there are not enough characters left in the buffer to fill the specified array. The portion of the array to fill may also be specified by slice.

The idiom for bulk copying between arrays is to fill the first array using relative puts, flip it, then copy to another array using relative gets. For instance, to use a `CharBuffer` to concatenate the values in an array, we might use[10]

```
String[] xs = new String[] { "a", "b", "c" };
CharBuffer cb = CharBuffer.allocate(1000);
for (String s : xs)
    cb.put(s);
cb.flip();
String s = cb.toString();
```

After the `put()` operations in the loop, the position is after the last character. If we were to dump to a string at this point, we would get nothing. So we call `flip()`, which sets the position back to zero and the limit to the current position. Then when we call `toString()`, we get the values between zero and the limit, namely, all the characters we appended. The call to `toString()` does not modify the buffer.

2.11.6   Thread Safety

Buffers maintain state and are not synchronized for thread safety. Read-write synchronization would be sufficient.

2.12   Charset Class

Conversions between sequences of bytes and sequences of characters are carried out by three related classes in the `java.nio.charset` package. A character encoding is represented by the confusingly named `Charset` class. Encoding characters as bytes is carried out by an instance of `CharsetDecoder` and decoding by an instance of `CharsetEncoder`. All characters are represented as usual in Java with sequences of `char` values representing UTF-16 encodings of Unicode.

Encoders read from character buffers and write to byte buffers, and decoders work in the opposite direction. Specifically, they use the `java.nio` classes `CharBuffer` and `ByteBuffer`. The class `CharBuffer` implements `CharSequence`.

2.12.1   Creating a Charset

Typically, instances of `Charset` and their corresponding encoders and decoders are specified by name and accessed behind the scenes. Examples include constructing strings from bytes, converting strings to bytes, and constructing `char` streams from `byte` streams.

---

[10]Actually, a `StringBuilder` is better for this job because its size doesn't need to be set in advance like a `CharBuffer`'s.

Java's built-in implementations of `Charset` may be accessed by name with
the static factory method `CharSet.forName(String)`, which returns the character encoding with a specified name.

It's also possible to implement subclasses of `Charset` by implementing the
abstract `newEncoder()` and `newDecoder()` methods. Decoders and encoders
need to define behavior in the face of malformed input and unmappable characters, possibly defining replacement values. So if you must have Morse code,
it's possible to support it directly.

2.12.2 Decoding and Encoding with a `Charset`

Once a `Charset` is obtained, its methods `newEncoder()` and `newDecoder()`
may be used to get fresh instances of `CharsetEncoder` and `CharsetDecoder`
as needed. These classes provide methods for encoding `char` buffers as `byte`
buffers and decoding `byte` buffers to `char` buffers. The `Charset` class also
provides convenience methods for decoding and encoding characters.

The basic encoding method is `encode(CharBuffer,ByteBuffer,boolean)`,
which maps the `byte` values in the `ByteBuffer` to `char` values in the
`CharBuffer`. These buffer classes are in `java.nio`. The third argument is a
flag indicating whether or not the bytes are all the bytes that will ever be coded.
It's also possible to use the `canEncode(char)` or `canEncode(CharSequence)`
methods to test for encodability.

The `CharsetEncoder` determines the behavior in the face of unmappable characters. The options are determined by the values of class
`CodingErrorAction`, also in `java.nio.charset`.[11] The three actions allowed are to ignore unmappable characters (static constant `IGNORE` in
`CodingErrorAction`), to replace them with a specified sequence of bytes
(`REPLACE`), or to report the error, either by raising an exception or through
a return value (`REPORT`). Whether an exception is raised or an exceptional return value provided depends on the calling method. For the replacement option, the bytes used to replace an unmappable character may be set on the
`CharsetEncoder` using the `replaceWith(byte[])` method.

The `CharsetDecoder` class is similar to the encoder class, only moving
from a `CharBuffer` back to a `ByteBuffer`. The way the decoder handles malformed sequences of bytes is similar to the encoder's handling of unmappable
characters, only allowing a sequence of `char` as a replacement rather than a
sequence of `byte` values.

The `CharsetEncoder` and `CharsetDecoder` classes maintain buffered
state and so are not thread safe. New instances should be created for each
encoding and decoding job, though they may be reused after a call to `reset()`.

---

[11]The error action class is the way type-safe enumerations used to be encoded before enums
were added directly to the language, with a private constructor and a set of static constant implementations.

2.12.3 Supported Encodings in Java

Each Java installation supports a range of character encodings, with one character encoding serving as the default encoding. Every compliant Java installation supports all of the UTF encodings of Unicode. Other encodings, as specified by `Charset` implementations, may be added at the installation level or implemented programmatically within a JVM instance.

The supported encodings determine what characters can be used to write Java programs, as well as which character encoding objects are available to convert sequences of bytes to sequences of characters.

The class `SupportedEncodings` illustrates how to display the default encoding and the complete range of other supported encodings. The first part of the main pulls out the default encoding using a static method of `java.nio.charset.Charset`,

```
Charset defaultEncoding = Charset.defaultCharset();
```

The code to pull out the full set of encodings along with their aliases is

```
Map<String,Charset> encodings = Charset.availableCharsets();
for (Charset encoding : encodings.values()) {
    Set<String> aliases = encoding.aliases();
```

The result of running the program is

```
> ant available-charsets
Default Encoding=windows-1252
Big5
    csBig5
...
x-windows-iso2022jp
    windows-iso2022jp
```

The program first writes out the default encoding. This is `windows-1252` on a Windows machine. It's typically `ISO-8859-1` on Linux installs in the United States. After that, the program writes all of the encodings, with the official name followed by a list of aliases that are also recognized. We elided most of the output, because there are dozens of encodings supported.

2.13 International Components for Unicode

The International Components for Unicode (ICU) provide a range of useful open-source tools for dealing with Unicode and internationalization (i18N).[12]

---

[12]The word *internationalization* contains 18 letters and therefore is abbreviated *i18N*. Internationalization refers to the applications that can be adapted to various languages and regions. Its logical counterpart is *localization* (L10n), the process of adapting an internationalized application

Mark Davis, the co-developer of Unicode and president of the Unicode Consortium, designed most of ICU including the Java implementation and is still active on its project management committee. The original implementation was from IBM, so the classpaths still reflect that for backward compatibility, though it is now managed independently. The home page for the package is

    http://icu-project.org/

ICU is licensed under its own non-restrictive open-source license

    http://source.icu-project.org/repos/icu/icu/trunk/license.html

The package has been implemented in both Java and C, with ICU4J being the Java version. There is javadoc, and the user guide section of the site contains extensive tutorial material that goes far beyond what we cover in this section. It is distributed as a Java archive (jar) file, icu4j-*Version*.jar, which we include in the javabook/lib directory of this book's distribution. There are additional jar files available on the site to deal with even more character encodings and locale implementations.

In this section we cover the Unicode utilities for normalization of character sequences to canonical representations and for auto-detecting character encodings from sequences of bytes. In section 2.14 we cover the ICU utilities for collation (sorting). ICU also contains a range of locale-specific formatting utilities, time calculations, utilities for deeper linguistic processing, including boundary detection for words, sentences, and paragraphs as well as transliteration between texts in different languages.

2.13.1 Unicode Normalization

ICU implements all the Unicode normalization schemes (see section 2.3.10). The class NormalizeUnicode shows how to use NFKC, the normalization form that uses compatibility decomposition, followed by a canonical composition.

```
Normalizer2 normalizer
    = Normalizer2.getInstance(null,"nfkc",Mode.COMPOSE);
String s1 = "\u00E0"; // a composed with grave
String s2 = "a\u0300"; // a followed by grave

String n1 = normalizer.normalize(s1);
String n2 = normalizer.normalize(s2);
```

The ICU class Normalizer2 is defined in the package com.ibm.icu.text. There is no public constructor, so we use the rather overloaded and confusing static factory method getInstance() to create a normalizer instance. The first argument is null, which causes the normalizer to use ICU's definitions

---
for a specific region or language.

of normalization rather than importing definitions through an input stream. The second argument, "nfkc", is an unfortunately named string constant indicating that we'll use NFKC or NFKD normalization. The third argument is the static constant COMPOSE, from the static nested class Normalizer2.Mode, which says that we want to compose the output, hence producing NFKC. Had we used the constant DECOMPOSE for the third argument, we'd get an NFKD normalizer. Finally, it allows case folding after the NFKC normalization by specifying the second argument as "nfkc_cf".

Once we've constructed the normalizer, using it is straightforward. We just call its normalize() method, which takes a CharSequence argument. We first created two sequences of Unicode characters, U+00E0 (small a with grave accent) and U+0061, U+0300 (small a followed by grave accent). After that, we just print out the char values from the strings.

```
> ant normalize-unicode
s1 (a composed with grave) char values=  e0
s2 (a followed by grave) char values=  61, 300
n1 (normalized s1) char values=  e0
n2 (normalized s2) char values=  e0
```

Clearly, the initial strings s1 and s2 are different. Their normalized forms, n1 and n2, are both the same as s1, because we chose the composing normalization scheme that recomposes compound characters to the extent possible.

2.13.2 Encoding Detection

Unfortunately, we are often faced with texts with unknown character encodings. Even when character encodings are specified, say, for an XML document, they can be wrong. ICU does a good job at detecting the character encoding from a sequence of bytes, although it supports only a limited range of character encodings, not including the pesky Windows-1252, which is highly confusable with Latin1 and just as confusable with UTF-8 as Latin1. It's also problematic for Java use, because the default Java install on Windows machines uses Windows-1252 as the default character encoding.

We created an example class DetectEncoding that begins its main() method by extracting (and then displaying) the detectable character encodings.

```
String[] detectableCharsets
    = CharsetDetector.getAllDetectableCharsets();
```

These are the only encodings that will ever show up as return values from detection.

The next part of the program does the actual detection.

```
String declared = "ISO-8859-1";
String s = "D\u00E9j\u00E0 vu.";
String[] encodings = { "UTF-8", "UTF-16", "ISO-8859-1" };
for (String encoding : encodings) {
    byte[] bs = s.getBytes(encoding);
    CharsetDetector detector = new CharsetDetector();
    detector.setDeclaredEncoding(declared);
    detector.setText(bs);
    CharsetMatch[] matches = detector.detectAll();
```

First, it assigns the name of the declared encoding, ISO-8859-1, to the string variable declared and assigns the string *Déjà vu* to the string variable s. Then it creates an array of encoding names. For each of those encodings, it sets the byte array bs to the result of getting the bytes from s using that encoding. Next, it creates an instance of CharsetDetector (in com.ibm.icu.text) using the no-arg constructor, sets its declared encoding, ands set its text to the byte array. Then it generates an array of matches using the detectAll() method on the detector. These matches are instances of CharsetMatch, in the same package. The rest of the the code just iterates through the matches and prints them.

```
for (CharsetMatch match : matches) {
    String name = match.getName();
    int conf = match.getConfidence();
    String lang = match.getLanguage();
    String text = match.getString();
```

For each match, it retrieves the name of the character encoding, the integer confidence value, which will range from 0 to 100, with higher numbers being better, and the ISO code for the inferred language. It also gets the string that results from using the specified character encoding to convert the bytes and prints the hex value of the characters. The result of running the code is:

```
> ant detect-encoding
Detectable Charsets=[UTF-8, UTF-16BE, UTF-16LE, UTF-32BE,
UTF-32LE, Shift_JIS, ISO-2022-JP, ISO-2022-CN, ISO-2022-KR,
GB18030, EUC-JP, EUC-KR, Big5, ISO-8859-1, ISO-8859-2,
ISO-8859-5, ISO-8859-6, ISO-8859-7, ISO-8859-8, windows-1251,
windows-1256, KOI8-R, ISO-8859-9, IBM424_rtl, IBM424_ltr,
IBM420_rtl, IBM420_ltr]

encoding=UTF-8 # matches=3
    guess=UTF-8 conf=80 lang=null
        chars= 44 e9 6a e0 20 76 75 2e
    guess=Big5 conf=10 lang=zh
```

```
            chars= 44 77c7 6a fffd 20 76 75 2e
   . . .

   encoding=UTF-16 # matches=4
       guess=UTF-16BE conf=100 lang=null
           chars= feff 44 e9 6a e0 20 76 75 2e
       guess=ISO-8859-2 conf=20 lang=cs
           chars= 163 2d9 0 44 0 e9 0 6a 0 155 0 20 0 ...
   . . .


   encoding=ISO-8859-1 # matches=0
```

Overall, it doesn't do such a good job on short strings like this. The only fully
correct answer is for UTF-8, which retrieves the correct sequence of char values.

The UTF-16BE encoding is the right guess, but it messes up the conversion to text by concatenating the two byte-order marks FE and FF, which indicate big-endian, into a single char with value 0xFEFF. The detector completely
misses the Latin1 encoding, which seems like it should be easy.

The language detection is very weak, being linked to the character encoding. For instance, if the guessed encoding is Big5, the language is going to be
Chinese (ISO code "zh").

Confidence is fairly low all around other than UTF-16BE, but this is mainly
because we have a short string. In part, the character set detector is operating
statistically by weighing how much evidence it has for a decision.

2.13.3   General Transliterations

ICU provides a wide range of transforms over character sequences. For instance, it's possible to transliterate Latin to Greek, to translate Unicode to
hexadecimal, and to remove accents from outputs. Many of the transforms
are reversible. Because transforms are mappings from strings to strings, they
may be composed. So we can convert Greek to Latin, then remove the accents,
then convert to hexadecimal escapes. It's also possible to implement and load
your own transforms. Using transliteration on strings is as easy as the other
interfaces in ICU. Just create the transliterator and apply it to a string.

Built-In Transliterations

We first need to know the available transliterations, the identifiers
of which are available programatically. We created an example class
ShowTransliterations in the package for this chapter that extracts and displays the detectable character encodings. We implemented the main() method
as follows:

```
Enumeration<String> idEnum = Transliterator.getAvailableIDs();
while (idEnum.hasMoreElements())
    System.out.println(idEnum.nextElement());
```

The ICU Transliterator class is imported from the package. com.ibm.icu.text. We use its static method getAvailableIDs() to produce an enumeration of strings, which we then iterate through and print out.[13] An abbreviated list of outputs (converted to two columns) is

```
> ant show-transliterations
Accents-Any                 Hiragana-Katakana
Amharic-Latin/BGN           Hiragana-Latin
Any-Accents                 ...
Any-Publishing              Persian-Latin/BGN
Arabic-Latin                Pinyin-NumericPinyin
...                         ...
Latin-Cyrillic              Any-Null
Latin-Devanagari            Any-Remove
Latin-Georgian              Any-Hex/Unicode
Latin-Greek                 Any-Hex/Java
...                         ...
Han-Latin                   Any-NFC
Hangul-Latin                Any-NFD
Hebrew-Latin                Any-NFKC
Hebrew-Latin/BGN            ...
```

The transliterations are indexed by script, not by language. Thus, there is no French or English, just Latin, because that's the script. There is only so much that can be done at the script level, but the transliterations provided by ICU are surprisingly good.

In addition to the transliteration among scripts such as Arabic and Hiragana, there are also transforms based on Unicode itself. For instance, the Any-Remove transliteration removes combining characters and thus may be used to convert accented characters to their deaccented forms across all the scripts in Unicode. There are also conversions to hexadecimal representation; for instance Any-Hex/Java converts to hexadecimal char escapes suitable for inclusion in a Java program. The normalizations are also available through Any-NFC and so on.

---

[13] The Enumeration interface in the package java.util from Java 1.0 has been all but deprecated in favor of the Iterator interface in the same package, which adds a remove method and shortens the method names but is otherwise identical.

Transliterating

The second demo class is `Transliterate`, also in the package for this chapter, which takes two command-line arguments, a string to transliterate and a transliteration scheme and prints the output as a string and as a list of `char` values. The body of the `main()` method performs the transliteration as follows.

```
String text = args[0];
String scheme = args[1];
Transliterator trans = Transliterator.getInstance(scheme);
String out = trans.transliterate(text);
```

First we collect the text and transliteration scheme from the two command-line arguments. Then, we create a transliterator with the specified scheme using the static factory method `getInstance()`. We apply the newly created transliterator's `transliterate()` method to the input to produce the output. Finally we write out both the transliterated string and its constituent char values in hex.

```
System.out.println("Output=" + out);
System.out.println("Output char values");
for (char c : out.toCharArray())
    System.out.printf("%5h",c);
```

To use this demo class to transliterate English into Greek and correctly display Greek letters on the terminal window, we need to do two things: set the encoding on the Java standard output stream `System.out` to UTF-8

```
System.setOut(new PrintStream(System.out,true,"UTF-8"));
```

and tell Ant to expect UTF-8 encoded output:

```
> export ANT_OPTS="-Dfile.encoding=UTF-8"
```

The Ant target `transliterate` uses the properties `text` and `scheme` for the text to transliterate and coding scheme, respectively.

```
> ant -Dtext="taxi cab" -Dscheme=Latin-Greek transliterate
```
```
Scheme=Latin-Greek
Input=taxi cab
Output=ταξι καβ
Output char values
   3c4   3b1   3be   3b9    20   3ba   3b1   3b2
```

If the output in the terminal window looks like ???? ???, then Ant is not configured for UTF-8. If the output looks like Figure 1.3 in section 1.3, then either your terminal is not configured properly or the Greek fonts are not installed on your machine. To get around rendering problems, we print the hexadecimal representations of the characters as well. The Unicode character U+03c4, GREEK SMALL LETTER TAU, is the character τ, and U+03b1, GREEK SMALL LETTER ALPHA, is α. The entire string is $\tau\alpha\xi\iota$ $\kappa\alpha\beta$, which, if you sound it out, is roughly the same as *taxi cab* in Latin.

To see how transliteration can be used for dumping out hex character values, consider

```
> ant -Dtext="abe" -Dscheme=Any-Hex/Java transliterate
Input=abe
Output=\u0061\u0062\u0065
```

The output may be quoted as a string and fed into Java. Translations are also reversible, so we can also do it the other way around:

```
> ant -Dtext="\u0061\u0062\u0065" -Dscheme=Hex/Java-Any\
>    transliterate
Input=\u0061\u0062\u0065
Output=abe
```

Filtering and Composing Transliterations

The scope of transforms may be filtered. For instance, if we write [aeiou] Upper, the lowercase ASCII letters are transformed to uppercase. For example, using our demo program, we have

```
> ant -Dtext="abe" -Dscheme="[aeiou] Upper" transliterate
Scheme=[aeiou] Upper
Input=abe
Output=AbE
```

Transforms may also be composed. For any transforms A and B, the transform A; B first applies the transform A, then the transform B. Filters are especially useful when combined with composition. For example, the transform:

```
NFD; [:Nonspacing Mark:] Remove; NFC
```

composes three transforms: NFD, [:Nonspacing Mark:] Remove, and NFC. The first transform performs canonical character decomposition (NFD), the second removes the non-spacing marks, such as combining characters, and the third performs a canonical composition (NFC). We can demo this with the string déjà, which we encode using Java escapes as \u0064\u00E9\u006a\u00E0, by first prefixing the transform with Hex/Java-Any to convert the escapes to Unicode. The output is

```
Scheme=Hex/Java-Any; NFD; [:Nonspacing Mark:] Remove; NFC
Input=\u0064\u00E9\u006a\u00E0
Output=deja
```

2.14   Ordering Strings: Sorting and Collation

When the goal of a sort is to present a set of natural language texts in alphabetical order, it is necessary to define what an alphabetical ordering is. This ordering may be different from the lexicographical ordering. The lexicographic ordering depends only on the contents of the String object. The alphabetical ordering depends on information about the application that is producing or consuming this text.

2.14.1   Lexicographical Sort

The lexicographic sort order over two or more String objects is determined by the byte values of the UTF-16 encoding of Unicode code points.

The Java String class implements the Comparable<String> interface. The Comparable<T> interface specifies a single method compareTo<T>. The method String.compareTo(String) compares two strings based on their underlying character sequences. In section 2.9.4 we showed how to implement this function.

The demo class CompareStrings takes two strings as command-line arguments and reports how they are ordered with respect to one another.

```
if (s1.compareTo(s2) == 0)
    System.out.println(s1 + " is equal to " + s2);
else if (s1.compareTo(s2) < 0)
    System.out.println(s1 + " is less than " + s2);
else if (s1.compareTo(s2) > 0)
    System.out.println(s1 + " is greater than " + s2);
```

We use the Ant target compare, which uses the properties s1 and s2 as the two string arguments.

```
> ant -Ds1=aa -Ds2=ab compare
aa is less than ab
```

Lexicographic sort is based on a simple comparison of the byte values of the constituent characters in the string. It provides a total ordering over all String objects. Two strings s1 and s2, which match character for character, are equal; otherwise, s1 is less than s2 and s2 is greater than s1 or vice versa.

Using the default lexicographic sort, capital letters are distinct from lowercase letters.

```
> ant -Ds1=a -Ds2=A compare
a is greater than A
```

Different decompositions of composed characters are distinct. For example, in section 2.3.10 we saw that the glyph *à* can be specified either as

U+00E0, LATIN SMALL LETTER A WITH GRAVE, or as U+0061, LATIN SMALL LETTER A, followed by U+0300, COMBINING GRAVE ACCENT. The demo class CompareComposites compares exactly this pair.

```
String s1 = "\u00E0"; // a composed with grave
String s2 = "a\u0300"; // a followed by grave
System.setOut(new PrintStream(System.out,true,"UTF-8"));
```

In order to illustrate the consequence of this, we print out both the UTF-8 and the byte codes, as we did in the transliterate example in section 2.13.3. As before, both the terminal window and the environment variable ANT_OPTS must be configured for the UTF-8 encoding. The Ant target compare2 runs this demo.

```
> ant compare2
à s1 is greater than à s2
s1 char values:    e0
s2 char values:    61 300
```

2.14.2 The Comparable<T> and Comparator<T> Interfaces

The Java String class implements the Comparable<String> interface. The Comparable<T> interface imposes a total ordering on the objects of classes that implement it. The java.util.Comparator<T> interface also provides a total ordering on objects of type T. This interface specifies two methods compare and equals. If the ordering called for by some application is not the natural ordering or when the class doesn't implement Comparable, use a Comparator object instead.

The java.util.Comparator<T> interface is part of the *Java Collections Framework (JCF)*. Collections are objects that hold other objects, such as lists, sets, and maps. Ordered collections implement the java.util.List interface. The class java.util.Collections consists of static methods that operate on collections. It has two methods for sorting a collection. The one-arg method sort(List l) is restricted to types that implement the Comparable interface and sorts the specified list into ascending order according to the ordering imposed by the implementation of the compareTo method for that type. The two-arg method sort(List l, Comparator<? super T> c) sorts the list according to the ordering induced by the specified comparator. The class java.util.Arrays provides methods for manipulating arrays including methods for sorting the array. It also contains methods for sorting arrays based on the natural ordering of the objects in the array as well as by using a supplied comparator.

The demo class NaturalSort sorts a list of strings.

```
List<String> words = new ArrayList<String>();
String letters = args[0];
Permutations.permute(letters,words);

Collections.sort(words);
```

The program reads in a string and then generates a list containing all permutations of the characters in the string. Then it uses the `Collections.sort(List)` method to sort a list of strings into ascending order based on the ordering imposed by the string's `compareTo(String)` method. It prints the list before and after sorting.

To run this demo we use the Ant target `lex-sort`, which uses the property `letters` for the input string.

```
> ant -Dletters=AaB lex-sort
unsorted items:
  aBA, BaA, BAa, ABa, aAB, AaB

sorted using java.lang.String natural sort order:
  ABa, AaB, BAa, BaA, aAB, aBA
```

ASCII uppercase letters precede lowercase ASCII letters. The hex value of A is 0x41, the value of B is 0x42, and the value of a is 0x61. Therefore, the first element of the sorted list of items is ABa and the last element of the list is aBA.

In order to sort a list of words in case-insensitive order, we need to supply the `Collections.sort` method with a comparator that ignores case. We could write our own, but the `String` class defines exactly this comparator, available from the field `String.CASE_INSENSITIVE_ORDER`. Here is the code from `String.java` that defines this function.

```
public static final Comparator<String> CASE_INSENSITIVE_ORDER
    = new CaseInsensitiveComparator();
private static class CaseInsensitiveComparator
    implements Comparator<String>, java.io.Serializable {
    // use serialVersionUID from JDK 1.2.2 for interoperability
    private static final long serialVersionUID
        = 8575799808933029326L;

    public int compare(String s1, String s2) {
        int n1 = s1.length();
        int n2 = s2.length();
        int min = Math.min(n1, n2);
        for (int i = 0; i < min; i++) {
            char c1 = s1.charAt(i);
            char c2 = s2.charAt(i);
```

```
                        if (c1 != c2) {
                            c1 = Character.toUpperCase(c1);
                            c2 = Character.toUpperCase(c2);
                            if (c1 != c2) {
                                c1 = Character.toLowerCase(c1);
                                c2 = Character.toLowerCase(c2);
                                if (c1 != c2) {
                                    // No overflow
                                    // because of numeric promotion
                                    return c1 - c2;
                                }
                            }
                        }
                    }
                    return n1 - n2;
                }
            }
```

The demo class `CaseFoldSort` uses this comparator. The code is the same as for `NaturalSort`, except that the method `Collections.sort` is supplied with the case insensitive comparator.

To run this demo we use the Ant target `case-fold-sort`, which also uses the property `letters` for the input string.

```
> ant -Dletters=AaB case-fold-sort
unsorted items:
  aBA, BaA, BAa, ABa, aAB, AaB

case-insentitive sort order:
  aAB, AaB, aBA, ABa, BaA, BAa
```

Both *aAB* and *AaB* are ordered before *aBA* and *ABa*. The comparator `String.CASE_INSENSITIVE_ORDER` doesn't impose any ordering between upper- and lowercase versions of a letter. Here *aAB* precedes *AaB* in the sorted list only because the former precedes the latter in the unsorted list. Running this example again with the Ant property `-Dletters=aBA` produces the other ordering of upper- and lowercase *A*.

2.14.3 Collations and Locales

The alphabetic or dictionary sort order on words in a language is based on the ordering of the characters or glyphs of that language. This ordering is called a *collation*. The central class for collation is `Collator`, which provides a `compare(String,String)` method, which returns an `int` value. When the first string precedes the second string alphabetically, this value is less than zero; when the two strings are equal, this value is zero; and when the first string follows the second string alphabetically , this value is greater than zero.

A collation is defined with respect to a *locale*. A `java.util.Locale` represents a specific geographical, political, or cultural region. It is used to format information according to the customs of that region. There are three constructors for a `Locale` object. The one-arg constructor creates a `Locale` object from a language code. The two-arg constructor takes a language code plus a country code, and the three-arg constructor takes a language, country, and variant code, where the variant covers dialectical differences not covered by the country code. The `Locale` class also contains a number of predefined constants for common locales, e.g., `Locale.ENGLISH` or `Locale.CANADA_FRENCH`.

To sort a list of strings alphabetically, we construct a `Collator` from a given `Locale` and pass this in to the `Collections.sort` method. The example class `CollateStrings` in the package for this chapter uses the ICU4J library.[14]

```
ArrayList<String> words = new ArrayList<String>();
String foo = "foo";
words.add(foo);
String foo_metal = "fo\u00F6";
words.add(foo_metal);
```

We start with words made up of characters in the Latin1 character set. We have chosen variants on the strings *foo*, *bar*, and *baz*. We define each `String` object and add it to an `ArrayList<String>` named words.

```
Collections.sort(words);
printItems("lexical sort order:",words);
Collections.sort(words,
              Collator.getInstance(Locale.FRENCH));
printItems("Locale.FRENCH sort order:",words);
Collections.sort(words,
              Collator.getInstance(new Locale("sv")));
printItems("Locale.SWEDISH sort order:",words);
```

First we sort the list using the natural sort ordering on strings and print the sorted list. To sort the list using the collation rules for French, we use the static method `Collator.getInstance(Local)` and specify `Local.FRENCH`, which is one of the predefined constants for common locales. To sort the list using the collations rules for Swedish, we need to create a new `Locale` object using the constructor `Locale(String language)` with string argument *sv* which is

---

[14] While the JDK itself provides a full set of collation functionality, the ICU implementations are both faster and more comprehensive. A detailed comparison is available at

`http://icu-project.org/charts/comparison/collation.html`

the language code for Swedish. This code is taken from the set of language tags defined by the Internet Engineering Task Force (IETF) document BCP 47 (http://tools.ietf.org/html/bcp47).

The Ant target `collate` runs this demo.

```
> ant collate
lexical sort order:
 BAZ, FOOT, bar, bàr, bár, báz,
 bär, foo, foö, oy, ÖOF

Locale.FRENCH sort order:
 bar, bár, bàr, bär, BAZ, báz,
 foo, foö, FOOT, ÖOF, oy

Locale.SWEDISH sort order:
 bar, bár, bàr, BAZ, báz, bär,
 foo, FOOT, foö, oy, ÖOF
```

The lexical sort order on these strings is based strictly on the values of the characters in the string. We have used the single composite characters for the vowels with diacritics. Uppercase ASCII letters precede lowercase ASCII letters, which precede the uppercase Latin1 composite characters, which precede the lowercase composite characters.

In French, vowels without an accent precede vowels with an accent and the acute accent (`) precedes the grave accent (´) although the Latin1 code point U+00E0, LATIN SMALL LETTER A WITH GRAVE, precedes the code point U+00E1, LATIN SMALL LETTER A WITH ACUTE.

In Swedish the letters *a* with umlaut and *o* with umlaut are different letters of the alphabet from *a* and *o* and are ordered after *z*. Therefore, *bär* is ordered after *BAZ* and *báz*, *föo* is ordered after *FOOT*, and *ÖOF* is ordered after *oy*. The grave accent is used only in loanwords in the language and is treated as a variant of *a*.

Within a language collation rules can vary according to country, region, and/or dialect. Collation rules also vary according to context. Phonebooks may use a different sort order than dictionaries. To address the need for custom collation rules, the Unicode consortium created the *Unicode Collation Algorithm*

```
http://www.unicode.org/reports/tr10/
```

These rules have been extended by the ICU project

```
http://userguide.icu-project.org/collation/customization
```

If your application calls for a custom sort order, we recommend using ICU4J to define a custom `Collator`, which can then be used with the sort methods available from the Java Collections Framework.

2.14.4 Strings That Represent Date and Time Information

The conventions for writing date and time expressions are locale specific. Java provides the class `java.util.Date`, which represents a specific instant in time, with millisecond precision. This internal representation is language independent. Using a `Date` object provides fast and universal sorting on date and time information.

Dates can be expressed as a string of either words or numbers. The names of the months of the year, days of the week, names of numbers, and the order and format of a date are all locale dependent. The `java.text` package provides classes and interfaces that can be used to format `Date` objects into text strings and parse text strings into dates. The class `java.text.SimpleDateFormat` provides a concrete implementation of a date and time formatter and parser. The following code fragment shows how to use a `SimpleDateFormat` object to parse a text string of the format day-of-week followed by a comma followed by month-of-year and day-of-month followed by a comma followed by the four digit year into a `java.util.Date` object:

```
String pattern = "EEEEE, MMMMM dd, yyyy";
SimpleDateFormat format
    = new SimpleDateFormat(pattern,Locale.ENGLISH);
Date date = format.parse("Sunday, February 29, 2032",
                         new ParsePosition(0));
```

The `java.text.SimpleDateFormat` class uses a pattern language that uses the letters A-z to represent date and time components. The full pattern language is described in the class javadoc. Case is significant: the letter M designates the month while the letter m designates minutes.

First we define the pattern for the (expected) format of the text string. The letter E designates the day of the week. The sequence EEEEE specifies the full name (e.g., *Sunday*) while the sequence EEE specifies the short form (e.g., *Sun*). The letter M designates the month. The sequence MMMMM specifies the full name (e.g., *December*) while the sequence MMM specifies the short form (e.g., *Dec*). The letter d designates the day of the month and the letter y designates the year. The sequence yy specifies the last two digits of the year and the sequence yyyy specifies the entire year. The commas and spaces in the pattern string match exactly to the commas and spaces in the text.

The method `parse` takes two arguments: the text string to parse and a `java.text.Position` object that specifies the position at which to begin parsing, and it returns a `java.util.Date` object if the text matches the pattern or `null` if it cannot match the pattern.

Chapter 3

Input and Output

Java provides a rich array of classes for dealing with input and output. At the basic level, input and output streams provide a means to transfer data consisting of a sequence of bytes. Data may be transferred among memory with memory-backed streams, the file system via file streams or memory-mapped files, the terminal via standard input and output streams, and remote servers via sockets. Stream filters may be put in place to compress or decompress data.

Some streams block awaiting input or output. For instance, file (network) input streams will block while waiting for the file system (network), which is much slower than Java code. Read requests from a console representing standard input will block awaiting the next input from a user. To handle pipes, which allow an input stream to read from an output stream, Java uses threads to allow reads to wait until writes are ready or vice versa.

Bytes may encode anything, but we are particularly interested in the case of natural language text data, with or without document structure. To support streams of `char` values, Java provides `char` streams as byte streams. In order to create a character stream from a byte stream, the character encoding must be known.

We are also interested in sequences of bytes that encode Java objects through serialization. Serialization allows us to save and reuse complex data objects such as language models and tokenizers that are necessary components of a sophisticated natural language processing system.

The programs for this chapter are in the example source code distribution subdirectory:

```
javabook/src/io
```

This directory contains an Ant `build.xml` file that has targets to compile and run the examples. The programs belong to package `com.colloquial.io`. The subdirectory `javabook/src/io/src` contains the Java source files.

3.1 Files

Java provides the class `File` in the `java.io` package for representing the files and directories of a hierarchical file system. Underlyingly, an instance of `File` is nothing more than a string representing a path coupled with a convenient set of utility methods, some of which access the underlying file system.

3.1.1 File Path Names

The `File` class operates over a system-independent view of hierarchical path names. A *path name* consists of an optional prefix string followed by a sequence of zero or more path names.

For Unix-like file systems the prefix string is a forward slash (/). In Windows the prefix string is either a drive letter followed by a colon-backslash (`:\`), as in `C:\`, or a Universal Naming Convention (UNC) network path. UNC path names begin with two backslashes (\\) followed by the name of the computer or device on the network.[1] For example, \\MONTAGUE is the root of the shared files on the network computer named MONTAGUE.

The last name in the sequence of path names is either a directory name or a file name. Of the preceding items in the sequence of path names, the first name in the sequence is either a directory name or a host name (in the case of Windows network path names). All intervening names are directory names. Files may be either relative or absolute. An absolute path name provides a full description of where to find a file on the system in question. A relative path picks out a file or directory starting from some other path name. By default the classes in the java.io package always resolve relative path names against the current user directory. This directory is named by the system property `user.dir`, which is typically the directory in which the Java virtual machine was invoked. A consequence of this behavior is that the empty string ("") is a path that picks out this directory.

Windows vs. Unix File Conventions

Due to the differing setup of the operating systems, `File` objects behave differently on different platforms. In all cases, they respect the conventions of the file system on which they are run, but it requires some care to create portable code.

The most critical difference is that in Windows, file names are not case sensitive. Thus, FOO, foo, and Foo will all pick out the same file.

The most prominent difference between the two operating systems is that Windows uses a backslash (\) whereas Unix uses a forward slash (/) to sepa-

---

[1]Technically, for UNC network path names, the prefix string is composed of the two backslashes (\\) and the hostname is the first name in the sequence of path names.

rate directories and file names in a path. The `File` class contains two fields: `char separatorChar` and `String separator` where the latter `String` contains exactly the `char separatorChar` for convenience. For portable code, `File.separator` should be used when generating strings that will be interpreted as path names during subsequent processing on the same platform.

The static method `File.listRoots()` provides an array of all of the available root directories. We wrote a simple demo in the class `ListRoots`, the heart of which is

```
File[] roots = File.listRoots();
for (File file : roots)
```

Running it on a Windows machine returns

```
> ant list-roots
Root Directories
    C:\
    D:\
    Z:\
```

Windows platforms have a root directory for each active drive. The root directories `C:\` and `D:\` correspond to physical drives connected to my machine. The root directory `Z:\` is a mapped network drive that has been mounted. `ListRoots` returns `Z:\` because it is syntactically indistinguishable from the path name of a local file. File objects containing UNC path names are not returned by this method. The name of the network storage device `\\ls-x15de` whose code share partition is mapped to drive `Z:\` is not returned by the `File.listRoots()` method.

In Unix, there is a single root directory for the file system, and absolute path names will start with a forward slash (/). Running `list-roots` on a Mac OS X machine returns

```
> ant list-roots
Root Directories
    /
```

3.1.2 Constructing a `File`

There are four `File` constructors. The simplest, `File(String)`, simply takes a path name to construct a file object. The string may be anything, but separator characters will be parsed and normalized.

Conveniently, Java lets you use either forward (Unix) or backward (Windows) slashes interchangeably, as does Ant. Thus, in Windows, I can use Unix-style forward slashes with the same effect as backward slashes. For example, `new File("c:/foo")` constructs the same object as `new File("c:\foo")`.

There are also two-argument constructors taking a parent directory and a file name. The parent may be specified as a string using the constructor `File(String,String)` or as a file itself, using the constructor `File(File,String)`.

URI/URL to File Conversion

There is a fourth `File` constructor that takes a uniform resource identifier (URI) argument, `File(URI)` (see section 3.19 for more information on URIs and URLs). The URI class is in the `java.net` package, which comes standard with Java.

URIs for files have the form `file://`*host*`/`*path*, where the (optional) *host* picks out a domain name and *path* a file path. If the *host* is not specified, the form devolves to `file:///`*path*, and the host is assumed to be the so-called localhost, the machine on which Java is running.

It is also possible to convert an instance of `File` to a URI, using the method `toURI()` in `File`.

It is also possible to get a uniform resource locator (URL) from a file, by first converting to a URI and then calling the URI method `toURL()`, which returns an instance of URL, also in `java.net`.

3.1.3 Getting a File's Canonical Path

The method `getCanonicalFile()` returns a `File` based on an absolute path with a conventionalized name. For instance, if I happen to be running in directory `c:\lpb` (on Windows), then the following two expressions return equivalent files

```
new File("c:\\lpb\\Foo").getCanonicalPath()
```

```
new File("foo").getCanonicalPath();
```

Note that this is not truly a unique normal form. The resulting files will have different capitalizations for `foo` in this case but will be equivalent running under Windows. Further note that the canonical path is not used for equality (see section 3.1.7).

3.1.4 Exploring File Properties

There are many methods on `File` objects that explore the type of a file. The method `exists()` tests whether it exists, `isAbsolute()` whether it denotes an absolute path, `isDirectory()` whether it's a directory, `isFile()` whether it's an ordinary file, and `isHidden()` whether it's hidden (starts with a period (.) in Unix or is so marked by the operating system in Windows).

What permissions an application has for a file can be probed with
`canExecute()`, `canRead()`, and `canWrite()`, all of which return boolean values.

The time it was last modified, available through `lastModified()`, returns
the time as a `long` denoting milliseconds since the epoch (the standard measure of time on computers and the basis of Java's date and calendar representations).

The number of bytes in a file is returned as a `long` by `length()`.

The name of the file itself (everything but the parent), is returned by
`getName()`. The methods `getParent()` and `getParentFile()` return the parent directory as a string or as a file, returning `null` if no parent was specified.

3.1.5 Listing the Files in a Directory

If a file is a directory, the method `listFiles()` returns an array of files that
the directory contains; it returns `null` if the file's not a directory. The files may
also be listed by name using `list()`.

File listings may be filtered with an implementation of `FileFilter`, which
is passed in to the `listFiles` method. `FileFilter` is an interface in `java.io`
specifying a single method `accept(File)` returning `true` if the file is acceptable.

Example Program to List and Filter the Files in a Directory

The example program `FilterFiles` takes two arguments: the name of a directory and a file suffix. To find the total number of files in the directory, it
invokes `listFiles()` with no arguments.

```
File dir = new File(args[0]);
File[] allFiles = dir.listFiles();
```

To find only those files in the directory that end with the specified suffix, we define a class `SuffixFileFilter` that implements a `FileFilter`.
A `SuffixFileFilter` object contains member variable `String mSfx`. The
accept method returns `true` for filenames that end in `mSfx` and `false` otherwise.

```
class SfxFileFilter implements FileFilter {
    private final String mSfx;
    public SfxFileFilter(String sfx) {
        mSfx = sfx;
    }
    public boolean accept(File pathname) {
        return pathname.getName().endsWith(mSfx);
```

```
        }
    }
```

To find only those files in the specified directory whose names end with the specified suffix, we first instantiate a `SuffixFileFilter` and then pass that filter into the `listFiles(FileFilter filter)` method.

```
String sfx = args[1];
FileFilter sfxFilter = new SfxFileFilter(sfx);
File[] sfxFiles = dir.listFiles(sfxFilter);
```

We use the Ant target `filter-files` and pass in the directory and suffix arguments as follows:

```
> ant -Ddir="/tmp" -Dsfx=".log" filter-files
directory name=|/tmp|
12 files total
2 files end with |.log|
amt3.log
swtag.log
```

3.1.6 Exploring Partitions

Each file in an operating system exists in a partition, which is a top-level root directory. This is of interest because a file can't be created in a partition that's larger than the available space in that partition.

There are methods in `File` for exploring partitions. The methods `getFreeSpace()`, `getTotalSpace()`, and `getUsableSpace()` return the respective amounts of space on the partition as a `long` value.

3.1.7 Comparison, Equality, and Hash Codes

Equality of `File` objects is based on the underlying platform's notion of equality. For instance, on Windows, a file created with `new File("Foo")` creates a file that is equal to `new File("foo")`. For better or worse, this comparison is based on the platform's convention for file comparison, not by constructing a canonical path and comparing that. For instance, if I happen to be running from directory `c:\lpb`, then `new File("foo")` is not equal to `c:\lpb\foo`, even though their canonical paths are the same.

3.1.8 Example Program Listing File Properties

We wrote a simple program `FileProperties`, which, given the name of a file as an argument, lists all of its properties, its canonical path, and its URI form and provides a listing if it is a directory. The code is just a litany of prints for all of the methods described above.

Calling it with the Ant target `file-properties`, it uses the `file.in` Ant property to specify an argument. We can call it on its own source file using a relative path,

```
> ant -Dfile.in=src/com/colloquial/io/FileProperties.java\
>    file-properties
arg=src/com/colloquial/io/FileProperties.java
toString()=src/com/colloquial/io/FileProperties.java
getcanonicalFile()=(...)/src/com/colloquial/io/FileProperties.java
getName()=FileProperties.java
getParent()=src/com/colloquial/io
toURI()=file:(...)/src/com/colloquial/io/FileProperties.java
toURI().toURL()=file:(...)/src/com/colloquial/io/FileProperties.java
exists()=true
isAbsolute()=false
isDirectory()=false
isFile()=true
isHidden()=false
hashCode()=224325808
lastModified()=1386280957000
new Date(lastModified())=Thu Dec 05 17:02:37 EST 2013
length()=2138
canRead()=true
canExecute()=true
canWrite()=true
getFreeSpace()=161185681408
getTotalSpace()=501312405504
getUsableSpace()=161185681408
listFiles()={    }
```

3.1.9 Creating, Deleting, and Modifying Files and Directories

In addition to inspecting files, the `File` class lets you modify files, too.

Calling `createNewFile()` creates an empty file for the path specified by the `File` on which it is called, returning `true` if a new file was created and `false` if it already existed.

The `delete()` method attempts to delete a file, returning `true` if it's successful. If applied to a directory, `delete()` will succeed only if the directory is empty.

The properties of a file may be modified using, for example, `setExecutable(boolean, boolean)`, which attempts to make a file exe-

cutable for everyone or just the owner of the file. Similar methods are available
for readability, writability, and last modification date.

Files may be renamed using `renameTo(File)`, which returns `true` if it succeeds.

The method `mkdir()` creates the directory corresponding to the file. This
method creates only the directory itself, so the parent must exist. The method
`mkdirs()` recursively creates the directory and all of its parent directories.

3.1.10   Temporary Files

It is sometimes useful to create a temporary file. One of the properties used
to create the Java virtual machine is a directory for "temporary" files. This is
typically a platform default directory, like `/tmp` in Unix or `C:\WINNT\TEMP` on
Windows, but it may be configured when the JVM starts up.

The static `File` method `createTempFile(String,String)` attempts to
create a temporary file in the default temporary file with the specified prefix
and suffix, and it returns the file that's created. After the file is created, it will
exist, but have length zero.

The temporariness of the file doesn't mean it'll be guaranteed to disappear.
It is a matter of whether you delete the file yourself or whether the operating
system occasionally cleans out the temp directory.

Invoking the method `deleteOnExit()` on a file tells the operating system
that the file should be deleted when the JVM exits. Unfortunately, this method
is buggy on Windows, so it should not be taken as providing strong cross-
platform guarantees. It's always a good idea to make sure to use a `finally`
block to clear out temporary files.

3.2   I/O Exceptions

Almost all of the I/O operations are declared to throw `IOException`, a checked
exception in the `java.io` package. Like all exceptions, I/O exceptions should
not be ignored. In most cases, methods should simply pass on exceptions
raised by methods they call. Thus, most methods using I/O operations will
themselves be declared to throw an `IOException`.

At some point, a method will have to step up and do something with an
exception. In a server, this may mean logging an error and continuing on. In a
short-lived command-line program, it may mean terminating the program and
printing an informative error message.

It is important to clean up system resources in a long-running program.
Thus, it is not uncommon to see code in a `try` with a `finally` block to clean
up even if an I/O exception is raised.

3.2.1 Catching Subclass Exceptions

Some methods are declared to throw exceptions that are instances of subclasses of `IOException`. For instance, the constructor `FileInputStream(File)` may throw a `FileNotFoundException`.

If you are passing on exceptions, don't fall into the trap of passing just a general `IOException`. Declare your method to throw a `FileNotFoundException` and to throw an `IOException`. This provides more information to clients of the method, who then have the option to handle the exceptions generically at the `IOException` level or more specifically, such as for a `FileNotFoundException`. It also helps readers of your Javadoc understand what specifically could go wrong with their method calls.

In general, it's a good idea to catch subclasses of exceptions separately so that error handling and error messages may be as specific as possible. If the methods called in the `try` block are declared to throw the more general `IOException`, you'll want to catch the `FileNotFoundException` first. For example, it's legal to write

```
try {
    in = new FileInputStream(file);
} catch (FileNotFoundException e) {
    // do something
}
```

In general, you have to order the catches from more specific to more general. If you try to catch the I/O exception before the file not found exception, the compiler will gripe that the file not found exception has already been caught.

3.3 Security and Security Exceptions

Almost all of the I/O operations that attempt to read or modify a file may also throw an unchecked `SecurityException` from the base package `java.lang`. Typically, such exceptions are thrown when a program attempts to overstep its permissions.

File security is managed through an instance of `SecurityManager`, also in `java.lang`. This is a very flexible interface that is beyond the scope of this book.

3.4 Input Streams

The abstract class `InputStream` in `java.io` provides the basic operations available to all byte input streams. Concrete input streams may be constructed in many ways, but they are all closed through the `Closeable` interface (see section 3.6).

3.4.1 Single Byte Reads

A concrete extension of the `InputStream` class need only implement the top-level `read()` method. The `read()` method uses the C programming language pattern of returning an integer representing an unsigned byte value between 0 (inclusive) and 255 (inclusive) as the value read, or -1 if the end of stream has been reached.

3.4.2 Byte Array Reads

It is usually too inefficient to access data one byte at a time. Instead, it is usually accessed in blocks through an array. The `read(byte[])` method reads data into the specified byte array and returns the number of bytes that have been read. If the return value is -1, the end of the input stream has been reached. There is a similar method that reads into a slice of an array given an offset and length.

3.4.3 Available Bytes

The method `available()` returns an integer representing the number of bytes available for reading without blocking. This is not the same as the number of bytes available. For one thing, streams may represent terabytes of data, and `available()` returns only an integer. More importantly, some streams may block waiting for more input. For instance, the standard input (see section 3.18) may block while waiting for user input and show no available bytes, even if bytes may later become available.

Because no bytes may be available without blocking, it's possible for the block read method to return after reading no bytes. This does not mean there won't be more bytes to read later. The `read()` methods will return -1 when there are truly no more bytes to be read.

3.4.4 Mark and Reset

The method `markSupported()` returns `true` for markable input streams. If a stream is markable, calling `mark()` sets the mark at the current position in the stream. A later call to `reset()` resets the stream back to the marked position.

3.4.5 Skipping

There is also a method `skip(long)`, which attempts to skip past the specified number of bytes, returning the number of bytes it actually skipped. The only reason to use this method is that it is often faster than actually reading the bytes and then throwing them away, because skipping bypasses all the byte assignments that would otherwise be required for a read.

3.5 Output Streams

The `OutputStream` abstract class in the package `java.io` provides a general interface for writing bytes. It is thus the complement to `InputStream`. Output streams implement the `Closeable` interface and should be closed in the same way as other closeable objects (see section 3.6).

OutputStream itself implements the array writers in terms of single byte writes, with the close and flush operations doing nothing. Subclasses override some or all of these methods for additional functionality or increased efficiency.

3.5.1 Single Byte Writes

A single abstract method needs to be implemented by concrete subclasses, `write(int)`, which writes a byte in unsigned notation to the output stream. The low-order byte in the integer is written and the three high-order bytes are simply ignored (see section A.1.5 for more on the byte organization of integers). Thus, the value should be an unsigned representation of a byte between 0 (inclusive) and 255 (inclusive).

3.5.2 Byte Array Writes

Arrays of bytes may be written using the method `write(byte[])` and a slice variant taking a byte array with a start position and length.

The behavior is slightly different from that for reads. When a write method returns, all of the bytes in the array (or specified slice thereof) will have been written. Thus, it is not uncommon for array writes to block if they need to wait for a resource such as a network, file system, or user console input.

3.5.3 Flushing Writes

The method `flush()` writes any bytes that may be buffered to their final destination. As noted in the documentation, the operating system may provide further buffering, for instance, to the network or to disk operations.

The `OutputStream` class is defined to implement `Flushable`, the interface in `java.io` for flushable objects. Like the general `close` method from the `Closeable` interface, it may raise an `IOException`.

Most streams call the `flush()` method from their `close()` method so that no bytes are left in the buffer as a result of closing an object.

3.6 Closing Streams

Because most streams impose local or system overhead on open I/O streams, it is good practice to close a stream as soon as you are done with it.

3.6.1 The `Closeable` Interface

Conveniently, all the streams implement the handy `Closeable` interface in the package `java.io`. The `Closeable` interface specifies a single method, `close()`, which closes a stream and releases any resources it may be maintaining.

Care must be taken in closing streams, as the `close()` method itself may throw an `IOException`. Furthermore, if the stream wasn't successfully created, the variable to which it was being assigned may be null.

The typical idiom for closing a `Closeable` may be illustrated with an input stream

```
InputStream in = null;
File file = null;
try {
    in = new FileInputStream(file);
    // do something
} finally {
    if (in != null)
        in.close();
}
```

Sometimes, the close method itself is wrapped to suppress warnings, as in

```
try {
    in.close();
} catch (IOException e) {
    /* ignore exception */
}
```

Note that even if the close method is wrapped, the operations in the `try` block may throw I/O exceptions. To remove these, I/O exceptions may be caught in a block parallel to the `try` and `finally`.

3.7 Readers

The `Reader` abstract base class is to char data as `InputStream` is to byte data. For instance, `read()` reads a single char coded as an `int`, with -1 indicating the end of the stream. There is a block reading method `read(char[])` that returns the number of values read, with -1 indicating end of stream, and a similar method taking a slice of an array of char values. There is also a `skip(int)` method that skips up to the specified number of char values, returning the number of values skipped. The `Reader` class implements the `Closeable` interface and, like the `InputStream` and `OutputStream` classes, has a single `close()` method. All of these methods are declared to throw `IOException`.

Unlike input streams, concrete subclasses must implement the abstract methods `close()` and the slice-based bulk read method `read(char[],int,int)`.

Some readers are markable, as indicated by the same `markSupported()` method, with the same `mark()` method to set the mark at the current position and `reset()` method to return to the marked position.

3.7.1 The `Readable` Interface

The `Reader` class also implements the `Readable` interface in `java.lang`. This interface has a single method `read(CharBuffer)` that reads char values into a specified buffer, returning the number of values read or -1 for the end of stream (see section 2.11 for more on `CharBuffer`).

3.8 Writers

Writers are to readers as output streams are to input streams. The method `write(int)` writes a single character using the two low-order bytes of the specified integer as a char.

Arrays of characters may be written using `write(char[])`, and there is a method to write only a slice of a character array. Strings and slices of strings may also be written.

Like other streams, `Writer` implements `Closeable` and is hence closed in the usual way using `close()`. Like other output streams, it implements `Flushable`, so calling `flush()` should try to write any buffered characters.

3.8.1 The `Appendable` Interface

The `Writer` class also implements the `Appendable` interface in `java.lang`. This is the same interface as is implemented by the mutable character sequence implementations `CharBuffer`, `StringBuilder`, and `StringBuffer`.

This interface specifies a method for appending a single character, `append(char)`, and for sequences, `append(CharSequence)`, as well as for slices of character sequences. The result specified in the `Appendable` interface is `Appendable`, so calls may be chained. The result specified by `Writer` is `Writer`; subclasses may declare more specific return types than their superclasses. Other implementations also declare their own types as their return types.

3.9 Converting Byte Streams to Characters

Resources are typically provided as byte streams, but programs manipulating language data require character streams. Given a character encoding, a byte stream may be converted to a character stream.

3.9.1 The `InputStreamReader` Class

Given an input stream and a character encoding, an instance of `InputStreamReader` may be constructed to read characters. The usual idiom given that `encoding` is an instance of `String` and `in` an instance of `InputStream` is

```
Reader reader = new InputStreamReader(in,encoding);
// do something
reader.close();
```

The operations elided in the middle may then use the reader to retrieve character-based data. Instances may also be constructed from an instance of `CharSet` or with a `CharSetDecoder`, both of which are in `java.nio.charset`; the string-based method is just a shortcut that creates a decoder for a character set behind the scenes. This decoder is used to convert the sequence of bytes from the underlying input stream into the `char` values returned by the reader.

The question remains as to whether to attempt to close the input stream itself given that the reader was closed. When an `InputStreamReader` is closed, the input stream it wraps will be closed.[2] As long as the reader was constructed, there should be no problem. For more robustness, the stream may be nested in a `try-finally` block to ensure it's closed. The reader should be closed first, and if all goes well, the stream should already be closed when the close in the `finally` block is reached. This second call should not cause problems, because the `Closeable` interface specifies that redundant calls to `close()` should have no effect on a closed object.

---

[2]This is not clear from the documentation but is clear from the source code. Perhaps we're meant to infer the behavior from the general contract for `close()` in `Closeable`, which specifies that it should release all of the resources it is holding.

3.9.2   The `OutputStreamWriter` Class

In the other direction, the class `OutputStreamWriter` does the conversion. The idiom for construction, use, and closure is the same, only based on a `CharSetEncoder` to convert sequences of characters to sequences of bytes for writing.

3.9.3   Illegal Sequences

The documentation for both of these classes lists their behavior in the face of illegal `byte` or `char` sequences. For instance, an `InputStreamReader` may be faced with a sequence of bytes that is not decodable with the specified character encoding. Going the other way, an `OutputStreamWriter` may receive a sequence of `char` values that is not a legal UTF-16 sequence or that contains code points that are not encodable in the specified character encoding.

In practice, an `InputStreamReader`'s behavior will be determined by its `CharSetDecoder` and an `OutputStreamWriter`'s by its `CharSetEncoder`. The encoders and decoders may be configured to allow exceptions to be raised for illegal sequences or particular substitutions to be carried out.

3.10   Transcoding Byte Streams Using Latin1

The example class `ByteToString` from section 2.9.14 converts an array of bytes to a `String` and prints the hex values of both the bytes and chars to the terminal. We saw that specifying Latin1 as the character encoding results in a one-to-one correspondence between the input bytes and the characters in the string.

We can use Latin1 to recover and/or preserve the raw bytes from an input stream. If we construct a `Reader` from an input stream with Latin1 as the specified encoding, we can always recover the original bytes by converting the chars back to bytes using Latin1 as the specified encoding. To output the original bytes we construct a `Writer` with Latin1 as the specified encoding.

This is useful when an application's default configuration doesn't match the encoding used for some data set. There is always a default encoding. If an application doesn't specify an encoding, the default system property *file.encoding* will be used to determine the `CharSet`.

One such mismatch between the encoding used by an application and the encoding used for some data occurs when we use Ant to execute some of the demo programs in this book. The Ant program executes each demo program. It reads the output from each program into a file and writes it out again to the terminal. The default system property *file.encoding* is used to read and write the program outputs. In previous sections we have overridden this setting by setting the Ant environment variable ANT_OPTS to the encoding used by the demo program (see section 1.3).

Since Ant is only reading the text in and writing it out again, we can also specify Latin1 as the file.encoding

> export ANT_OPTS="-Dfile.encoding=Latin1"

To see that this setting works, run the export command and then run the example program Transliterate from section 2.13.3 in the example directory javabook/src/chars:

```
> ant -Dtext="taxi cab" -Dscheme=Latin-Greek transliterate
Scheme=Latin-Greek
Input=taxi cab
Output=ταξι καβ
Output char values
  3c4   3b1   3be   3b9    20   3ba   3b1   3b2
```

As long as the terminal window encoding is UTF-8 and the Greek-language fonts are installed, the output of this program will look like ταξι καβ.

Setting the ANT_OPTS environment variable in this way has the advantage of ensuring that Ant won't corrupt the outputs of any target we use it to run no matter what encodings that target may use for System.out.

3.11   File Input and Output Streams

Streaming access to files is handled by the subclasses FileInputStream and FileOutputStream, which extend the obvious base classes.

3.11.1   Constructing File Streams

A file input stream may be constructed with either a file using the constructor FileInputStream(File) or the name of a file, using FileInputStream(String).

Similarly, output streams may be constructed using FileOuptutStream(File) and FileOuptutStream(String). If constructed this way, if the file exists, it will be overwritten and resized to the output produced by the output stream. To append to a file, construct an output stream using FileOuptutStream(File,boolean), where the boolean flag specifies whether to append.

The constructors are declared to throw the checked exception FileNotFoundException, in package java.io, which is a subclass of IOException.

3.11.2 Finalizers

Both the input and output file streams declare finalizer methods that may release any system resources when the related stream is no longer in scope. The problem with finalization is that it's not guaranteed to happen until the JVM on which the code was running is terminated.

In any case, whether it exits normally or not, the operating system will recover any process-specific file handles. Thus, short-lived processes such as simple commands do not need to be as careful about recovering file-based resources as long-running server processes. In any case, the best the code can do is close all streams as soon as they are no longer needed, even in the face of exceptions.

3.11.3 File Descriptors

The `FileDescriptor` class in `java.io` provides an encapsulation of a file input or output stream. Every time a file input or output stream is created, it has an associated file descriptor. The file descriptor may be retrieved from a file input stream or file output stream using the method `getFD()`. A new input or output stream may be constructed based on a file descriptor.

3.11.4 Examples of File Streams

Counting the Bytes in a File

We wrote a demo program `FileByteCount` that opens a file input stream and then reads all of its content, counting the number of instances of each byte. The work is done with

```
public static void main(String[] args)
    throws FileNotFoundException, IOException {

    File file = new File(args[0]);
    InputStream in = new FileInputStream(file);
    long[] counts = new long[256];
    int b;
    while ((b = in.read()) != -1)
        ++counts[b];
```

Note that the `main()` method is declared to throw both a `FileNotFoundException` and its superclass `IOException` (see section 3.2 for more information on I/O exceptions and their handling).

The body of the method creates an instance of `File` using the command-line argument, then an input stream, based on the file. It then allocates an array of `long` values the size of the number of bytes, which is used to store the counts (recall that primitive numbers are always initialized to 0 in Java,

including in arrays). Then we use the C-style read method to read each bye
into the integer variable b. If the value is -1, indicating the end of stream (end
of file here), the loop is exited. In the body of the read loop, the count for the
byte just read is incremented.

We call the method using the Ant target `file-byte-count`, specifying the
`file.in` property for the file to be counted. Here we call it on its own source
code,

```
> ant -Dfile.in=src/com/colloquial/io/FileByteCount.java\
>    file-byte-count
Dec   Hex      Count
  10    a         33
  32    20       189
  33    21         1
...
 123    7b         2
 125    7d         2
```

Because the file is encoded in ASCII, these bytes can be read as characters. For
instance, character hexadecimal value 0A is the line feed, 20 is a newline, 32
is the digit 2, up through 7D, which is the right curly bracket (}). We can infer
that the file has 34 lines, because there are 33 line feeds.

Copying from One File to Another

Our next sample program, `CopyFile`, copies the bytes in one file into another
file and illustrates the use of array-based reads and writes. After reading in the
command-line arguments, the work is carried out by

```
InputStream in = new FileInputStream(fileIn);
OutputStream out = new FileOutputStream(fileOut);
byte[] buf = new byte[8192];
int n;
while ((n = in.read(buf)) >= 0)
    out.write(buf,0,n);
out.close();
in.close();
```

We first create the file input and output streams. We've assigned them to variables of type `InputStream` and `OutputStream` rather than to their specific
subclasses because we do not need any of the functionality specific to file
streams. We then allocate an array `buf` of bytes to act as a buffer and declare
a variable `n` to hold the count of the number of bytes read. The loop continually reads from the input stream into the buffer, assigning the number of
bytes read to `n` and exiting the loop if the number of bytes read is less than

zero (signaling end of stream). In the body of the loop, we write the bytes in the buffer to the output stream, being careful to specify that we want to write only n bytes. Unlike reads, writes either succeed in writing all their bytes (perhaps having to block) or throw an exception. When we're done, we close both streams.[3]

Character Encoding Conversion

As a third example, we'll show how to wrap our file-based streams in readers and writers in order to carry out character encoding conversion. Here we use a character buffer to do the transfer,

```
InputStream in = new FileInputStream(fileIn);
InputStreamReader reader = new InputStreamReader(in,encIn);
OutputStream out = new FileOutputStream(fileOut);
OutputStreamWriter writer = new OutputStreamWriter(out,encOut);
char[] buf = new char[4096];
for (int n; (n = reader.read(buf)) >= 0; )
    writer.write(buf,0,n);
writer.close();
reader.close();
```

The program may be called with the Ant target `file-decode-encode` with arguments given by properties `file.in`, `enc.in`, `file.out`, and `enc.out`.

3.12 Buffered Streams

Some sources of input, such as an HTTP connection or a file, are most efficiently dealt with in larger chunks than a single byte. In most cases, when using such streams, it is more efficient to buffer the input or output. Both byte and character streams may be buffered for both input and output. For byte streams, the classes are `BufferedInputStream` and `BufferedOutputStream` and for character streams `BufferedReader` and `BufferedWriter`.

3.12.1 Constructing Buffered Streams

The constructor `BufferedInputStream(InputStream,int)` wraps the specified input stream in a buffered input stream with specified buffer size (in

---

[3]We don't need elaborate `try-finally` logic to close the file streams because they are closed automatically when the command-line program exits. We could get into trouble if another program were to call this `main()` without exiting the JVM after the call. A more robust version of this program might catch I/O exceptions thrown by the write method and delete the output stream rather than leaving a partial copy. We've shown what this would look like in the source file for `CopyFile` in a parallel method named `main2()`.

bytes). The constructor `BufferedOutputStream(OutputStream,int)` performs the same role for output streams. There are also one-argument constructors for which the buffer sizes may be dropped, in which case a default
size is used.

For example, we may create a buffered input stream from a file input stream
given a `File` instance `file` with

```
InputStream in = new FileInputStream(file);
InputStream bufIn = new BufferedInputStream(in);
```

The variable `bufIn` is then used where the unbuffered stream `in` would've been
used. By assigning all these streams of different types to a base `InputStream`,
it makes it easier to change the code later.

The constructors only save a pointer to the underlying stream and create a
buffer, so they don't throw I/O exceptions, because they're not doing any I/O.

3.12.2   Sizing the Buffer

There is often a measurable performance improvement from getting the buffer
size right for the underlying platform and application, but performance mea-
surement and tuning is a tricky business.

3.12.3   Closing a Buffered Stream

When a buffered stream is closed, it closes the contained stream. See the discussion in section 3.9.1 concerning writing robust stream closing idioms. The
close will also flush any bytes or characters currently being buffered.

3.12.4   Built-in Buffering

Many of the streams (or readers and writers) have built-in buffering. For instance, the gzip input and output streams have built-in buffers. In these cases,
there's no need to buffer twice for efficiency's sake.

If you are eventually going to wrap a byte stream in a buffered reader
or writer, the byte stream doesn't itself need to be buffered. The buffering,
through use of block reads and writes, carries itself through.

Similarly, if your own code does buffering, as in our example in `CopyFile`
(see section 3.11.4), there's no need to buffer the file input or output streams.

By this same line of reasoning, if a byte stream is converted to a character stream or vice versa, buffering is not required at both places. Usually, the
buffer is placed later in the chain, around the reader or writer, as in the following examples.

```
InputStream in = new FileInputStream(file);
Reader reader = new InputStreamReader(in,"UTF-8");
BufferedReader bufReader = new BufferedReader(reader);

OutputStream out = new FileOutputStream(file);
Writer writer = new OutputStreamWriter(out,"UTF-8");
BufferedWriter bufWriter = new BufferedWriter(writer);
```

3.12.5 Line-Based Reads

The BufferedReader class implements a method to read lines. The method readLine() returns a String corresponding to the next line of input read, not including the end-of-line markers. If the end of stream has been reached, this method will return null.

This class recognizes three end-of-line markers: a line feed (\n), a carriage return (\r), or a line feed followed by a carriage return (\n\r).

3.13 Array-Backed Input and Output Streams

The array-backed input streams and readers read from arrays of data held in memory. The array-backed output streams and writers buffer the bytes or characters written to them and provide access to them as an array at any time.

3.13.1 The ByteArrayInputStream Class

The class ByteArrayInputStream wraps a byte array to produce an in-memory input stream. The constructor ByteArrayInputStream(byte[]) creates the input stream. The byte array is not copied, so changes to it will affect the input stream.

Byte array input streams support the mark() and reset() methods.

Closing a byte array input stream has no effect whatsoever.

3.13.2 The CharArrayReader Class

The class CharArrayReader performs the same service, creating a Reader from an array of characters. They support the same range of methods with almost all the same behaviors, only for char data rather than byte data. Inconsistently, close() behaves differently, releasing the reference to the underlying character array and causing all subsequent calls to read methods to throw I/O exceptions.

There is also a class StringReader that does the same thing as a character array reader for string input.

3.13.3   The `ByteArrayOutputStream` Class

A `ByteArrayOutputStream` provides an in-memory output stream that buffers any bytes written to it. Because it uses arrays, the maximum amount of data that can be written to an output stream is `Integer.MAX_VALUE` bytes.

There is a no-argument constructor and one that specifies the initial capacity of the buffer.

The method `size()` returns the number of bytes that are buffered.

All of the bytes written to a byte array output stream are available as a byte array using the method `toByteArray()`. The returned array is a copy of the bytes buffered in an underlying array, so changes to it do not affect the output stream. Calling this method does not remove the returned bytes from the buffer.

Calling `reset()` removes all of the currently buffered bytes, allowing a byte array output stream to be reused.

Closing a byte-array output stream has no effect. In particular, the bytes that have been buffered will still be available.

3.13.4   The `CharArrayWriter` Class

A `CharArrayWriter` does the same thing for characters, implementing methods of the same name as byte-array output streams.

3.14   Compressed Streams

In many cases, resources are compressed to save storage space or transfer bandwidth. The standard Java package `java.util.zip` supports a general pair of streams, `DeflaterInputStream` and `InflaterInputStream`, for compressing and decompressing sequences of bytes. Although new implementations may be written, Java builds in support for Gnu zip (gzip) compression and for the zip format for compressing archives consisting of multiple hierarchically named streams as an archive. Java's own Java archive (jar) files are essentially zipped archives and are also implemented.

3.14.1   Gzip Input and Output Streams

The gzip input and output streams are constructed by wrapping another stream and optionally specifying a buffer size. After construction, they behave just like any other stream.

The sample program `FileGZIP` wraps a file output stream in a gzip output stream in order to implement a simple compression command-line program. The work in the `main()` method is done by

```
InputStream in = new FileInputStream(fileIn);
OutputStream out = new FileOutputStream(fileOut);
OutputStream zipOut = new GZIPOutputStream(out);

byte[] bs = new byte[8192];
for (int n; (n = in.read(bs)) >= 0; )
    zipOut.write(bs,0,n);

in.close();
zipOut.close();
```

Aside from the creation of the compressed stream, the rest is just a buffered stream copy.

The sample program `FileUnGZIP` uncompresses one file into the other, with all the work being done in the creation of the streams,

```
InputStream in = new FileInputStream(fileIn);
InputStream zipIn = new GZIPInputStream(in);
OutputStream out = new FileOutputStream(fileOut);
```

After the streams are created, the input is copied to the output as before. Both programs print the input and output file lengths for convenience.

The Ant target `file-gzip` calls the program with arguments the value of properties `file.uncompressed` and `file.gzipped`. It's conventional to name a compressed file the same thing as the original file with a suffix denoting the type of compression, which for gzip is `gz`. Here we compress the build file `build.xml`, which, being XML, is highly redundant and hence highly compressible.

```
> ant -Dfile.uncompressed=build.xml\
>    -Dfile.gzipped=build.xml.gz file-gzip
Original Size=6697        Compressed Size=1236
```

We can uncompress in the same way, calling the `file-ungzip` target, which takes as command-line arguments the values of properties `file.gzipped` and `file.ungzipped`.

```
> ant -Dfile.ungzipped=build.xml.copy\
>    -Dfile.gzipped=build.xml.gz file-ungzip
Original Size=1236        Expanded Size=6697
```

The round trip results in `build.xml.copy` containing exactly the same bytes as `build.xml`. You may verify that the files contain the same content using the `diff` program from the command line,

```
> diff build.xml build.xml.copy
```

which prints no output when the files being compared are the same. Listing the directory contents shows the sizes,

```
> ls -l build.xml*
6697 Dec  5 16:54 build.xml
6697 Dec  5 16:58 build.xml.copy
1236 Dec  5 16:58 build.xml.gz
```

Along the same lines, you may verify that command-line versions of gzip, such as gunzip, can handle the compressed file.[4]

If you try to compress a stream that isn't in gzip format, the input stream will throw an I/O exception with an explanatory message.

3.14.2   Zip Input and Output Streams

Zip streams enable the representation of compressed archives. A zip archive consists of a sequence of entries. Each entry contains meta information and data. The data are accessed through an input stream for reading and an output stream for writing. The pattern for using the zip streams is somewhat unusual, so we will provide an example.

The ZIPEntry Class

The meta-information for an entry is encapsulated in an instance of ZIPEntry in the java.util.zip package. Information about the entry including compressed size, CRC-32 checksum, time last modified, comments, and entry name is available through methods.

Zip archives may be arranged hierarchically. Directory structure is described through entry names, with the forward slash (/) acting as the separator. The method isDirectory() is available to determine whether an entry is a directory, which is signaled by its ending in a forward slash.

For the purpose of creating archives, the ZIPEntry values may be set with setter methods corresponding to the get methods. This entails that the ZIPEntry class is mutable.

Creating a Zip Archive with Ant

To provide a zip file for experimental purposes, we've written an Ant target example-zip that builds a zipped archive using Ant's built-in mkdir, echo, and zip tasks. The Ant code is straightforward,

```
<property name="file.in.zip"
          value="build/demo-archive.zip"/>
```

---

[4]We recommend working in a temporary directory so as not to destroy the original build.xml file. The command-line compressors and uncompressors typically work by creating an output file that adds or removes the compression format's standard suffix.

```
<target name="example-zip">
  <mkdir dir="build/archive/dir"/>
  <echo message="Hello."
        encoding="UTF-8"
        file="build/archive/hello.txt"/>
...
  <zip destfile="${file.in.zip}"
       basedir="build/archive"
       encoding="UTF-8"/>
</target>
```

It uses the property file.in.zip to define the zipped archive's location. The
mkdir task makes a working directory in our build directory, which will be
cleaned the next time the clean target is invoked. The echo task writes text to
a file with a specified encoding. The elided tasks write two more files. We then
call the zip target, specifying the target file, the directory that is being zipped
up, and the encoding to use for file names.

The demo file creation target needs to be run before the demo so there's
something to unzip.

```
> ant example-zip
Building zip: c:\lpb\src\io\build\demo-archive.zip
```

Reading a Zip Archive

A ZIPInputStream is created, and then the archive is read entry by entry.
The method getNextEntry() returns the ZIPEntry object for the next entry
to be read, or null if there are no more entries. For each entry, we read its
meta-information from the entry object and its data from the input stream.

We provide a sample program FileZipView that reads a zip archive from
a file and displays its properties and contents. The work in the main() method
is done by

```
InputStream in = new FileInputStream(fileZipIn);
ZipInputStream zipIn = new ZipInputStream(in);
byte[] bs = new byte[8192];
while (true) {
    ZipEntry entry = zipIn.getNextEntry();
    if (entry == null) break;
    printEntryProperties(entry);
    for (int n; (n = zipIn.read(bs)) >= 0; )
        System.out.write(bs,0,n);
}
zipIn.close();
```

To get going, the file input stream is wrapped in a ZipInputStream. The buffer bs is used for writing. This loop uses the while-true-break idiom to run until a condition discovered in the middle of the body is discovered. Here, we assign the entry variable to the next entry. If it's null, we break out of the loop. Otherwise, we print the properties of the entry using a subroutine with the obvious implementation, and then read the bytes from the zip input stream and write them to standard output.

We have an Ant target file-zip-view that dumps out the contents of a zip archive specified through the file.in.zip property.

```
> ant -Dfile.in.zip=build/demo-archive.zip file-zip-view
getName()=abc/       isDirectory()=true
getSize()=0       getCompressedSize()=0
new Date(getTime())=Tue Jul 20 18:21:36 EDT 2010
getCrc()=0       getComment()=null
--------------------------
getName()=abc/bye.txt       isDirectory()=false
getSize()=7       getCompressedSize()=9
new Date(getTime())=Tue Jul 20 18:21:36 EDT 2010
getCrc()=3258114536       getComment()=null
Goodbye
--------------------------
. . .
--------------------------
getName()=hello.txt       isDirectory()=false
. . .
Hello
```

We've moved lines together to save space and elided the third entry and part of the fourth. Each division is for an entry, and the commands used to access the properties are printed. For instance, the first entry is a directory named abc/, and the second entry is an ordinary entry named abc/bye.txt, implying containment in the first directory by naming. The final entry is another ordinary entry named hello.txt, which isn't in any directory. Note that the compressed size is larger than the uncompressed size, which is not unusual for a short (or random, or already compressed) sequence of bytes.

After printing out all the properties for each entry, the program prints the contents by simply writing the bytes read directly to the standard output. For example, the entry named abc/bye.txt contains the UTF-8 bytes for Goodbye.

Creating a Zip Archive

Zip archives may be created programmatically using ZipOutputStream by reversing the process by which they are read. That requires creating ZipEntry objects for each entry in the archive and setting their properties. The entry meta-information is then written to the archive using the `putNextEntry()` method on the zip output stream, and then writing the bytes to the stream. The method `setMethod(int)` may be used with argument constants `STORED` for uncompressed entries and `DEFLATED` for compressed entries.

3.15   Tape Archive (Tar) Streams

The archaically named tape archive (tar) format is popular, especially among Unix users, for distributing data with a directory structure. Tar files themselves are typically compressed using gzip (see section 3.14.1). The Ant build library contains classes for manipulating tar streams, so we will be importing the Ant jar for compiling and running the examples in this section.

3.15.1   Reading Tar Streams

The way in which data may be read out of a tar file is easy to see with an example.

Code Walkthrough

We provide a demo class `FileTarView` that reads from a tar file that has optionally been gzipped. The `main()` method is defined to throw an I/O exception and read a file `tarFile` and boolean flag `gzipped` from the first two command-line arguments. The code begins by constructing the tar input stream.

```
InputStream fileIn = new FileInputStream(tarFile);
InputStream in = gzipped
    ? new GZIPInputStream(fileIn)
    : fileIn;
TarInputStream tarIn = new TarInputStream(in);
```

We first create a file input stream. Then we wrap it in a gzip input stream if the gzipped flag has been set. Then, we just wrap the input stream in a `TarInputStream`, from package `org.apache.tools.tar`.

We then use a read loop, inside which we access the properties of the entries and read the entry data.

```
while (true) {
    TarEntry entry = tarIn.getNextEntry();
    if (entry == null) break;

    boolean isDirectory = entry.isDirectory();
    String name = entry.getName();
```

```
String userName = entry.getUserName();
String groupName = entry.getGroupName();
int mode = entry.getMode();
Date date = entry.getModTime();
long size = entry.getSize();

ByteArrayOutputStream out = new ByteArrayOutputStream();
byte[] copyBuf = new byte[1024*8];
int numBytes;
while ((numBytes = tarIn.read(copyBuf)) > 0)
    out.write(copyBuf,0,numBytes);
byte[] bs = out.toByteArray();
```

We use the `getNextEntry()` method of the tar input stream to get the next instance of `TarEntry`, also from `org.apache.tools.tar`. If the entry is null, the stream has ended and we break out of the loop.

If the tar entry exists, we then access some of its more prominent properties including whether or not it's a directory, the name of the entry, the name of the user and group for whom it was created, the mode (usually specified as octal, so we print it out in octal), the date the entry was last modified, and the entry's size.

We read the data in the entry from within a `while` loop. Note that as for zip input streams, this is done by reading to the end of the tar input stream. The tar input stream is then reset. After we're done with the tar input stream, we close it through the closeable interface.

```
tarIn.close();
```

Tar input streams implement Java's `Closeable` interface, so we close it through the `close()` method. Although not documented, closing a tar input stream will close any contained stream other than `System.in`. Here, this closes the gzip input stream, which in turn closes the file input stream.

Running the Demo

The Ant target `file-tar-view` runs the command, passing the value of properties `tar.file` and `gzipped` as command-line arguments.

```
> ant -Dtar.file=../../data/20news-bydate.tar.gz\
>    -Dgzipped=true file-tar-view
-----------------------------------
name=20news-bydate-test/    isDirectory=true
userName=jrennie    groupName=    mode=755
date=Tue Mar 18 07:24:56 EST 2003
size=0    #bytes read=0
```

```
------------------------------------
name=20news-bydate-test/alt.atheism/    isDirectory=true
userName=jrennie    groupName=    mode=755
date=Tue Mar 18 07:23:48 EST 2003
size=0    #bytes read=0
------------------------------------
name=20news-bydate-test/alt.atheism/53265    isDirectory=false
userName=jrennie    groupName=    mode=644
date=Tue Mar 18 07:23:47 EST 2003
size=1994    #bytes read=1994
...
name=20news-bydate-train/    isDirectory=true
userName=jrennie    groupName=    mode=755
date=Tue Mar 18 07:24:55 EST 2003
size=0    #bytes read=0
------------------------------------
name=20news-bydate-train/alt.atheism/    isDirectory=true
...
```

Note that we first see the directory `20news-bydate-test`. The user name is `jrennie`, there is no group name, and the mode indicating permissions is 755 (octal). The last-modified date is in 2003. The size of the directory is zero, and the number of bytes read is zero. The next directory looks similar, only its name is `test/alt.atheism`, indicating that it is nested in the previous entry. In this corpus, it also indicates that the directory contains postings from the `alt.atheism` newsgroup. The `TarEntry` object lets you access all the entries for the files or directories it contains, but that won't let you read the data.

After the two directories, we see a file, with name `bydate-test/alt.atheism/53265` and mode 644 (octal). The reported size matches the number of bytes read, 1994.

After the files in the `alt.atheism` directory, there are 19 more test newsgroup directories. Then, we see the training data directory `20news-bydate-train`, which also has a set of 20 named newsgroup sub-directories.

3.16 Accessing Resources from the Classpath

When distributing an application, it is convenient to package all the necessary files along with the compiled classes in a single Java archive (jar). This is particularly useful in the context of servlets, which are themselves packaged in web archives (war), a kind of jar with extra meta-information.

3.16.1   Adding Resources to a Jar

Resources that will be accessed programmatically are added to an archive file just like any other file. We provide an Ant target `example-resource-jar` that may be used to create a jar at the path picked out by the property `resource.jar`.

```
<property name="resource.jar"
          value="build/demo-text.jar"/>

<target name="example-resource-jar">
  <mkdir dir="build/resources/com/colloquial/io"/>
  <echo message="Hello from the jar."
        encoding="UTF-8"
        file="build/resources/com/colloquial/io/hello.txt"/>
  ...
  <jar destfile="${resource.jar}">
    <fileset dir="build/resources"
             includes="**/*.txt"/>
  </jar>
</target>
```

We define the default for the property `resource.jar` to be a file of the same name in the `build` directory (which is subject to cleaning by the `clean` target). The target that builds the jar first makes a directory under `build/resources` into which files will be placed. These are created by `echo` tasks, for instance, creating a file `/com/colloquial/io/hello.txt` under `build/resources`. After the directory structure to be archived is created in `build/resources`, a `jar` task creates it, specifying that the archive should include all the files in `build/resources` that match the pattern `**/*.txt`, which is all files ending in `.txt`. The `example-resource-jar` target should be invoked before the demo in the next section.

```
> ant -Dresource.jar=build/demo-text.jar example-resource-jar
Building jar: (...)/javabook/src/io/build/demo-text.jar
```

3.16.2   Resources as Input Streams

One of the ways in which an input stream may be accessed is by specifying a resource. The system will then look for the resource on the classpath in a number of prespecified locations based on its name.

The sample program `ResourceInput` reads the content of a resource from the classpath and writes it to the standard output. The part of the `main()` method that gets the resource as an input stream is:

```
String resourceName = args[0];
InputStream in
    = ResourceInput.class
    .getResourceAsStream(resourceName);
```

The name of the resource is read in as the first command-line argument. Then the method `getResourceAsStream(String)` is called with the name of the resource. It is called on the `Class` instance for the `ResourceInput` class, specified by the static constant `ResourceInput.class`. The calling class is also important because the rules for locating the resource depend on the particular class loader used to load the class.

If the name begins with a forward slash (/), it is taken to be an absolute path name (absolute in the classpath, not in the file system). Otherwise, it is a relative path. Relative paths are interpreted relative to the package name of the class from which the get method was called. Specifically, the package name of the class using forward slashes as separators is used a prefix for the name.

The Ant target `resource-input` looks for a resource with the name given by property `resource.name`, adding the archive named by property `resource.jar` to the classpath. The jar from which we are reading needs to be on the classpath. How it gets there doesn't matter: you could put it on the command line, set an environment variable read by the JVM, use a servlet container's classpath, etc. Here, we just add the jar named by property `resource.jar` to the classpath in the Ant target. Very often, we just bundle resources we want to read from the classpath along with the compiled classes for an application. This is convenient for everything from document type definitions (DTDs) to compiled statistical models.

We run the program using the resource named `hello.txt` and the jar we created in the last section.

```
> ant -Dresource.jar=build/demo-text.jar\
>    -Dresource.name=hello.txt resource-input
Hello from the jar.
```

Note that we would get the same result if we specified the `resource.name` property to be the absolute path `/com/colloquial/io/hello.txt` (note the initial forward slash).

Once the stream is retrieved from the resource, it may be manipulated like any other stream. It may be buffered, converted to a reader or object input stream, interpreted as an image, etc.

3.17   Print Streams and Formatted Output

A print stream is a very flexible output stream that supports standard stream output, conversion of characters to bytes for output, and structured C-style formatting. This provides most of the functionality of a Writer's methods, while extending the base class InputStream.[5]

3.17.1 Constructing a Print Stream

A print stream may be constructed by wrapping another input stream or providing a file to which output should be written. The character encoding and whether auto-flushing should be carried out may also be specified. We recommend restricting your attention to the constructors PrintStream(File,String), which writes to a file given a specified encoding, and PrintStream(OutputStream,boolean,String), which prints to the specified output stream, optionally using auto-flushing, using a specified character encoding. The other constructors are shorthands that allow the parameters for character encoding and auto-flushing to be dropped, in which case the default character encoding is the default charset for the instance of the JVM in which the code is running and the default auto-flush value is false.

3.17.2 System.out Is a Print Stream

System.out is a PrintStream stream that corresponds to the Unix standard out (stdout) device. The javadoc specifies that all characters printed by a PrintStream are converted into bytes *using the platform's default character encoding* (emphasis added). This may be problematic when using stdout for monitoring or debugging.[6] In order to ensure that data sent to the console are correctly encoded, we wrap System.out in an OutputStreamWriter and explicitly specify the character encoding. Then we create a new PrintWriter that preserves the character encoding and has the same functionality as System.out.

```
OutputStreamWriter outWriter
    = new OutputStreamWriter(System.out,"UTF-8");
PrintWriter out
    = new PrintWriter(outWriter,true);
```

3.17.3 Exception Buffering

The second unusual feature of print streams is that none of their methods is declared to throw an I/O exception. Instead, they implement an exception

---

[5]It's not possible in Java to be both a Writer and a InputStream because these are both abstract base classes, and a class may extend only one other class. In retrospect, it'd be much more convenient if the streams were all defined as interfaces.

[6]Debug by printf is surprisingly effective.

buffering pattern, only without an actual buffer.[7] In cases where other streams would raise an I/O exception, the print stream methods exit quietly, while at the same time setting an error flag. The status of this flag is available through the method `checkError()`, which returns `true` if a method has caught an I/O exception.

3.17.4 Formatted Output

One of the most convenient aspects of print streams is their implementation of C-style `printf()` methods for formatted printing. These methods implicitly use an instance of `Formatter` in `java.util` to convert a sequence of objects into a string.

Format syntax is very elaborate, and for the most part, we restrict our attention to a few operations. The method's signature is `printf(Locale,String,Object...)`, where the string is the formatting string and the variable-length argument `Object...` is zero or more objects to format. How the objects are formatted depends on the format string and the `Locale` (from `java.util`). The locale is optional; if it is not supplied, the default locale will be used. The locale impacts the printing of things such as dates and decimal numbers, which are conventionally printed differently in different places. Although we are obsessive about maintaining unadulterated character data and work in many languages, a discussion of the intricacies of application internationalization is beyond the scope of this book.

For example, the sample program `FileByteCount` (see section 3.11.4) uses string, decimal, and hexadecimal formatting for strings and numbers.

```
System.out.printf("%4s %4s %10s\n","Dec","Hex","Count");
for (int i = 0; i < counts.length; ++i)
    if (counts[i] > 0L)
        System.out.printf("%4d %4h %10d\n",i,i,counts[i]);
```

The first `printf()` has the format string `"%4s %4s %10s\n"`, which says to write the first string using four characters, the second string using four characters, and the third string using 10 characters; if they are too short, they align to the right, and if they are too long, they run over their allotted space. The second `printf()` uses %4d for a four-place integer (right aligned), and %4h for a four-digit hexadecimal representation. Note that auto-boxing (see section A.2.6) converts the integers i and `counts[i]` to instances of `Integer` to act as inputs to `printf()`. Formatted prints do not automatically occupy a line; we have manually added Unix-style line boundary with the line feed character escape \n.

---

[7]This pattern is sometimes implemented so that the actual exceptions that were raised are accessible as a list.

Finally, note that the two `printf()` statements intentionally use the same width so that the output is formatted like a table with headings aligned above the columns.

3.18   Standard Input, Output, and Error Streams

In many contexts, the environment in which a program is executed provides streams for input, output, and error messages. These streams are known as standard input, standard output, and standard error. Standard Unix pipelines direct these streams in two ways. They can direct the standard input to be read from a file or the standard output or error to be written to a file. Second, they can pipe processes together, so that the standard output from one process is used for the standard input of the next process. Shell scripts and scripting languages such as Python manage standard input and output from processes in a similar way to shells.[8]

3.18.1   Accessing the Streams

Java provides access to these streams through three static variables in the class `System` in the package `java.lang`. The variable `System.in` is of type `InputStream` and may be used to read bytes from the shell's standard input. The standard and error output streams, `System.out` and `System.err`, are provided constants of type `PrintStream` (see section 3.17 for more information on print streams). The standard output and error print streams use the platform's default encoding (see below for how to reset this).

3.18.2   Redirecting the Streams

The standard input and output streams may be reset using the methods `setIn(InputStream)`, `setOut(PrintStream)`, and `setErr(PrintStream)`. This is convenient for writing Java programs that act like Python or shell scripts.

The mutability of the output and error streams enables a Java program to reset their character encodings. For example, to reset standard output to use UTF-8, insert the following statement before any output is produced,

```
System.setOut(new PrintStream(System.out,true,"UTF-8"));
```

---

[8]Java provides an implementation of Unix-style pipes through piped streams and readers and writers. These are based on the classes `PipedInputStream`, `PipedOutputStream`, `PipedReader`, and `PipedWriter` in the standard `java.io` package. These classes are multi-threaded so that they may asynchronously consume the output of one process to provide the input to the next, blocking if need be to wait for a read or write.

The value `true` enables auto-flushing. The new standard output wraps the old standard output in a new print stream with the desired encoding.

The output streams may be similarly redirected to files by using a `PrintStream` constructed from a file in the same way. For example,

```
System.setErr(new PrintStream("stdout.utf8.txt","UTF-16BE"));
```

sends anything the program writes to the standard error stream to the file `stdout.utf8.txt`, using the UTF-16BE character encoding to convert characters to bytes.

The standard input stream may be wrapped in an `InputStreamReader` or `BufferedReader` to interpret byte inputs as characters. Standard output and error may be wrapped in the same way, which is an alternative to resetting the streams.

3.18.3 Unix-like Commands

Commands in Unix are often defined to default to writing to the standard output if a file is not specified. This idiom is easy to reconstruct for Java commands. Suppose we have a variable `file` that is initialized to a file or `null` if the command is to write an output

```
PrintStream out
    = (file != null)
    ? new PrintStream(new FileOutputStream(file))
    : System.out;
```

If the file is non-null, an output stream for it is wrapped in a print stream; otherwise, the standard output is used. The same can be done for input.

3.19 URIs, URLs, and URNs

A uniform resource identifier (URI) picks out something on the web by name. This is a very general notion, but we will need only a few instances in this book. The specifications for these standards are quite complex and beyond the scope of this book.

3.19.1 Uniform Resource Names

There are two (overlapping) subtypes of URIs, based on function. A uniform resource name (URN) is a URI that provides a name for something on the web but may not say how or where to get it. A typical instance of a URN is the Digital Object Identifier (DOI) system, which is becoming more and more widely used to identify text resources such as journal articles. For example, the DOI

`doi:10.1016/j.jbi.2003.10.001` picks out a paper that has the alternative
URN `PMID:15016385`, which uses a PubMed identifier (PMID) instead of a DOI.

3.19.2 Uniform Resource Locators

A uniform resource locator (URL) provides a means of locating (a concrete instance of) an item on the web. A URL indicates how to get
something by providing a scheme name, such as `file://` for files
or `http://` for the hypertext transport protocol (HTTP). For example, the URL `http://dx.doi.org/10.1016/j.jbi.2003.10.001` is for the
same paper as above but specifies a web protocol, HTTP, and host,
`dx.doi.org`, from which to fetch a specific embodiment of the resource.
There may be many URLs that point to the same object. For instance,
`http://linkinghub.elsevier.com/retrieve/pii/S1532046403001126` is
a URL for the same paper, which links to the publisher's site.

3.19.3 URIs and URLs in Java

The standard `java.net` package has a class `URI` for URIs and a class `URL` for
URLs. Both of them may be constructed using a string representation of the
resource. Once constructed, the classes provide a range of structured access
to the fields making up the resource. For instance, both objects have methods such as `getHost()` and `getPort()`, which may return proper values or
indicators such as `null` or `-1` if there is no host or port.

   The demo program `UrlProperties` constructs a URL from a command-line
argument and prints out its available properties. The beginning of the `main()`
method is

```
public static void main(String[] args)
    throws MalformedURLException {

    String url = args[0];
    URL u = new URL(url);
    System.out.println("getAuthority()=" + u.getAuthority());
```

The rest of the program just prints out the rest of the properties. The `main()`
method throws a `MalformedURLException`, a subclass of `IOException`, if the
URL specified on the command line is not well formed. This ensures that once
a URL is constructed, it is well formed. There are no exceptions to catch for
the get methods; they operate only on the string representations and are guaranteed to succeed if the URL was constructed.

   The Ant target `url-properties` calls the command supplying as an argument the value of the property `url.in`.

```
> ant -Durl.in="http://google.com/webhp?q=dirichlet" url-properties
```

```
getAuthority()=google.com
getDefaultPort()=80
getFile()=/webhp?q=dirichlet
getHost()=google.com
getPath()=/webhp
getPort()=-1
getProtocol()=http
getQuery()=q=dirichlet
getRef()=null
getUserInfo()=null
toExternalForm()=http://google.com/webhp?q=dirichlet
toString()=http://google.com/webhp?q=dirichlet
```

Looking over the output shows how the URL is parsed into components such as host, path, and query.

3.19.4 Reading from URLs

URLs know how to access resources. These resources may reside locally or remotely. Wherever they reside and whatever their content, resources are all coded as byte streams. Java provides built-in support for protocols http, https, ftp, file, and jar.

Once a URL is created, the method openStream() returns an InputStream that may be used to read the bytes from the URL. Depending on the URL itself, these bytes may be from a local or networked file, a local or remote web server, or elsewhere. Opening the stream may throw an I/O exception, as a connection is opened to the URL. Once the input stream is opened, it may be used like any other stream.

The sample program ReadUrl shows how to read the bytes from a URL and relay them to standard output.

```
URL u = new URL(url);
InputStream in = u.openStream();

byte[] buf = new byte[8096];
int n;
while ((n = in.read(buf)) >= 0)
    System.out.write(buf,0,n);

in.close();
```

The code between the stream creation and its closing is just a generic buffered stream copy.

The Ant target read-url is configured to call the sample program using as URL the value of the property url.in.

```
> ant -Durl.in=http://lingpipe.com url-read
```

```
<?xml version="1.0" encoding="UTF-8"?>
<!DOCTYPE html ...
<html ...
<head>
<title>LingPipe Home</title>
<meta http-equiv="Content-type"
      content="application/xhtml+xml; charset=utf-8"/>
...
pageTracker._trackPageview();
} catch(err) {}</script></body>
</html>
```

As with most pages these days, LingPipe's home page starts with a title, content type, and cascading stylesheet (CSS) declaration and ends with some Javascript. Whether you can see all of the output of a page depends on your shell; you can save the output to a file and then view it in a browser.

A file URL may be used as well as an HTTP-based URL. This allows an abstraction over the location of the bytes being read.

3.19.5   URL Connections

The output stream method we used above, `getOutputStream()`, is just a convenience method for calling the `openConnection()` method to get an instance of `URLConnection` and calling its `getOutputStream()` method. URL connections allow various properties of the connection to be inspected and set.

Although the URL method `openConnection()` is declared to return a `URLConnection`, if the URL uses the HTTP protocol, the documentation specifies that a `HttpURLConnection` will be returned. Thus, the `URLConnection` may be cast to `HttpURLConnection` at run time. The HTTP-based connection provides additional methods for manipulating HTTP headers and responses, such as content types, last-modified dates, character encodings, handling redirected web pages, fetching HTTP response codes, managing timeouts and keep-alive times for the connection, and other intricacies of HTTP management.

A URL connection may also be used to write to a URL. This makes it possible to attach data for a POST-based request and thus implement general web services. This is covered in more detail in chapter 5.

3.20   The Input Source Abstraction

The class `InputSource`, in standard Java package `org.xml.sax`, provides an input abstraction for XML documents with a rather awkward mutable implementation. An input source specifies the source of its input as a URL, an input stream, or a reader.

There is a constructor for each mode of input specification. `InputSource(String)` may be used with a system identifier in the form of a URL, and `InputSource(InputStream)` and `InputSource(Reader)` may be used for stream data. Although input sources are not immutable, we recommend using a detailed constructor rather than a simple constructor followed by setters.

There is also a no-argument constructor `InputSource()` and setters for each of the input types. The setters `setSystemId(String)`, `setByteStream(InputStream)`, and `setCharacterStream(Reader)` correspond to the three contentful constructors.

The system ID may be used to resolve relative paths within an XML document. Thus, setting a system ID may be useful even when a byte stream or a character stream has been specified.

Before using an input source, a character encoding may be specified using the `setEncoding(String)` method. A further awkwardness arises because this method makes sense only in conjunction with an input stream or URL; readers supply already converted `char` values.

It is up to the consumer of the input source to gather data from whatever source is specified. Typically, consumers will try the reader, then the input stream, then the URL. Because of the mutability of the class through the setters, an input source may have an input stream and a reader and a URL specified.

3.21 File Channels and Memory-Mapped Files

As an alternative to streaming I/O, memory mapping essentially provides a random-access interface for files by providing an array-like access abstraction on top of files. It is then up to the operating system's file manager to deal with actual commits to and reads from disk.

Memory-mapped files are great for random access to data on disk. For instance, databases and search engines make heavy use of memory mapping.

Both the file input and file output stream classes implement a `getChannel()` method that returns an instance of `FileChannel`. File channels are part of the "new" I/O, rooted at package name `java.nio`, specifically in the package `java.nio.channels`.

File channels support reading and writing into `ByteBuffer` instances. Byte buffers and other buffers are in the `java.nio` package. Byte buffers may be wrapped to act as character buffers or other primitive-type buffers. See section 2.11 for a basic overview of buffers focusing on character buffers.

File channels may also be used to produce a `MappedByteBuffer`, which creates a memory-mapped file accessible as a `ByteBuffer`. The other way to create a file that which may be used to produce a memory-mapped buffer is through the `RandomAccessFile` class in `java.io`. The `RandomAccessFile` class implements the `DataInput` and `DataOutput` interfaces, which provide utilities to write arbitrary primitives and strings in addition to bytes.

3.22   Object and Data I/O

Java provides built-in support for writing objects to streams through the classes `ObjectInputStream` and `ObjectOutputStream` in the package `java.io`. Object input and output streams implement the `ObjectInput` and `ObjectOutput` interfaces, which extend the `DataInput` and `DataOutput` interfaces. The object streams deal with writing objects and the data streams with writing primitive types and strings. Only objects with a runtime class that implements the `Serializable` interface in package `java.io` may be written or read. We first provide an example and then discuss how to implement the `Serializable` interface.

3.22.1   Example of Object and Data I/O

The sample program `ObjectIo` provides an example of using object input and output streams to write objects and primitive objects and then reconstitute them. The `main()` method begins by writing the objects and primitive types,

```
ByteArrayOutputStream bytesOut = new ByteArrayOutputStream();
ObjectOutput out = new ObjectOutputStream(bytesOut);

out.writeObject(new File("foo"));
out.writeUTF("bar");
out.writeInt(42);

out.close();
```

Note that a byte array output stream is created and assigned to the appropriate variable. We use a byte array for convenience; it could've been a file output stream, a compressed file output stream, or an HTTP write in either direction. The output stream is then wrapped in an object output stream and assigned to a variable of the interface type, `ObjectOutput`. The object output is then used to write a file object using the `writeObject()` method from the `ObjectOutput` interface. Next, a string is written using the `writeUTF(String)` method from the `DataOutput` interface. This does not write the string as an object, but using an efficient UTF-8-like encoding scheme. Lastly, an integer is written; the `DataOutput` interface provides write methods for all of the primitive types. Finally, the output stream is closed in the usual way through the `Closeable` interface method `close()`.

We then reverse the process to read the object back in.

```
byte[] bytes = bytesOut.toByteArray();
InputStream bytesIn = new ByteArrayInputStream(bytes);
ObjectInput in = new ObjectInputStream(bytesIn);

@SuppressWarnings("unchecked")
File file = (File) in.readObject();
String s = in.readUTF();
int n = in.readInt();

in.close();
```

First, we get the bytes that were written from the byte array output stream and use them to create a byte array input stream.[9] Then we wrap that in an object input stream, which we use to read the object, string, and primitive integer value. Then we close the input stream. The result of the object read must be upcast to `File` because the `readObject()` method is declared to return `Object`.[10] Because the class may not be found or the class loader may fail to load the class for the object, the `readObject()` method is also declared to throw a `ClassNotFoundException`, which we simply declare on the `main()` method rather than handle. The result of running the program is

```
> ant object-io
file.getCanonicalPath()=(...)/javabook/src/io/foo
s=bar
n=42
```

3.22.2 The `Serializable` Interface

The `Serializable` interface in package `java.io` is what's known as a marker interface. The marker pattern involves an interface, such as `Serializable`, which declares no methods. The interface is used to treat classes that implement it differently in some contexts. The object input and output classes use the `Serializable` marker interface to determine whether a class can be serialized or not.

When a class is serialized, its fully qualified path name is written out as if by the `writeUTF()` method. A 64-bit serial version identifier is also written. Then data representing the state of the class are written.

All that is strictly necessary to make a class serializable is to declare it to implement the `Serializable` interface, although it must also meet a few

---

[9]Note that we assign variables to the most general type possible; the input stream had to be assigned to `ByteArrayInputStream` because we needed to call the `toByteArray()` method on it.

[10]The `@SuppressWarnings` annotation is used to suppress the unchecked warning that would otherwise be generated by the compiler for the runtime cast. Although the cast can't fail in this context, because we know what we wrote, it may fail in a runtime context if the expected input format is not received.

additional conditions described below. If nothing else is specified, the serial version identifier will be computed from the class's signature, including the signature of its parents and implemented interfaces. If nothing else is done, the state of the class is serialized by serializing each of its member objects and writing each of its primitive member variables, including all those inherited from parent classes.

The first condition for default serializability is that all of the class's member variables (including those of its superclasses) implement the `Serializable` interface or are declared to be `transient`. If that is the case, the object output method uses reflection to write out each object and primitive member variable in turn.

The second requirement on a class for default serializabilty is that it must implement a public no-argument constructor. If that is the case, reconstituting an object will also happen by reflection, first calling the no-argument constructor, and then reading and setting all the member variables.

The third requirement is that the same version of the class be used for reading and writing. There are two parts to this requirement. The first version requirement is that the signature of the class used to read in the serialized instance must be the same as that used to write the objects. If you change the member variables, method declarations, subclasses, etc., it will interfere with deserialization. The second version requirement is that the major version of Java being used to deserialize must be at least as great as that used to serialize. Thus, it is not possible to serialize in Java version 7 and deserialize in version 6.

3.22.3 The Serialization Proxy Pattern

Java allows classes to take full control over their serialization and deserialization, which we take advantage of to overcome the limitations of default serialization, such as the restrictions on superclass behavior, backward compatibility with changing signatures, and the ability to create immutable objects without no-arg constructors.

Our recommended approach to serialization is to use the serialization proxy pattern, which we describe in this section by example, with an implementation in `SerialProxied` defined here. The class begins by declaring it implements `Serializable`, and then defining two final member variables in a single two-argument constructor.

```java
public class SerialProxied implements Serializable {

    private final String mS;
    private final int mCount;
    private final Object mNotSerializable = new Object();

    public SerialProxied(String s, int count) {
```

```
            mS = s;
            mCount = count;
    }
```

The finality of the variables means that instances of the class are immutable in the sense that once they are constructed they will never change. Immutable classes are easy to reason about, especially in multi-threaded environments, because they are well formed when constructed and never change behavior.

The `writeReplace()` Method

Before applying default serialization, the object write methods first check, using reflection, whether a class implements the `writeReplace()` method. If it does, the return result of calling it is serialized instead of the class itself.

The `SerialProxied` class implements the `writeReplace()` method by returning a new instance of the `Serializer` class.

```
private Object writeReplace() {
    return new Serializer(this);
}
```

Note that the method is declared to be private, so it will not appear in the documentation for the class and may not be called by clients. Reflection is still able to access the method even though it's private.

Serialization Proxy Implementation

The rest of the work's done in the class `Serializer`. We declare the class within the `SerialProxied` class as a static nested class, `Serializer`.

```
private static class Serializer implements Externalizable {
    SerialProxied mObj;
    public Serializer() { }
    Serializer(SerialProxied obj) {
        mObj = obj;
    }
```

The class itself is declared to be private and static. The full name of would be `com.colloquial.io.SerialProxied.Serializer`, but given its privacy, we can access it only from within `SerialProxied`.

As we will shortly see, the `Externalizable` interface it implements extends `Serializable` with the ability to take full control over what is written and read. The variables and methods within it are package protected, though they could also all be private. There are two constructors, a no-arg constructor

required to be public for deserialization, and a one-argument constructor used
by the `writeReplace()` method shown above for serialization.

The rest of the methods in the `Serializer` class are

```
public void writeExternal(ObjectOutput out)
    throws IOException {

    out.writeUTF(mObj.mS);
    out.writeInt(mObj.mCount);
}

public void readExternal(ObjectInput in) throws IOException {
    String s = in.readUTF();
    int count = in.readInt();
    mObj = new SerialProxied(s,count);
}

Object readResolve() {
    return mObj;
}
```

We describe them in turn below.

The `writeExternal()` Method

The first method is the `writeExternal()` method, which writes to the specified object output. In this case, it uses its within-class private access to retrieve
and write the member variables of the `SerialProxied` object mObj.

The `readExternal()` Method

The next method is the `readExternal()` method. This method and its sister
method, `writeExternal()`, are specified in the `Externalizable` interface as
public so they must be public here.[11]

The read method first reads the serialized string and integer from the specified object input. Then it uses these to construct a new `SerialProxied` instance based on the string and count and assigns it to the object variable
mObj.

The `readResolve()` Method

Finally, the `readResolve()` method is used to return the object that was read
in. This method is the deserialization counterpart to `writeReplace()`. After

---

[11]The `readExternal()` method is also declared to throw a `ClassNotFoundException` to deal
with cases when it fails to deserialize an object using the object input's `readObject()` method. We
don't need it here because we are only using the data input methods `readUTF()` and `readInt()`.

the readExternal() method is called, if readResolve() is defined, its return value is returned as the result of deserialization. Thus, even though the
Serializer is the one being serialized and deserialized, it is not visible at all
to external clients.

Serial Version Variable

The final piece of the puzzle to take control over is the computation of the
serial version identifier. This allows serialization to bypass the computation
of this identifier by inspecting the serialized object's signature by reflection.
This is not only more efficient, but it also allows the signatures to be changed
without affecting the ability to deserialize already serialized instances.

If a class has already been fielded without declaring a serial version ID,
the command-line program serialver, which is shipped with the Sun/Oracle
JDK, may be used to compute the value that would be computed by reflection
during serialization. It needs only the classpath and full name of the class.

```
> serialver -classpath build/tj-io-1.0.jar\
>   com.colloquial.io.SerialProxied
static final long serialVersionUID = -688378786294424932L;
```

The output is a piece of Java code declaring a constant serialVersionUID
with the current value of the identifier as computed by serialization. We just
insert that into the class SerialProxied class. Technically, we may use whatever number we like here; it's checked for consistency only during serialization. We also need to insert the version ID constant into the nested static class
SerialProxied.Serializer.

Chapter 4

Regular Expressions

Generalized regular expressions, as implemented in Java and scripting languages such as Perl and Python, provide a general means for describing spans of text. Given a regular expression (regex) and some text, basic regex functionality allows us to test whether a string matches the regex or find non-overlapping substrings of a string matching the regex.

We start with the classes and methods in package `java.util.regex` and build a series of short example programs. Then we cover the syntax for regular expressions in Java using our example programs to show how different constructions behave. Our discussion of regular expressions is limited. We recommend *Mastering Regular Expressions, 3rd Edition* by Jeffrey E.F. Friedl, O'Reilly and Associates, 2006, for a comprehensive treatment of regular expressions in theory and practice.

The programs for this chapter are in the example source code distribution subdirectory:

`javabook/src/regex`

This directory contains an Ant `build.xml` file with targets to compile and run these programs. The programs belong to package `com.colloquial.regex`. The subdirectory `javabook/src/regex/src` contains the Java source files.

4.1 The `java.util.regex` Package

Despite the rich functionality of regexes, Java's `java.util.regex` package contains only two classes, `Pattern` and `Matcher`. An instance of `Pattern` provides an immutable representation of a regular expression. An instance of `Matcher` represents the state of the matching of a regular expression against a string.

4.1.1 Matching Entire Strings

It's easiest to start with an example of using a regular expression for matching, which we wrote as the example class RegexMatch:

```
String regex = args[0];
String text = args[1];

Pattern pattern = Pattern.compile(regex);
Matcher matcher = pattern.matcher(text);
boolean matches = matcher.matches();
```

First, we read the regex from the first command-line argument, then the text from the second argument. We then use the regular expression to compile a pattern, using the static factory method pattern.compile(). This pattern is reusable. We next create a matcher instance, using the method matcher() on the pattern we just created. Finally, we assign a boolean variable matches the value of calling the method matches() on the matcher. And then we print out the result.

Regular expressions may consist of strings, in which case they simply carry out exact string matching. We use simple strings as the regex for the examples in this section. In the following sections we go through the regex syntax and rerun these programs with more powerful regexes.

To test our program, we try to match the regex aab against string *aabb*. There is an Ant target regex-match that feeds the command-line arguments to our program. For the example at hand, we have

```
> ant -Dregex="aab" -Dtext="aabb" regex-match
Regex=|aab|    Text=|aabb|    Matches=false
```

The test fails because there isn't an exact match against the entire string. On the other hand, the regex abc does match the string *abc*.

```
> ant -Dregex="abc" -Dtext="abc" regex-match
Regex=|abc|    Text=|abc|    Matches=true
```

Note that we have used the vertical bar to mark the boundaries of the regular expression and text in our output. These vertical bars are not part of the regular expression or the text. This is a useful trick in situations where space may appear as the prefix or suffix of a string. It may get confusing if there is a vertical bar within the string, but the outer vertical bars are always the ones dropped.

4.1.2 Finding Matching Substrings

The second main application of regular expressions is to find substrings of a string that match the regular expression. The main method in our class

RegexFind illustrates this. We read in two command-line arguments into string variables `regex` and `text` as we did for `RegexMatch` in the previous section. We begin by compiling the pattern and creating a matcher for the text just as in `RegexFind`.

```
Pattern pattern = Pattern.compile(regex);
Matcher matcher = pattern.matcher(text);
while (matcher.find()) {
    String found = matcher.group();
    int start = matcher.start();
    int end = matcher.end();
```

The first call of the `find()` method on a matcher returns `true` if there is a substring of the text that matches the pattern. If `find()` returned `true`, then the method `group()` returns the substring that matched, and the methods `start()` and `end()` return the span of the match, which is from the start (inclusive) to the end (exclusive).

Subsequent calls to `find()` return `true` if there is a match starting on or after the end position of the previous calls. Thus, the loop structure in the program above is the standard idiom for enumerating all the matches.

To run examples, we use the Ant target `regex-find`. Like `regex-match`, it takes a regex and a text string as arguments. We find the regex `aa` in the string *aaaaab* (five *a* s followed by one *b*).

```
> ant -Dregex="aa" -Dtext="aaaaab" regex-find
Found |aa| at (0,2)    Found |aa| at (2,4)
```

As before, the vertical bars are delimiters, not part of the matching substring. The string *aa* actually shows up in four distinct locations in *aaaaab*, at spans (0,2), (1,3), (2,4), and (3,5). Running find returns only two of them. The matcher works from the start to the end of the string, returning the first match it finds after the first call to `find()`. In this case, that's the substring of *aaaaab* spanning (0,2). The second call to `find()` starts looking for a match at position 2, succeeding with the span (2,4). Next, it starts looking at position 4, but there is no substring starting on or after position 4 that matches *aa*.

4.1.3 Find-and-Replace Operations

A common usage pattern for regular expressions is to find instances of one pattern and replace them with another. We provide a sample program `RegexReplace`. The `main()` method illustrates replacement.

```
Pattern pattern = Pattern.compile(regex);
Matcher matcher = pattern.matcher(text);
String result = matcher.replaceAll(replacement);
```

The pattern and matcher are created as usual. Then, we create a string by replacing all the matches of the pattern in the text provided to the matcher with the specified replacement. We could also use `replaceFirst()` to return the result of replacing only the first match.

The Ant target `regex-replace` takes three arguments: a regex, a replacements string, and a text string.

```
> ant -Dregex="a" -Dreplacement=z -Dtext="abc abc" regex-replace
regex=|a|        replacement=|z|
text=|abc abc|   result=|zbc zbc|
```

How the `Matcher.replaceAll` Method Works

The `Matcher.replaceAll` method is a convenience method that makes repeated calls to the methods `find`, `appendReplacement`, and `appendTail`. The Java SE 7 javadoc provides the following example

```
Pattern p = Pattern.compile("cat");
Matcher m = p.matcher("one cat two cats in the yard");
StringBuffer sb = new StringBuffer();
while (m.find()) {
    m.appendReplacement(sb, "dog");
}
m.appendTail(sb);
System.out.println(sb.toString());
```

This code writes one dog two dogs in the yard to the standard-output stream.

These methods use a `StringBuffer` to store the intermediate results. `StringBuffer` objects are thread safe, and therefore, this operation incurs a certain amount of processing overhead due to synchronization.

4.2   Empty Regex

The simplest regular expression is the empty regular expression. It matches only the empty string. For example, the expression `Pattern.compile("").matcher("").matches()` evaluates to `true`. Using our test code from the command line proves tricky, because we have to escape the quotes if we want to assign environment variables, as in

```
> ant -Dregex=\"\" -Dtext=\"\" regex-match
Regex=||    Text=||    Matches=true
```

```
> ant -Dregex=\"\" -Dtext="a" regex-match
Regex=||    Text=|a|    Matches=false
```

The empty regex matches everywhere in a string, as the following example shows.

```
> ant -Dregex=\"\" -Dtext="aa" regex-find
Found || at (0,0)    Found || at (1,1)    Found || at (2,2)
```

Replacing the empty regex inserts the replacement string between every existing character in a string.

```
> ant -Dregex=\"\" -Dreplacement=z -Dtext="aa" regex-replace
regex=||    replacement=|z|
text=|aa|   result=|zazaz|
```

4.3 Character Regexes

The most basic regular expressions describe single characters. Some characters have special meanings in regexes and thus need to be escaped for use in regular expressions.

4.3.1 Characters as Regexes

A single character may be used a regular expression. A regular expression consisting of a single character matches only that single character. For instance, `Pattern.compile("a").matcher("a").matches()` would evaluate to `true`. Using our Ant match target,

```
> ant -Dregex="b" -Dtext="b" regex-match
Regex=|b|    Text=|b|    Matches=true
```

```
> ant -Dregex="b" -Dtext="c" regex-match
Regex=|b|    Text=|c|    Matches=false
```

Within a Java program, Java character literals may be used within the string denoting the regex. For instance, we may write `Pattern.compile("\u00E9")` to compile the regular expression that matches the character U+00E9, LATIN SMALL E WITH ACUTE, which would be written as é.

Unicode Escapes

Arbitrary Unicode characters may be escaped in the same way as in Java. That is, \u*hhhh* is a regular expression matching the character with Unicode code point U+*hhhh*. For example,

```
> ant -Dregex="\u0041" -Dtext="A" regex-match
Regex=|\u0041|    Text=|A|    Matches=true
```

Note that we did not have to escape the backslash for the shell because the following character, u, is not an escape. Unicode escapes are useful for matching the period character, U+002E, FULL STOP, which is a reserved character in regexes representing wildcards (see section 4.4.1).

```
> ant -Dregex="\u002E" -Dtext="." regex-match
Regex=|\u002E|    Text=|.|    Matches=true
```

In a Java program, we'd still have to write `Pattern.compile("\\u002E")`.

Unicode escapes in regexes are confusing, because they use the same syntax as Java Unicode literals. Further complicating matters, the literal for backslashes in Java programs, `\\`, is the same as the regex literal escape. There is a world of difference between the patterns produced by `Pattern.compile("\u002E")` and `Pattern.compile("\\u002E")`. The former is the same as `Patten.compile(".")` and matches any character; the latter uses a regex escape and matches only the period character.

Other Escapes

In order to match a character which is used as a metacharacter in a Java `Pattern` construct, it must be escaped by the backslash character. There are also other built-in escapes, such as `\n` for newline and `\\` for a backslash character.

We must be careful to distinguish regex escapes in a `Pattern` construct from escapes needed for string literals in Java. Because Java string literals also use a backslash for escapes, to specify a single backslash we write `\\` and to specify an escape character that contains a backslash such as newline `\n` we write `\\n`. To create the regex `\\`, we need to use two backslash escapes in our string literal, writing `Pattern.compile("\\\\")`.

Running this example from the command line is problematic. The shell itself is a scripting language with its own set of escape characters, one of which is the backslash. Usually we use double quotes to enclose the arguments and prevent the shell from expanding special characters, but `\"` is a valid escape sequence for the shell, which means that the closing double quotes on the command-line arguments aren't interpreted correctly. We use single quotes instead because the shell treats all text enclosed by single quotes as a literal.[1]

To invoke the regex-match program with a regex consisting of the backslash literal, we need to set up the call `Pattern.compile("\\\\")` and match it against a text consisting of the backslash literal `\\`.

---

[1]Different implementations of the bash shell parse the command line differently. Try this on your machine using double quotes or no quotes around the arguments.

```
> ant -Dregex='\\\\' -Dtext='\\' regex-match
Regex=|\\|    Text=|\|    Matches=true
```

Our Java program gets a value for `regex` consisting of a length-two string made up of two backslashes and a value for `text` consisting of a single backslash. The match succeeds because the regex \\ is the escaped backslash character, which matches a single backslash.

4.4 Character Classes

Regular expressions provide a range of built-in character classes based on ASCII or Unicode, as well as the ability to define new classes. Each character class matches a set of characters. A familiar example of a character class is the `digits` class, which comprises the ASCII digits {0,1,2,3,4,5,6,7,8,9}. In Java this class can be specified either explicitly as [0-9] or by the predefined character class \d. We strongly recommend the use of the predefined classes whenever possible. They make your code easier to read and eliminate errors introduced by incomplete or malformed definitions.

Application-specific character classes are specified as a set of character alternatives enclosed in brackets. For example, [aA] specifies the character class that matches both the upper- and lowercase letter A. This syntax is confusing because within the square brackets aA is interpreted as the set resulting from the union of these two atomic characters, but outside of this context the aA is interpreted as the concatenation of these two characters. Trying to do an exact match between the regex and [aA] and the string aA fails.

```
> ant -Dregex="[aA]" -Dtext="aA" regex-match
Regex=|[aA]|    Text=|aA|    Matches=false
```

Because character classes may appear within other character classes, these alternatives need not be single characters. We discuss compound character classes later in this section.

4.4.1 The Wildcard as the Universal Character Class

A singe period (.) is a regular expression that matches any single character. We may think of it as the universal character class. For instance, the regex . matches the string *a*, and a.c matches *abc*.

```
> ant -Dregex="a.c" -Dtext="abc" regex-match
Regex=|a.c|    Text=|abc|    Matches=true
```

Whether or not a wildcard matches an end-of-line sequence depends on whether or not the DOTALL flag is set (see section 4.14.1); if it is set, the wildcard matches end-of-line sequences. The following two expressions evaluate to `true`,

```
Pattern.compile(".").matcher("A").matches();
Pattern.compile(".",DOTALL).matcher("\n").matches();
```

whereas the following expression evaluates to `false`,

```
Pattern.compile(".").matcher("\n").matches();
```

4.4.2 Unicode Classes

Unicode defines a range of categories for characters, such as the category Lu of uppercase letters (see section 2.3.9 for more information). The regular expression \p{*X*} matches any unicode character belonging to the Unicode category *X*. For example, the class Lu picks out uppercase letters, so we have

```
> ant -Dregex="\p{Lu}" -Dtext="A" regex-match
Regex=|\p{Lu}|    Text=|A|    Matches=true
```

Using a capital letter complements the category; for instance, \p{Lu} matches uppercase letters, whereas \P{Lu} matches any character except an uppercase letter.

4.4.3 ASCII Classes

There are character classes built in for ASCII characters. For instance, \d is for digits, \s for whitespace, and \w for alphanumeric characters. For example,

```
> ant -Dregex="\d" -Dtext="7" regex-match
Regex=|\d|    Text=|7|    Matches=true
```

For these three ASCII classes, the capitalized forms match ASCII characters that don't match the lowercase forms. So \D matches non-digits, \S non-whitespace, and \W non-alphanumeric characters.

There are a range of built-in ASCII classes from the POSIX standard built in. They use the same syntax as the Unicode classes described in the previous section. For example, \p{ASCII} matches any ASCII character and \p{Punct} matches ASCII punctuation characters.

The ASCII characters must be used with care, because they will not have their described behavior when interpreted over all of Unicode. For example, there are whitespaces in Unicode that don't match \s and digits that don't match \d.

4.5 Compound Character Classes

Character classes may be built up from single characters and/or other character classes using set operations such as union, intersection, and negation.

The syntax for compound character classes uses brackets around a character class expression. The atomic character class expressions are single characters such as a or character class set names such as \p{Lu} (any uppercase Unicode letter character).

Character classes may be unioned within the brackets using a concatenation syntax. This can be confusing, especially in complex regular expressions that contain both character classes and compound regexes. For instance, [aeiou] is the character class picking out the ASCII vowels. It is composed of the union of character class expressions a, e, ..., u.

```
> ant -Dregex="[aeiou]" -Dtext="i" regex-match
Regex=|[aeiou]|    Text=|i|    Matches=true
```

Class escapes may be used, so that [\p{Lu}\p{N}] picks out uppercase letters and numbers.

The use of range notation may be used as shorthand for unions. For instance, [0-9] picks out the ASCII digits *0, 1, ..., 9*. For example,

```
> ant -Dregex="[I-P]" -Dtext="J" regex-match
Regex=|[I-P]|    Text=|J|    Matches=true
```

Character classes may be complemented. The syntax involves a caret, with [^A] picking out the class of characters not in class *A*. The expression *A* must be either a range or a sequence of character class primitives. For instance, [^z] represents the class of every character other than *z*.

```
> ant -Dregex="[^z]" -Dtext="z" regex-match
Regex=|[^z]|    Text=|z|    Matches=false
```

```
> ant -Dregex="[^z]" -Dtext="a" regex-match
Regex=|[^z]|    Text=|a|    Matches=true
```

Unlike the usual rules governing the logical operations disjunction, conjunction, and negation, the character class complementation operator binds more weakly than union. Thus, [^aeiou] picks out every character that is not an ASCII vowel.

Character classes may also be intersected. The syntax is the same as for logical conjunction, with [A&&B] picking out the characters that are in the classes denoted by both *A* and *B*. For instance, we could write [[a-z]&&[^aeiou]] to pick out all lowercase ASCII characters other than the vowels,

```
> ant -Dregex="[[a-z]&&[^aeiou]]" -Dtext="i" regex-match
Regex=|[[a-z]&&[^aeiou]]|    Text=|i|    Matches=false
```

As described in the Javadoc for `Pattern`, the order of attachment for character class operations is

Order	Expression	Example
1	Literal Escape	`\x`
2	Grouping	`[...]`
3	Range	`0-9`
4	Union	`ace`
5	Intersection	`a-z&&[^aeiou]`

Thus, the square brackets act like grouping parentheses for character classes. As mentioned earlier, within square brackets `union` is implicit whereas otherwise concatenation is implicit.

Complementation must be treated separately. Complementation applies only to character groups or ranges and must be closed within brackets before being combined with union or intersection or the scope may not be what you expect. For instance, `[^a[c-e]]` is not equivalent to `[^acde]` but rather is equivalent to `[[^a][c-e]]` and can be specified this way to avoid confusion.

4.6 Concatenating Regexes

The regexes in our very first examples consisted of concatenated characters, as we saw in section 4.1.1 using regexes such as aab. With a list of characters (or strings) being concatenated, the boundary case is the concatenation of an empty list (see section 4.2).

Two regular expressions x and y may be concatenated to produce a compound regular expression xy. The regex xy matches any string that can be decomposed into a string that matches x followed by a string that matches y. For example, if we have a regex `[aeiou]` that matches vowels and a regex `0-9` that matches digits, we can put them together to produce a regex that matches a vowel followed by a digit.

```
> ant -Dregex="[aeiou][0-9]" -Dtext="i7" regex-match
Regex=|[aeiou][0-9]|   Text=|i7|    Matches=true
```

Concatenation is associative, meaning that if we have three regexes x, y, and z, the regexes $(xy)z$ and $x(yz)$ match exactly the same set of strings. Because parentheses may be used for groups (see section 4.12), the two regexes do not always behave exactly the same way.

4.7 Disjunction

If x and y are regular expressions, the regular expression $x|y$ matches any string that matches either x or y (or both). For example,

```
> ant -Dregex="ab|cd" -Dtext="ab" regex-match
Regex=|ab|cd|     Text=|ab|      Matches=true

> ant -Dregex="ab|cd" -Dtext="cd" regex-match
Regex=|ab|cd|     Text=|cd|      Matches=true

> ant -Dregex="ab|cd" -Dtext="bc" regex-match
Regex=|ab|cd|     Text=|bc|      Matches=false
```

Concatenation takes precedence over disjunction, so that ab|cd is read as (ab)|(cd), not a(b|c)d.

The order of disjunctions doesn't matter for matching (other than for efficiency), but it matters for the find operation. For finds, disjunctions are evaluated left to right and the first match is returned.

```
> ant -Dregex="ab|abc" -Dtext="abc" regex-find
Found |ab| at (0,2)

> ant -Dregex="abc|ab" -Dtext="abc" regex-find
Found |abc| at (0,3)
```

Because complex disjunctions are executed through backtracking, disjunctions that have to explore many branches can quickly lead to inefficient regular expressions. Even a regex as short as (a|b)(c|d)(e|f) has $2^3 = 8$ possible search paths to explore. Each disjunction doubles the size of the search space, leading to exponential growth in the search space in the number of interacting disjunctions. In practice, disjunctions often fail earlier. For instance, if there is no match for a|b, further disjunctions are not explored.

4.8 Parentheses for Scoping

If *A* is a regular expression, (*A*) is a regular expression that matches exactly the same strings as *A*. Note that parentheses come in matched pairs, and each picks out the unique subexpression *A* it wraps.

Parentheses play the usual role of grouping in regular expressions and may be used to disambiguate what would otherwise be misparsed. For instance, the expression (a|b)c is very different from a|(bc), but the expressions gray|grey and gr(a|e)y are equivalent.

Parentheses also play the role of identifying the subexpressions they wrap. This is covered in section 4.12.

4.9   Greedy Quantifiers

There are operators for optionality or multiple instances that go under the general heading of "greedy" because they match as many times as they can. In this section, we explore the behavior of these greedy quantifiers. In the next section, we consider their "reluctant" counterparts that do the opposite.

4.9.1   Optionality

The simplest greedy quantifier is the optionality marker. The regex *A*? matches a string that matches *A* or the empty string. For example,

```
> ant -Dregex="a?" -Dtext="a" regex-match
Regex=|a?|    Text=|a|    Matches=true
```

```
> ant -Dregex="a?" -Dtext=\"\" regex-match
Regex=|a?|    Text=||    Matches=true
```

   The greediness of the basic optionality marker, which tries to match before trying to match the empty string, is illustrated using `regex-find`,

```
> ant -Dregex="a?" -Dtext="aa" regex-find
Found |a| at (0,1)    Found |a| at (1,2)    Found || at (2,2)
```

The first two substrings found are matches to a rather than to the empty string. Only when we are at position 2, at the end of the string, do we match the empty string because we can no longer match a.

   The greediness of optionality means that the *A*? behaves like the disjunction (*A*|) of *A* and the empty string. Because it is the first disjunct, a match against *A* is tried first.

4.9.2   Kleene Star

A regular expression *x* may have the Kleene-star operator[2] applied to it to produce the regular expression *A*∗. The regex *A*∗ matches a string if the string is composed of a sequence of zero or more matches of *A*. For example, [01]∗ matches any sequence composed only of 0 and 1 characters,

```
> ant -Dregex="[01]*" -Dtext="00100100" regex-match
Regex=|[01]*|    Text=|00100100|    Matches=true
```

It will also match the empty string but will not match a string with any other character.

   Using find, the standard Kleene-star operation is greedy in that it consumes as much as it can during a `find()` operation. For example, consider

---

[2] Named after Stephen Kleene, who invented regular expressions as a notation for his characterization of regular languages.

```
> ant -Dregex="[01]*" -Dtext="001a0100" regex-find
Found |001| at (0,3)    Found || at (3,3)
Found |0100| at (4,8)   Found || at (8,8)
```

The first result of calling `find()` consumes the expression [01] as many times as possible, consuming the first three characters, 001. After that, the expression matches the empty string spanning from 3 to 3. It then starts at position 4, finding 0100 and then the empty string again after that. Luckily, `find()` is implemented cleverly enough that it returns the empty string only once.

Kleene star may also be understood in terms of disjunction. The greedy Kleene star regex *A** behaves like the disjunction of *A*(*A**) and the empty regex. Thus, it first tries to match *A* followed by another match of *A** and only failing that tries to match the empty string. For instance, the two regexes in the following patterns match exactly the same strings.

```
Pattern p1 = Pattern.compile("(xyz)*");
Pattern p2 = Pattern.compile("(xyz(xyz)*)|");
```

Kleene star interacts with disjunction in the expected way. For example, matching consumes an entire string, as with

```
> ant -Dregex="(ab|abc)*" -Dtext="abcab" regex-match
Regex=|(ab|abc)*|    Text=|abcab|    Matches=true
```

while finding returns only an initial match,

```
> ant -Dregex="(ab|abc)*" -Dtext="abcab" regex-find
Found |ab| at (0,2)    Found || at (2,2)
Found |ab| at (3,5)    Found || at (5,5)
```

This is a result of the greediness of the Kleene-star operator and the evaluation order of disjunctions. If we reorder, we get the whole string because we first match abc against the disjunction and then continue trying to match (abc|ab)*, which matches ab.

```
> ant -Dregex="(abc|ab)*" -Dtext="abcab" regex-find
Found |abcab| at (0,5)    Found || at (5,5)
```

4.9.3 Kleene Plus

The Kleene-plus operator is like the Kleene star but requires at least one match. Thus, *A*+ matches a string if the string is composed of a sequence of one or more matches of *A*. The Kleene-plus operator may be defined in terms of Kleene star and concatenation, with *A*+ behaving just like *AA**. Use Kleene plus instead of star to remove those pesky empty string matches.

```
> ant -Dregex="(abc|ab)+" -Dtext="abcab" regex-find
Found |abcab| at (0,5)
```

4.9.4 Match Count Ranges

We can specify an exact number or a range of possible numbers of matches. The regular expression $A\{m\}$ matches any string that may be decomposed into a sequence of m strings, each of which matches A.

```
> ant -Dregex="a{3}" -Dtext="aaa" regex-match
Regex=|a{3}|    Text=|aaa|     Matches=true
```

There is similar notation for spans of counts. The regex $A\{m,n\}$ matches any string that may be decomposed into a sequence of between m (inclusive) and n (inclusive) matches of A. The greediness comes in because it prefers to match as many instances as possible. For example,

```
> ant -Dregex="a{2,3}" -Dtext="aaaaa" regex-find
Found |aaa| at (0,3)     Found |aa| at (3,5)
```

The first result found matches the regex a three times rather than twice.

There is also an open-ended variant. The regex $A\{m,\}$ matches any string that can be decomposed into m or more strings, each of which matches A.

4.10 Reluctant Quantifiers

There are a range of reluctant quantifiers that parallel the more typical greedy quantifiers. For matching, the reluctant quantifiers behave just like their greedy counterparts, whereas for find operations, reluctant quantifiers try to match as little as possible.

The reluctant quantifiers are written like the greedy quantifiers followed by a question mark. For instance, $A*?$ is the reluctant version of the Kleene-star regex $A*$, $A\{m,n\}?$ is the reluctant variant of the range regex $A\{m,n\}$, and $A??$ is the reluctant variant of the optionality regex $A?$.

Reluctant quantifiers may be understood by reversing all the disjuncts in the definitions of the greedy quantifier equivalents. For instance, we can think of $A??$ as $(\,|A)$ and $A*?$ as $(\,|AA*?)$.

Here we repeat some key examples of the previous section using reluctant quantifiers.

```
> ant -Dregex="a??" -Dtext="aa" regex-find
Found || at (0,0)     Found || at (1,1)     Found || at (2,2)
```

```
> ant -Dregex="(abc|ab)+?" -Dtext="abcab" regex-find
Found |abc| at (0,3)     Found |ab| at (3,5)
```

```
> ant -Dregex="a{2,3}?" -Dtext="aaaaa" regex-find
Found |aa| at (0,2)     Found |aa| at (2,4)
```

4.11   Possessive Quantifiers

The third class of quantified expression is the possessive quantifier. Possessive quantifiers will not match a fewer number of instances of their pattern if they can match more. Procedurally, they commit to a match once they've made it and do not allow backtracking.

The syntax for a possessive quantifier follows the quantifier symbol with a plus sign (+); for instance, ?+ is possessive optionality and *+ is greedy Kleene star. Consider the difference between a greedy Kleene star

```
> ant -Dregex="[0-9]*1" -Dtext="1231" regex-match
Regex=|[0-9]*1|    Text=|1231|     Matches=true
```

which matches, and a possessive Kleene star,

```
> ant -Dregex="[0-9]*+1" -Dtext="1231" regex-match
Regex=|[0-9]*+1|    Text=|1231|     Matches=false
```

which does not match. Even though [0-9]* indicates a greedy match, it is able to back off and match only the first three characters of the input, 123. The possessive quantifier, once it has matched 1231, does not let it go, and the overall match fails.

4.11.1   Independent Group Possessive Marker

If *A* is a regex, then (?>A) is a regex that matches the same thing as *A* but groups the first match possessively. That is, once (?>A) finds a match for *A*, it does not allow backtracking. We can see this with a pair of examples.

```
> ant -Dregex="(?>x+)xy" -Dtext="xxy" regex-match
Regex=|(?>x+)xy|    Text=|xxy|     Matches=false
```

This doesn't match, because the x+ matches both instances of *x* in the text being matched and doesn't allow backtracking. Contrast this with

```
> ant -Dregex="(?>x+)y" -Dtext="xxy" regex-match
Regex=|(?>x+)y|    Text=|xxy|     Matches=true
```

The parentheses in this construction do not count for grouping (see section 4.12).

4.12   Parentheses, Groups, and Capturing

Parentheses come in matched pairs, and each picks out the unique subexpression *A* it wraps. The pairs of parentheses in a regular expression are numbered from left to right, beginning with 1. There is an implicit pair of parentheses around the entire pattern, with group number 0. The identities of the groups are used for pulling out substring matches. They are also used as back references in regexes (see section 4.12.1) and for replace operations based on regexes (see section 4.1.3). The following example shows how this numbering works:

```
a(b(cd)(e))
 0 1 2   3
```

We have lined up the identifier of each parentheses group with the opening paren. Group 1 is b(cd)(e), group 2 is cd, and group 3 is e. The entire expression is group 0.

The Matcher class contains the method group(int), which picks out the subsequence of match captured by the specified group number. The group() method is equivalent to group(0). The start and end position of a group may also be retrieved, using start(int) and end(int). The methods start() and end() are just shorthand for start(0) and end(0). If there hasn't been a match or the last find did not succeed, attempting to retrieve groups or positions raises an illegal state exception.

The example class RegexGroup builds on RegexMatch in that it takes a pattern and a string as arguments and looks for a match. If the string matches the pattern, it prints out all capturing groups.

```
if (matcher.matches()) {
    int ct = matcher.groupCount();
    for (int i = 0; i<=ct; i++) {
        String found = matcher.group(i);
        int start = matcher.start(i);
        int end = matcher.end(i);
```

When we use this program to match the string abcde against the pattern a(b(cd)(e)), the result corresponds to our numbering above.

```
> ant -Dregex="a(b(cd)(e))" -Dtext="abcde" regex-group
Group: 0 captures: |abcde| at (0,5)
Group: 1 captures: |bcde| at (1,5)
Group: 2 captures: |cd| at (2,4)
Group: 3 captures: |e| at (4,5)
```

A typical linguistic example would be to look for the word *Mr* and try to get the following name. We consider a few examples and concoct the following regex: Mr((\s(\p{Lu}\p{L}*))+). This regex specifies that after the *Mr* we expect to find a series of initials or proper names. The innermost regex (\p{Lu}\p{L}*), group 3, specifies an uppercase letter followed by zero or more letters. Group 2 consists of whitespace followed by group 3. Group 1 consists of one or more of these.

```
> ant -Dregex="Mr((\s(\p{Lu}\p{L}*))+)" -Dtext="Mr J Smith"\
> regex-group
Group: 0 captures: |Mr J Smith| at (0,10)
Group: 1 captures: | J Smith| at (2,10)
Group: 2 captures: | Smith| at (4,10)
Group: 3 captures: |Smith| at (5,10
```

The captured input associated with a group is always the subsequence that the group most recently matched. Therefore, in this example, group 3 matches just the surname and group 2 matches the surname and the whitespace immediately preceding it. Try running this example with the text *Mr JJ John Jacob Jingleheimer Schmidt.*

This regex is relatively brittle. A more complex regex would deal with the extra leading space, allow optional periods after the *Mr* with the appropriate escape, and also deal with periods in names. Matching complicated patterns with regexes is a tricky business.

4.12.1 References to Capturing Groups

The regex \n is a back reference to the match of the *n*-th capturing group before it. We can use matching references to find pairs of duplicate words in text. For instance, consider

```
> ant -Dregex="(\d+).*(\1)" -Dtext="10 out of 10" regex-group
Group: 0 captures: |10 out of 10| at (0,12)
Group: 1 captures: |10| at (0,2)
Group: 2 captures: |10| at (10,12)
```

The regex \1 will match whatever matched group 1. Group 1 is (\d+), and group 2 is (\1); both match the expression *10*, only at different places. The text *9 out of 10* doesn't match.

```
> ant -Dregex="(\d+).*(\1)" -Dtext="9 out of 10" regex-group
Regex=|(\d+).*(\1)|
Text=|9 out of 10|
Not matched
```

If the match index is out of bounds for the number of groups, matching fails without raising an exception.

Here is a more complex regex that finds and displays the version number on a jarfile:

```
> ant -Dregex="(\w+)\-([\d\.]+)\.jar" -Dreplacement='\$1.jar v\$2'\
> -Dtext="foo-7.6.jar" regex-replace
```

```
regex=|(\w+)\-([\d\.]+)\.jar|
replacement=|$1.jar v$2|
text=|foo-7.6.jar|
result=|foo.jar v7.6|
```

Note that we had to escape the literal hyphen and period characters in the regex. Furthermore, we had to use single quotes and escape the group reference $n in order to prevent the shell from interpreting the references.[3] The class \w is for word characters, which are alphanumerics and the underscore.

Capturing groups can be referenced from within the `Matcher.replaceAll` method. The sequence $n references the n-th capturing group in the current match.[4]

```
matcher.replaceAll("$3");
```

In the linguistic example above, this statement changes *Mr J J Smith* to *Smith*. In general, this construction is used to mask or omit all of the matched text save for specific substrings.

4.12.2 Named References

As of Java 7, a capturing group can be assigned a name so that it can be back-referenced later by name instead of by number. The regex (?<NAME>A) specifies a capturing group with name *NAME* that matches regex *A*. Group names must start with a letter and may contain only ASCII letters and digits.

The regex \\k<NAME> can be used to reference this group within the regex. The sequence ${NAME} references the named group in the `replaceAll` method.

4.13 Non-capturing Regexes

Some regexes match virtual positions in an input without consuming any text themselves. Boundary matchers match specific sequences, but do not consume any input themselves. Non-capturing groups are enclosed by parentheses, but these parentheses aren't counted by the `Matcher.groupCount` method, nor can they be referenced.

4.13.1 Begin- and End-of-Line Matchers

The caret (^) is a regular expression that matches the end of a line, and the dollar sign ($) is a regular expression that matches the beginning of a line. For

---

[3]This is necessary for the Mac OS X Bash shell interpreter.
[4]Therefore, any occurrences of the character $ in the string argument to `replaceAll` must be escaped.

example,

```
> ant -Dregex="^abc$" -Dtext="abc" regex-match
Regex=|^abc$|    Text=|abc|    Matches=true

> ant -Dregex="ab$c" -Dtext="abc" regex-match
Regex=|ab$c|    Text=|abc|    Matches=false
```

The begin- and end-of-line regexes do not themselves consume any characters.

These begin-of-line and end-of-line regexes do not match newlines inside of strings unless the MULTILINE flag is set (see section 4.14.1). By default, these regexes match newline sequences for any platform (Unix, Macintosh, or Windows) and many more (see the table below). If the UNIX_LINES flag is set, they match only Unix newlines (see section 4.14.1).

Line Terminators and Unix Lines

Code Point(s)	Description	Java
U+000A	LINE FEED	\n
U+000D	CARRIAGE RETURN	\r
U+000D, U+000A	CARRIAGE RETURN,LINE FEED	\r\n
U+0085	NEXT LINE	\u0085
U+2028	LINE SEPARATOR	\u2028
U+2029	PARAGRAPH SEPARATOR	\u2029

4.13.2 Begin and End of Input

Because begin of line and end of line have variable behavior, there are regexes \A for the beginning of the input and \z for the end of the input. These will match the begin and end of the input no matter what the match mode is. For instance,

```
> ant -Dregex="\A(mnp)\z" -Dtext="mnp" regex-group
regex=|\A(mnp)\z|
text=|mnp|
Group  0=|mnp| at (0,3)
Group  1=|mnp| at (0,3)
```

Here we use the demp program RegexGroup which shows the positions at which the grouping parentheses match. We go into more detail on grouping in section 4.12.

4.13.3 Word Boundaries

The regex \b matches a word boundary and \B a non-word boundary, both
without consuming any input. Word boundaries are the usual punctuation and
spaces and the begin and end of input. For example,

```
> ant -Dregex="\b\w+\b" -Dtext="John ran quickly." regex-find
Found |John| at (0,4)
Found |ran| at (5,8)
Found |quickly| at (9,16)
```

4.13.4 Non-capturing Groups

Non-capturing regexes are enclosed by parentheses, but the parentheses aren't
counted as capturing groups. In all cases the opening parenthesis is immediately followed by a question mark. Note that named capturing groups (see
section 4.12.2) begin with a question mark; all other groups that begin with
a question mark are non-capturing. The regex (?>A) is one example (see section 4.11.1).

   If x is a regex, then (?:x) matches the same things as x, but the parentheses are not treated as capturing and so they aren't counted by the method
groupCount(). To see this, we re-run the match-group example in section 4.12, changing the expression a(b(cd)(e)) to a(b(?:cd)(e)):

```
> ant -Dregex="a(b(?:cd)(e))" -Dtext="abcde" regex-group
Regex=|a(b(?:cd)(e))|
Text=|abcde|
Group: 0 captures: |abcde| at (0,5)
Group: 1 captures: |bcde| at (1,5)
Group: 2 captures: |e| at (4,5)
```

4.13.5 Positive and Negative Lookahead

Often you want to match something only if it occurs in a given context. If
A is a regex, then (?=A) is the positive lookahead and (?!A) the negative
lookahead regular expression. These match a context that either matches or
doesn't match the specified regular expression. They must be used following
other regular expressions.

   One reason to use lookahead is that further finds can match the material
that the lookahead matched; this material is beyond the offset returned by
the Matcher.end method. The example class RegexFindVerbose shows how
a matcher consumes the input string.

```
matcher.appendReplacement(sb,"");
sb.setLength(0);
matcher.appendTail(sb);
```

We use the methods `Matcher.appendReplacement` and `appendTail` (see section 4.1.3) to get the input string from the matcher, using a `StringBuffer` for intermediate storage. We reset the length of the buffer to zero before calling the `appendTail` method, so that the only text we collect is the text that has not yet been consumed by the matcher.

If we want to find instances of numbers preceding periods, we specify

```
> ant -Dregex="\d+(?=\.)" -Dtext="12.3 45.6" regex-find-verbose
Regex=|\d+(?=\.)|
Text=|12.3 45.6|
matched: |12| at (0,2)
remaining: |.3 45.6|
matched: |45| at (5,7)
remaining: |.6|
```

How does this work? Positive lookahead finds the period. The matcher has only *looked* ahead. If we change this regex to \d+(\.) (without positive lookahead), we see that the match includes the period.

```
> ant -Dregex="\d+(\.)" -Dtext="12.3 45.6" regex-find-verbose
Regex=|\d+(\.)|
Text=|12.3 45.6|
matched: |12.| at (0,3)
remaining: |3 45.6|
matched: |45.| at (5,8)
remaining: |6|
```

To find numbers not preceding periods, we could use:[5]

```
> ant -Dregex='\d+(?!\.)' -Dtext="12.3" regex-find
Found |1| at (0,1)
Found |3| at (3,4)
```

4.13.6 Positive and Negative Lookbehind

There are backward-facing variants of the positive and negative lookahead constructs (?<=x) and (?<!x). These are more limited in that the regular expression *x* must expand to a simple sequence and thus may not contain

---

[5]Note the use of single quotes in order to prevent the shell from expanding the exclamation point character (!) in the negative lookahead regular expression.

the Kleene-star or Kleene-plus operations. They must be used preceding other regular expressions.

For example, the following example finds sequences of digits that do not follow periods or digits.

```
> ant -Dregex='(?<![\.\d+])\d+'-Dtext="12.3 .45 67" regex-find
Found |12| at (0,2)
Found |67| at (9,11)
```

In this example, the regular expression specifies a compound character class that consists of either a single period or any sequence of digits. The greedy quantifier + attaches to the character class \d.

4.14   Pattern Compilation

Pattern objects are immutable and therefore thread safe. Since all of the state of the matching of a regular expression against a string resides in the Matcher object, many matchers can and should share a compiled Pattern since this reuse has the potential to improve program efficiency.

4.14.1   Pattern Match Flags

In Figure 4.1 we list the set of flags, all represented as static integer constants in Pattern, that may be supplied to the pattern compiler factory method Pattern.compile(String,int) to control the matching behavior of the compiled pattern.

The flags are defined using a bit-mask pattern whereby multiple flags are set by taking their bitwise-or value.[6] For instance, the expression DOTALL | MULTILINE allows the wildcard to match anything and the line-terminator expressions to match internal newlines. More than two flags may be set this way, so we could further restrict to Unix newlines with DOTALL | MULTILINE | UNIX_LINES.

Even stronger matching than canonical equivalence with unicode case folding can be achieved by writing the regular expression using compatibility normal forms and using the ICU package to perform a compatibility decomposition on the input (see section 2.3.10).

---

[6]Although bitwise-or looks like addition for flags like these with only one bit on, it breaks down when you try to set flags twice. Thus, DOTALL + MULTILINE evaluates to the same thing as DOTALL | MULTINE, and DOTALL + DOTALL evaluates to the same thing as UNICODE_CASE, whereas DOTALL | DOTALL evaluates to the same thing as DOTALL.

Constant	Value	Description
DOTALL	32	Allows the wildcard (.) expression to match any character, including line terminators. If this mode is not set, the wildcard does not match line terminators.
MULTILINE	8	Allows the begin of line (^) and end of line ($) to match internal line terminators. If this is not set, they match only before the first and after the last character. The full Java notion of newline is used unless the flag UNIX_LINES is also set.
UNIX_LINES	1	Treat newlines as in Unix, with a single U+000A, LINE FEED, Java string escape \n, representing a newline. This affects the behavior of wildcard (.) and begin-of-line (^) and end-of-line ($) expressions.
CASE_INSENSITIVE	2	Matching is insensitive to case. Case folding is only for the ASCII charset (U+0000 to U+007F) unless the flag UNICODE_CASE is also set, which uses the Unicode definitions of case folding.
UNICODE_CASE	64	If this flag and the CASE_INSENSITIVE flag are set, matching ignores case distinctions as defined by Unicode case folding rules.
CANON_EQ	128	Matches are based on canonical equivalence in Unicode (see section 2.3.10).
LITERAL	16	Treats the pattern as a literal (i.e., no parsing).
COMMENTS	4	Allows comments in patterns and causes pattern-internal whitespace to be ignored.

Fig. 4.1: *Regex Pattern Match Flags*

4.14.2   Pattern Construction Exceptions

Attempting to compile a regular expression with a syntax error raises a runtime exception, `PatternSyntaxException` from the `java.util.regex` package. The parser tries to provide a helpful warning message. For instance, here's what we see if we inadvertently add a right parenthesis to our regex.

```
> ant -Dregex="aa)" -Dtext="aaab" regex-find
Exception in thread "main"
    java.util.regex.PatternSyntaxException:
    Unmatched closing ')' near index 1
```

4.15   Thread Safety, Serialization, and Reuse

4.15.1   Thread Safety

Because instances of `Pattern` are immutable, it is safe to use them concurrently in multiple threads. Because instances of `Matcher` contain the state of the current match, it is not thread safe to use matchers concurrently without synchronization.

4.15.2   Serialization

Patterns are serializable. The string representing the pattern and the compilation flags are stored and the version read back in is an instance of `Pattern` behaving just like the original. Often patterns do not need to be serialized because they're effectively singletons (i.e., constants).

4.15.3   Reusing Matchers

Matchers may be reused, although the typical usage pattern is to construct them for a text, use them once, and then discard them. When reusing matchers, the `reset()` method is called on a matcher to reset it to behave as if it had just been constructed with its given pattern and character sequence. The character sequence may be changed. The pattern may also be changed on the fly, without changing the current position. This may be useful if you alternately match first one pattern and then another.

4.16   String Methods That Use Regexes

There are many utility methods in the `String` class that are based on regular expressions.

The method `matches(String)` returns `true` if the string matches the regex specified by the argument. The call:

```
str.matches(regex)
```

yields exactly the same result as the expression:

```
Pattern.matches(regex, str)
```

The method `replaceAll(String,String)` takes as arguments a string representing a regex and a replacement string. It returns the result of replacing all the substrings in the string matching the regex with the replacement string. The call:

```
str.replaceAll(regex, repl)
```

yields exactly the same result as the expression:

```
Pattern.compile(regex).matcher(str).replaceAll(repl)
```

Therefore, the replacement may contain references to match groups.[7] There is also a corresponding `replaceFirst(String,String)` method. The call:

```
str.replaceFirst(regex, repl)
```

yields exactly the same result as the expression:

```
Pattern.compile(regex).matcher(str).replaceFirst(repl)
```

One of the more useful utilities is `split(String)`, which splits a string around the matches of a regular expression, returning an array as a result. For example, the call:

```
"foo12bar177baz".split(\d+)
```

splits on digits, returning the string array:

```
{ "foo", "bar", "baz" }
```

Note that the matching numbers are removed.

The method `split(String,int)` takes a second `int` parameter that limits the number of times the pattern is applied and therefore controls the length of the resulting array. If the limit n is greater than zero, then the pattern will be applied at most n - 1 times, the array's length will be no greater than n, and the array's last entry will contain all input beyond the last matched delimiter. If n is less than zero, then the pattern will be applied as many times as possible and the array can have any length. If n is zero then the pattern will be applied as many times as possible, the array can have any length, and trailing empty strings will be discarded.

---

[7] If the replacement string contains backslashes (\) and dollar signs ($) that are intended to be treated as literal replacements, they must be quoted. Therefore, to replace all forward slashes in `String str` with a backslash, we write `str.replaceAll("/","\\\\")`.

The method `split(String)` is shorthand for `split(String,0)`. The call:

`str.split(regex,n)`

yields the same result as the expression:

`Pattern.compile(regex).split(str,n)`

Therefore, the call:

`str.split(regex)`

is equivalent to:

`Pattern.compile(regex).split(str,0)`

In the OpenJDK reference implementation of the `String` class, the methods `matches`, `replaceAll`, `replaceFirst`, and `split` all call the corresponding methods in the pattern class directly. Here is the implementation of the one-arg and two-arg `String.split` methods:

```
public String[] split(String regex) {
    return split(regex, 0);
}
public String[] split(String regex, int limit) {
    return Pattern.compile(regex).split(this, limit);
}
```

Each call to the `String.split` requires creating and compiling a new `Pattern` object as well as a `Matcher`.

4.17 Regexes for Dates and Times

In section 2.14.4 showed how to use the `java.text.SimpleDateFormat` class to parse a `String` into a `java.util.Date` object. We advise against trying to use Java regexes to parse date and time information from text. Use the `java.text` package classes instead!

Chapter 5

Character Data for the Web

In this chapter we examine the intersection of Java character encoding and web technologies by showing the processing steps involved in sending character data via HTTP between Java programs. The programs and data files for this chapter are in the example source code distribution subdirectory:

```
javabook/src/webchars
```

This directory contains an Ant `build.xml` file that has targets to compile and run the examples. The programs belong to package `com.colloquial.webchars`. The subdirectory `javabook/src/webchars/src` contains the Java source files.

5.1 Character Data Transport Via HTTP

The HTTP protocol is used to send data between web servers and clients. The notion of client and server is relative. The client sends an HTTP request to the server, and the server sends an HTTP response back to the client. Web browsers are but one kind of client. Data can be sent between many web services. Data interchange formats developed for data feeds include XML formats such as RSS, ATOM, as well as JSON, the Javascript Object Notation.

How is character data sent via HTTP? This is a misleading question. HTTP sends and receives streams of bytes via sockets. It is up to the client and server programs to map these bytes to characters. Without knowing the character set and encoding scheme used to generate these bytes, we cannot reliably interpret the data.

An HTTP message, whether a request or a response, consists of a header and an optional message body. HTTP/1.1 is the version of the protocol in common use today.

The header consists of a series of fields. A field is a key-value pair in clear text format separated by a colon character and terminated by a carriage-return line-feed (CR-LF). A field may have multiple values, in which case the values are separated by spaces therefore, a value may not contain spaces. The key must be ASCII text. Non-ASCII values are allowed provided they are encoded.[1] The header is terminated by a blank field, that is, two consecutive CR-LF sequences. The message body, if any, follows the header. Here is an example of the header of an HTTP request:

```
GET / HTTP/1.1[CRLF]
Host: colloquial.com[CRLF]
User-Agent: Web-sniffer/1.0.44 (+http://web-sniffer.net/)[CRLF]
Accept-Encoding: gzip[CRLF]
Accept: text/html,application/xhtml+xml;q=0.9,*/*;q=0.8[CRLF]
Accept-Language: en-US,en;q=0.5[CRLF]
Accept-Charset: ISO-8859-1,UTF-8;q=0.7,*;q=0.7[CRLF]
Cache-Control: no-cache[CRLF]
Referer: http://web-sniffer.net/[CRLF]
[CRLF]
```

And this is the header of the HTTP response

```
Status: HTTP/1.1 200 OK[CRLF]
Date: Mon, 22 Apr 2013 15:09:07 GMT[CRLF]
Server: Apache[CRLF]
Accept-Ranges: bytes[CRLF]
Content-Length: 868[CRLF]
Connection: close[CRLF]
Content-Type: text/html[CRLF]
[CRLF]
```

For text data, the header fields of interest are the `Content-Length` and `Content-Type` fields. The `Content-Length` field specifies the number of bytes in the body. The `Content-Type` field consists of a MIME type optionally followed by a semicolon followed by parameters of the form `attribute=value`. Here is an example of a `Content-Type` field with a `charset` parameter

```
Content-Type: text/html; charset=ISO-8859-4
```

This example specifies that message body is HTML encoded using ISO-8859-4, the Latin4 character set. The HTTP/1.1 protocol specifies that if the `Content-Type` field is missing from the header, the default MIME type is text/plain and the default character encoding is ISO-8859-1, Latin1 (see section 2.4.2).

---

[1] See Internet Engineering Task Force (IETF) RFC 5987 for details.

5.1.1 Using `java.net` for HTTP Requests and Responses

The `java.net` package contains classes used to implement networking applications. We start by using `java.net.URL` and `java.net.URLConnection` objects to send and receive HTTP requests and responses via the example class `EchoHttpHeader`.

```
URL url = new URL(args[0]);
URLConnection connection
    = (URLConnection)url.openConnection();
connection.connect();
```

First we create a URL object from the first command-line argument. If the argument doesn't start with a known protocol such as `http`, `ftp`, `file`, `jar`, or if it is null, the constructor will throw a `MalformedURLException`. Next we create a `URLConnection` by calling the `openConnection()` method on the URL object. Despite its name, this method doesn't connect to the specified website it just creates a `URLConnection` object, to which setup parameters and general request properties can be modified and added. When the `connect()` method is invoked, the request is sent and the remote object becomes available.

```
Map<String,List<String>> headerFields
    = connection.getHeaderFields();
```

The method `getHeaderFields` parses the HTTP header into a map of field names to values. The first line of the HTTP header is the `Status-Line`, which gives the HTTP-version, status-code, and reason-phrase, e.g., HTTP/1.1 200 OK. We run this program with the Wikipedia home page as the URL:

```
> ant -Durl="http://www.wikipedia.org" http-headers
URL: http://www.wikipedia.org
successful connection
HTTP Response header fields:
field name: null value: HTTP/1.0 200 OK
field name: Age value: 30
field name: Content-Length value: 46388
field name: Last-Modified value: Fri, 21 Dec ...
field name: X-Cache-Lookup values : HIT from ...
field name: Connection value: keep-alive
field name: Server value: Apache
field name: X-Cache values : HIT from cp1017.eqia...
field name: Cache-Control value: s-maxage=3600, ...
field name: X-Content-Type-Options value: nosniff
field name: Date value: Tue, 15 Jan 2013 21:13:43 GMT
field name: Vary value: Accept-Encoding
field name: Content-Type value: text/html; charset=utf-8
```

This is the universal Wikipedia page which consists of links to all the language-specific Wikipedias.

We run this program again, and this time we request the Japanese Wikipedia homepage, which has the URL http://ja.wikipedia.org:

```
> ant -Durl="http://ja.wikipedia.org" http-headers
URL: http://ja.wikipedia.org
successful connection
HTTP Response header fields:
field name: null value: HTTP/1.0 200 OK
field name: Age value: 139
field name: Content-Language value: ja
field name: Content-Length value: 86186
field name: Last-Modified value: Tue, 15 Jan 2013 ...
field name: Connection value: keep-alive
field name: X-Cache-Lookup values : MISS from cp1003.eqia...
field name: X-Cache values : MISS from cp1003.eqiad.wmnet, ...
field name: Server value: Apache
field name: X-Content-Type-Options value: nosniff
field name: Cache-Control value: private, s-maxage=0, ...
field name: Date value: Tue, 15 Jan 2013 21:13:05 GMT
field name: Vary value: Accept-Encoding,Cookie
field name: Content-Type value: text/html; charset=UTF-8
```

The field Content-Language is specified for the Japanese home page but not for the universal Wikipedia page. The contents of these pages are different; and this is reflected in the different values for the Content-Length field. Both pages have the same Content-Type value: text/html; charset=UTF-8. Using a UTF encoding means that the message body may contain all the widely used characters in most of the world's languages. On my browser, most of the Wikipedia languages display in their proper font, excepting a few uncommon ones such as Dhivehi and Gutisk.

We use the header information to process the message body. The example class EchoHttpBody retrieves the bytes from the message body and uses the charset parameter in the Content-Type field to convert them to characters. This program reads in the URL from the command line and creates a URLConnection, as in the previous example. Next it looks for the Content-Type field and parses out the charset name.

```
String charset = "ISO-8859-1";
String contentType =
    connection.getContentType();
if (contentType != null) {
    Pattern pattern = Pattern.compile(".*charset=(.*)");
    Matcher matcher = pattern.matcher(contentType);
```

```
    if (matcher.matches()) {
        charset = matcher.group(1);
    }
}
```

The convenience method URLConnection.getContentType() returns the entire contents of the Content-Type field. We use a simple regex to extract the value of the charset parameter. If no header field is present or the charset parameter is not specified, then the encoding defaults to Latin1.

```
InputStream in = connection.getInputStream();
ByteArrayOutputStream bytesOut = new ByteArrayOutputStream();
int b;
while ((b = in.read()) != -1) {
    bytesOut.write((byte)b);
}
in.close();
byte[] respBytes = bytesOut.toByteArray();
bytesOut.close();
String respString = new String(respBytes,charset);
```

Next we read in the bytes from the body and convert them to a string using the specified charset to correctly map bytes to characters.

```
OutputStreamWriter charsetWriter
    = new OutputStreamWriter(System.out, charset);
PrintWriter out
    = new PrintWriter(charsetWriter, true);
out.println(respString);
```

In order to write this string to the terminal we need to use a java.io.Writer that has the same character encoding as that of the string. We construct one using Java's Standard.out, which is a PrintStream that writes to the standard output stream. To demonstrate, we use this program to fetch the French Wikipedia home page, which has the URL http://fr.wikipedia.org:

```
> ant -Durl="http://fr.wikipedia.org" http-body
URL: http://fr.wikipedia.org
Content-Type: text/html; charset=UTF-8
charset: UTF-8
HTTP Response body:
<!DOCTYPE html>
<html lang="fr" dir="ltr" class="client-nojs">
<head>
<meta charset="UTF-8" />
<title>Wikipédia, l'encyclopédie libre</title>
```

The first four lines of output are diagnostics printed by the `EchoHttpBody` program itself. The rest of the output is the HTML for the French Wikipedia homepage. We only show the first several lines of HTML for this page.

5.2 MIME Types and the `charset` Parameter

MIME types are specified as type/subtype pairs optionally, followed by a parameter. MIME type `text/*` includes type/subtypes:

```
text/plain
text/html
text/xml
```

It may take a `charset` parameter. The MIME-type standard[2] specifies that the default `charset` parameter for type `text` is ASCII (see section 2.4.1).

The type `text/xml` is a legacy type; for XML data the type `application/xml` is preferred. Data in a defined dialect of XML are specified accordingly. For example, RSS feed data should be of type `application/rss+xml`. Examples of MIME-types for XML and dialects of XML include:

```
application/xml
application/rss+xml
application/xhtml+xml
```

The MIME type `application/xml` and the MIME types for other XML dialects can take an optional `charset` parameter. If no `charset` parameter is present, then it is up to the application to guess the character encoding used based on rules laid out in the XML 1.0 Recommendation. See `http://www.w3.org/TR/REC-xml/#sec-guessing`.

5.2.1 MIME Type `application/x-www-form-urlencoded`

The MIME type `application/x-www-form-urlencoded` is so named because it is the default encoding used by the browser to send a POST request from a web form element. This encoding allows URLs that contain non-ASCII characters to be sent via an HTTP request.

A URL encoded string contains only alphanumeric ASCII characters plus the characters hyphen, underscore, period, and asterisk. The percent character is allowed but is interpreted as the start of a special escaped sequence. To encode a string, spaces are converted to '+' and all other characters are converted by taking their byte value (the UTF-8 character encoding is recommended) and

---

[2]The MIME-type standard available from: `http://www.ietf.org/rfc/rfc2046.txt`.

converting each byte to the sequence *%xy*, where *xy* corresponds to the two-digit hex value of the 8 bits. Because the percent character is meaningful, if it occurs in the data, it will be URL encoded as %25.

The `Java.net` package contains two convenience classes, `URLEncoder` and `URLDecoder`, which provide static methods to encode and decode strings. The example class `EncodeDecodeUrl` encodes and decodes a string.

```
String s1 = "\u00c0 votre sant\u00e9!";
String s2 = URLEncoder.encode(s1,"UTF-8");
String s3 = URLDecoder.decode(s2,"UTF-8");
```

We construct the string literal *À votre santé* using the hexadecimal representation of the Unicode code points for the non-ASCII characters. We use the static method `URLEncoder.encode` to create a URL-encoded version and then decode that. Finally we print out all three strings, using a `PrintWriter` whose character encoding is UTF-8.

```
> ant url-encode
string: À votre santé!
url encoded: %C3%80+votre+sant%C3%A9%21
decoded: À votre santé!
```

5.3 XML

In this section we focus on processing text data in XML documents. There are many good books on XML processing. We particularly recommend *Java and XML* by McLaughlin et al. published by O'Reilly.

5.3.1 XML Character Encoding

The character encoding used for the XML document is of primary importance. It is specified in the opening XML declaration, e.g.,

```
<?xml version="1.0" encoding="UTF-8" ?>
```

The encoding declaration is optional. The default character encoding is UTF-8.

XML was designed for Unicode data. Even if the document's declared encoding is a legacy encoding such as Latin1 (ISO-8859-1), the document can contain any legal Unicode character. Characters outside of the declared encoding can be represented by numerical character references (NCR) or predefined entity references, which we discuss in this section.

When XML is sent as the body of an HTTP message, the HTTP `Content-Type` header should match the declared encoding. If the HTTP `Content-Type` header is unspecified, the message body encoding defaults to

Latin1. If the body is decoded using the wrong character encoding, then either the message may be corrupted or an exception may be thrown.

Allowed Characters

As we saw in section 2.3, not all Unicode characters are legal XML characters. ASCII control characters are not legal Unicode, excepting tab, carriage return, and line feed. XML also disallows some Unicode characters in the surrogate code blocks. XML documents that have been created from non-UTF data, such as legacy data encoded in Latin1 (ISO-8859-1) or Windows-1252, may sometimes contain characters that fall outside of the allowed values. This is likely to cause a parser error, especially if the legacy character encoding is not declared in the opening XML declaration.

Characters and Entity References

XML entity references are used in place of characters, either as a way of escaping reserved characters that would otherwise be interpreted as markup or when the character symbol is not available. The XML syntax markers cannot be used as regular characters in text; use the following set of predefined entities instead: < for < (open tag), > for > (close tag), & for &, ' for ' (single quote), and &quot for " (double quote).

Many other characters have named entity references. The full list of entity definitions for characters is maintained by the W3C and is available from:

```
http://www.w3.org/TR/xml-entity-names/
```

All permitted Unicode characters may be represented with a numeric character reference. The numerical character reference is the value of the Unicode code point expressed in either decimal or hex, prefixed by ampersand and followed by a semicolon. Decimal values start with # (hashcode), and hexadecimal values start with #x. For example, the Greek capital letter Sigma has Unicode code point U+03A3 (hex value 3A3, decimal value 931). In XML (and HTML) this is written as either Σ, Σ, Σ, or Σ.

Parsed and Unparsed Character Data

An XML document must contain a single top-level element. Within this element, text is either character data or markup. The markup consists of the angle brackets (<>) and the names inside them. All text that is not markup is character data.

By default, XML processors parse all text in an XML document in order to find markup and entity references. CDATA is unparsed character data within an XML element. A CDATA section starts with <![CDATA[and ends with]]>.

Nested CDATA sections are not allowed. The sequence]]> is always inter-preted as the close of a CDATA section. If this sequence occurs in the text itself, it must be placed outside of the CDATA section, and if more text fol-lows, then a new CDATA section is opened.

CDATA sections may be useful in situations where the contents of an ele-ment contain many instances of the XML syntax markers, for example, when the contents are a Javascript or HTML fragments. In a CDATA sections, these characters can be used directly, instead of using entity references. However, because the CDATA contents are unparsed, no entity references can be used. Thus, the contents of the CDATA section are restricted to only the legal XML characters in the declared encoding.

5.3.2 DOM and SAX APIs for XML

An XML document consists of a single top-level element that contains nested XML elements. There are two approaches to processing XML: DOM and SAX.

The DOM (Document Object Model) approach to XML maps the XML docu-ment into a tree structure and then navigates that tree. Once fully constructed, any part of the tree can be accessed and the structure of the tree itself can be modified. The DOM tree for large documents will require large amounts of memory.

SAX, the Simple API for Java, is an event-based sequential access parser API. It is a streaming interface. Applications using SAX receive event notifica-tions about the XML document being processed as each element and attribute are encountered in sequential order, starting at the top of the document and ending with the closing of the ROOT element. The application must imple-ment handlers to deal with the different events. SAX parsers can process XML in linear time and are memory efficient.

Here is the "Hello world" XML document:

```
<?xml version="1.0"?>
<!DOCTYPE foo SYSTEM "foo.dtd">
<foo><bar>Hello, world!</bar></foo>
```

An event-based parser treats this as a series of linear events that are reported to the calling application as

```
start document
start element: foo
start element: bar
characters: "Hello, world!"
end element: bar
end element: foo
end document
```

5.3.3   SAX Example: Trace Events and Get Characters

The example class TraceSaxEvents illustrates how the SAX parser/handler
pattern works. It uses the parsers and handlers in the org.xml.sax package
to report on parsing events, and it echoes all characters found in the elements
in that document.

```
static class TraceHandler extends DefaultHandler {
    public void characters(char[] cs, int start, int len) {
        System.out.println("characters: |"
                            + new String(cs,start,len)
                            + "|");
    }
    public void startDocument() {
        System.out.println("startDocument");
    }
    public void startElement(String namespaceURI,
                             String localName,
                             String qName,
                             Attributes atts) {
        System.out.println("startElement: " + qName);
    }
    public void endDocument() {
        System.out.println("endDocument");
    }
    public void endElement(String namespaceURI,
                           String localName,
                           String qName) {
        System.out.println("endElement: " + qName);
    }
}
```

First we create a class TraceHandler. The class DefaultHandler in package org.sax.xml.helpers provides default implementations for the callback
methods of the core SAX2 handler classes. The TraceHandler class overrides
the methods startDocument, endDocument, codestartElement, endElement,
and characters so that these events are reported to the console. The
characters method prints the characters enclosed by the vertical bar (|) char-
acter.

```
InputSource in = new InputSource(args[0]);
XMLReader reader = XMLReaderFactory.createXMLReader();
reader.setContentHandler(new TraceHandler());
reader.parse(in);
```

We use the XMLReaderFactory to get an XMLReader. We set the XMLReader's content handler to a new instance of TraceHandler. The XMLReader parses the input. The handler's callback methods are called as the parser encounters XML markup.

XML elements may contain text interleaved with other elements. The example source code distribution directory for this chapter includes the example data file sometext.xml that contains the following:

```
<?xml version="1.0"?>
<foo>
 tok1
 <bar> tok2 </bar>  tok3
 <bar> tok4
          tok5 </bar>
</foo>
```

We run TraceSaxEvents via the Ant target trace-sax. To specify the data file sometex.xml as the argument, we set a Java environment variable named url. The URL protocol for a local file is file://.

```
> ant trace-sax -Durl="file:///full/path/to/sometext.xml"
startDocument
startElement: foo
characters: |
 to|
characters: |k1
 |
startElement: bar
characters: | tok2 |
endElement: bar
characters: |  tok3
 |
startElement: bar
characters: | tok4
          tok5 |
endElement: bar
characters: |
 |
endElement: foo
endDocument
```

The XMLReader parses data from the InputSource as it becomes available. There are two consecutive callbacks to the characters method to retrieve the initial content that includes whitespace, the string *tok1*, another space plus a newline. All characters and whitespace that are outside of XML markup tags are returned by the characters method.

5.3.4   DOM Example: Encode Characters for XML

The example class `JDomGenerateXml` generates an XML document that contains text content in several languages. The character encoding is specified by the user. Depending on the specified encoding, different subsets of the character data must be escaped. This program uses the open-source API JDOM2 from `http://www.jdom.org` to create a document and write it out to disk. The JDOM2 jar file is included in the `lib` subdirectory of `javabook/src/webchars`. The Ant `build.xml` file includes this jar file in classpath specification.

This program takes two command-line arguments. The first argument specifies the character encoding and is stored as the `String` object `encoding`. The second argument the name of the output file and is stored as the `String` object `fileName`.

We construct an XML document in a top-down fashion by first creating the root XML element and adding it to a new XML document. The top-level element of this document is a `<toast_set>`. It contains multiple `<toast>` elements that have an attribute named `lang` and whose text content consists of a toast in the language.

```
Element root = new Element("toast_set");
Document document = new Document(root);
```

Then we add toasts in English, French, Russian, and Korean.

```
Element e1 = new Element("toast");
e1.setAttribute("lang","English");
e1.addContent(new Text(CHEERS));
root.addContent(e1);

Element e2 = new Element("toast");
e2.setAttribute("lang","French");
e2.addContent(new Text(SANTE));
root.addContent(e2);

Element e3 = new Element("toast");
e3.setAttribute("lang","Russian");
e3.addContent(new Text(NAZDROV));
root.addContent(e3);

Element e4 = new Element("toast");
e4.setAttribute("lang","Korean");
e4.addContent(new Text(GAMBAE));
root.addContent(e4);
```

These toasts are specified as `String` objects. Unicode escapes are used for all non-ASCII characters.

```
public static String CHEERS = "cheers!";
public static String SANTE = "sant\u00e9!";
public static String NAZDROV = "\u041d\u0430 " +
    "\u0437\u0434\u043e\u0440\u0432\u044c!";
public static String GAMBAE = "\uac74\ubc30!";
```

The following sequence of statements outputs this newly created XML document in an easy-to-read format:

```
Format format = Format.getPrettyFormat();
format.setEncoding(encoding);
FileOutputStream fileOut
    = new FileOutputStream(fileName);
OutputStreamWriter writer
    = new OutputStreamWriter(fileOut,encoding);
BufferedWriter bufWriter
    = new BufferedWriter(writer);
XMLOutputter outputter
    = new XMLOutputter(format);
outputter.output(document,bufWriter);
```

The `org.jdom2.output.XMLOutputter` outputs the contents of an XML document as a stream of bytes. A `org.jdom2.output.Format` object controls the encoding used to do this conversion. The method `setEncoding(String encoding)` overrides the default encoding. The encoding argument is also used to set the character encoding on the `OutputStreamWriter` that the `XMLOutputter` is writing to. This is necessary because a `Writer` configuration cannot be queried or controlled by the `XMLOutputter`.

`Format.getPrettyFormat()` returns a new `Format` object that performs whitespace beautification with 2-space indents, uses the UTF-8 encoding, doesn't expand empty elements, includes the declaration and encoding, and uses the default entity escape strategy. An escape strategy encapsulates the logic that determines which characters should be formatted as character entities. The set of syntax markers are always formatted as character entities (see section 5.3.1). The method `canEncode` in class `java.nio.charset.CharsetEncoder` is used to identify characters whose Unicode code point is not mapped into a character in the specified encoding (see section 2.12.2).

To see how entities are escaped under different encodings, we run `JDomGenerateXML` via the Ant target `gen-xml`. The Ant `build.xml` file uses the properties named `encoding` and `file` to specify the program arguments.

First we generate an XML file in UTF-8, then we count the total number of entity escapes. In the UTF-8 file, there are no character entity escapes because UTF-8 contains character mappings for all Unicode code points.

```
> ant gen-xml -Dencoding="UTF-8" -Dfile="enc-utf8.xml"
Encoding: UTF-8
Output file: enc-utf8.xml

> grep -o "\&#x" enc-utf8.xml | wc -l
     0
```

To count the number of escaped entities, we use the Unix command-line utilities grep and wc. We run grep over the output file looking for matches to the pattern \&#x, which is the prefix of a numerical character reference. The grep -o flag tells grep to print only the matching part of the line. This has the nice side effect that when the pattern matches multiple times in a line, all matches are printed out, one match per line. By piping the grep output through the wc utility with the -l flag, we get the total number of matches.

Next we generate an XML file with encoding ASCII and repeat our counting procedure.

```
> ant gen-xml -Dencoding="ASCII" -Dfile="enc-ascii.xml"
Encoding: ASCII
Output file: enc-ascii.xml

> grep -o "\&#x" enc-ascii.xml | wc -l
    11
```

The four different toasts contain a total of 11 characters outside of the ASCII range: one character in the French-language toast, the eight Cyrillic letters in the Russian-language toast, and the two ideographs in the Korean-language toast.

KOI8 is the legacy encoding for the Cyrillic alphabet. We repeat this exercise for this encoding.

```
> ant gen-xml -Dencoding="KOI8" -Dfile="enc-koi8.xml"
Encoding: KOI8
Output file: enc-koi8.xml

> grep -o "\&#x" enc-koi8.xml | wc -l
     3
```

The KOI8 encoding contains characters corresponding to the code points for ASCII and Cyrillic characters but not é or the two Korean ideographs.

5.4 HTML

HTML is a markup language used for documents sent via HTTP from web servers to web browsers (or other web clients, collectively known as User-Agent programs). Bytes are sent via HTTP; characters are displayed by the browser.

HTML meta-tags are used either to emulate the use of the HTTP response header or to embed additional metadata within the HTML document. These tags have the form `<meta http-equiv="foo" content="bar">`. In the following example these tags emulate the `charset` parameter of the `Content-Type` header field:

```
<meta http-equiv="Content-Type" content="text/html; charset=UTF-8">
<meta charset="UTF-8">
```

However, the browser controls the character encoding. Even if the `charset` information is present in the HTTP response header or in metadata tags in the HTML document itself, the browser can choose to ignore or override it.

5.4.1 HTML Character and Entity References

As in XML, the characters that are syntax markers cannot be used directly in text, and the corresponding predefined entities must be used instead: `&lt;` for < (open tag), `&gt;` for > (close tag), `&amp;` for &, `&apos;` for ' (single quote), and `&quot` for " (double quote). The HTML specification defines a large set of character entity references:

```
http://www.w3.org/TR/html4/sgml/entities.html
```

```
http://www.w3.org/TR/html5/syntax.html#named-character-references
```

Numeric character references may also be used. The numerical character reference is the value of the Unicode code point expressed in either decimal or hex, prefixed by an ampersand and followed by a semicolon. This is the same format used for XML numeric character references (see section 5.3.1).

```
<html>
<head>
<meta http-equiv="Content-Type" content="text/html; charset=UTF-8">
</head>
<body>
<h4>Hello World in Japanese</h4>
<ul>
  <li>escaped HTML: &#x4eca;&#x65e5;&#x306f;&#x4e16;&#x754c;!
  <li>plain text: 今日は世界!
</ul>
</body>
</html>
```
```
U:--- hello_jp.html  All (9.0)  SVN:1023  (Fundamental)
```

Fig. 5.1: *Contents of page* `hello_jp.html`

We use the example HTML page `hello_jp.html` to explore the behavior of the browser, which is included with the source code for example programs for this chapter. Figure 5.1 shows the contents of this web page as displayed by the emacs editor. This web page contains two different ways of creating a web page that displays the Japanese word for *hello*. First we use numeric character references for the hex value of the Unicode code points of each character. Next we just include the Japanese characters as regular text.[3] Figure 5.2 shows

```
Hello World in Japanese

  • escaped HTML: 今日は世界!
  • plain text: ä»Šæ—Ÿā¯ä¸ç·Œ!
```

Fig. 5.2: *Viewing* `hello_jp.html` *in a browser using encoding ISO-8859-1*

the contents of this web page as displayed in a web browser after using the browser controls to set the character encoding to ISO-8859-1. The browser ignores the HTML meta-tags. The first version of Japanese "hello" displays correctly, while the plain-text version is seriously corrupted.

While the safest way to insure that character data always renders correctly is to use entity references for all non-ASCII characters, this approach has several drawbacks: the web page is all but unreadable outside of a browser, a numeric character reference uses five characters to encode a single character, and the browser has to do more work to render a page.

5.4.2   Parsing HTML

Parsing HTML documents is challenging because although standards have been developed for HTML, they are often not met. Therefore, applications that mine HTML documents for text data must be able to handle ill-formed HTML. When we need to extract text data from an HTML document, we use the NekoHTML parser.

NekoHTML is a simple HTML scanner and tag balancer. It can handle (some but not all) missing and mismatched element tags. NekoHTML is distributed under the Apache 2.0 license. It can be downloaded from

```
http://nekohtml.sourceforge.net/
```

NekoHTML is written using the Apache Project's Xerces Native Interface (XNI).[4] The NekoHTML binary distribution includes jar files for Xerces as well. The jar file `xercesMinimal.jar` contains only those classes that are needed for

---

[3]This word and its unicode encoding are taken from chapter 13 of *Java Servlet Programming, Second Edition*, by Jason Hunter, O'Reilly Books. See example 13-5 and figure 13-4, *A Japanese hello*

[4]See `http://xerces.apache.org/xerces2-j/xni.html` for details.

NekoHTML. Both `nekohtml.jar` and `xercesMinimal.jar` are included in the `lib` subdirectory of `javabook/src/webchars`, and the Ant `build.xml` file includes them in the classpath specification.

NekoHTML provides convenience classes for both DOM and SAX parsers. The demo class `NekoHtmlParse` uses the class `DOMParser` in package `org.cyberneko.html.parsers`.

```
DOMParser parser = new DOMParser();
parser.parse(args[0]);
printTextNodes(parser.getDocument());
```

The `main` method of `NekoHtmlParse` reads in the name of an HTML file from the command line, instantiates a DOM parser, and calls the `parse(String)` method to parse the HTML document into a DOM tree, and then it calls a helper method `printTextNodes(Node)` that walks over a DOM tree and prints the results.

```
public static void printTextNodes(Node node) {
    if (Node.TEXT_NODE == node.getNodeType()
        && node.getTextContent().trim().length() > 0) {
        System.out.println(node.getParentNode().getNodeName());
        System.out.println("|" + node.getTextContent() + "|");
    }
    Node child = node.getFirstChild();
    while (child != null) {
        printTextNodes(child);
        child = child.getNextSibling();
    }
}
```

The method `printTextNodes(Node)` walks over all nodes in the DOM tree. When it finds a text node that contains non-whitespace text, it prints the name of the parent node and the text. We use the vertical bar symbol as a delimiter around the text to show how whitespace is processed.

The example source code distribution directory for this chapter includes the example HTML file `toast.html` that contains the following:

```
<html>
<head>
<meta http-equiv="Content-Type"
     content="text/html; charset=ISO-8859-1">
</head>
<body>
<p>In English we say: cheers!
<p>In French we say: santé
</body>
</html>
```

We run `NekoHtmlParse` via the Ant target `parse-html` using the Ant property `html.file` to specify the input file.

```
> ant parse-html -Dhtml.file=toast.html
P
|In English we say: cheers!
|
P
|In French we say: santé

|
```

This example explicitly specifies a character encoding using HTML meta-tags. If this encoding is missing, NekoHTML will use the default encoding Windows-1252.

The demo class `NekoHtmlEncoding` shows how to explicitly specify both the default encoding and whether or not to use the encoding specified by the HTML meta-tags by setting properties on the parser. Like `NekoHtmlParse`, `NekoHtmlEncoding` uses a DOM Parser to process an HTML file. It takes an additional command-line argument that specifies the encoding used by the parser.

```
String encoding = args[1];
parser.setFeature("http://cyberneko.org/html/features/scanner/"
                +"ignore-specified-charset",
                true);
parser.setProperty("http://cyberneko.org/html/properties/"
                +"default-encoding",
                encoding);
```

The call to the parser's `setFeature` method tells it to ignore the encoding specified by any HTML meta-tags. The call to `setProperty` sets the new default encoding.

We run `NekoHtmlEncoding` via the Ant target `parse-encoding` using the Ant property `html.file` to specify the input file and the property `encoding` to specify the encoding. `NekoHtmlEncoding` reports the encoding used to parse the document and then prints the text, as in NekoHtmlParse.

```
> ant parse-encoding -Dhtml.file=toast.html -Dencoding=ASCII
```

When the encoding is set to ASCII, the final letter *é* of *santé* is outside of the ASCII character set and so NekoHTML replaces it with the missing character symbol, a question mark inside a black diamond.

5.5 JSON

JavaScript Object Notation (JSON) is a lightweight, text-based, language-independent data interchange format. It defines a small set of formatting rules for the portable representation of structured data. The JSON format is described in this RFC

```
http://tools.ietf.org/html/rfc4627
```

The website `http://json.org/` provides a good introduction to JSON and also lists tools and packages for many different programming languages. In this section we use the `org.json` package from JSON-java, Douglas Crockford's free reference implementation. JSON-java's license specifies that "the Software shall be used for Good, not Evil." Full details are available here:

```
http://www.json.org/license.html
```

The source code can be downloaded from:

```
https://github.com/douglascrockford/JSON-java
```

A jar file compiled from this source is included in the `lib` subdirectory of `javabook/src/webchars`. The Ant `build.xml` file includes this jar file in classpath specification.

5.5.1 JSON Syntax

JSON has four primitive types: strings, numbers, booleans, and *null*. It allows two data structures: objects and arrays. An array is an ordered sequence of zero or more values. An JSON object consists of zero or more name-value pairs. The corresponding Java object is `Map<String,Object>`, since the name must be a string and the value can be any JSON data type and the fields are unordered.

JSON consists of Unicode characters, and the default encoding is UTF-8. JSON has three literals: `null` and the boolean values `true` and `false`. JSON has six *structural characters*:

```
: , [ ] { }
```

The colon character is the separator between the name and value of an object. The comma is the separator between values in an object or array. The open and close square brackets are the array begin and end symbols, and the open and close curly brackets are the object begin and end symbols.

Strings are enclosed in double quotes. A string consists of zero or more Unicode characters. When a string contains double quotes or structural characters, these are escaped by the backslash \, as is the backslash character itself. Unicode characters may be written as is or as the hex value of the Unicode

code point preceded by \u. Unicode characters outside of the Basic Multilingual Plane must be written out as the UTF-16 surrogate pair. For example, a string containing only the G clef character (U+1D11E) is written "\uD834\uDD1E".

Imagine that we have an application that registers personal information and uses JSON as the data interchange format. Here is an example of the external string representation of a JSON object for this application:

```
{ "name" : "fifty-cent",
  "nicknames" : [ "fiddy", "50\u00a2" ],
  "lucky_number" : 2.99792458e8,
  "phone" : [ { "h" : "212-555-1234" },
              { "m" : "646-555-5678" },
              { "f" : null } ] }
```

This object has four unordered member fields. The value of field name is a string. The value of field nicknames is an array of strings. The value of field lucky_number is a number in scientific notation. The value of field phone is an array of objects.

5.5.2 Generating Data in JSON Format

The example program GenJson creates a JSON object that contains the information in the above example.

```
JSONObject fiddy = new JSONObject();
fiddy.put("name","fifty-cent");
JSONArray nicknames = new JSONArray();
nicknames.put("fiddy");
nicknames.put("50\u00a2");
fiddy.put("nicknames",nicknames);
```

The process of creating a JSON object is straightforward. We make successive calls to the 0-arg constructors of JSONObject and JSONArray. There are several put methods defined for both JSONObject and JSONArray. The put methods for JSONObject add a key/value pair to the object. The put methods for JSONObject add another value to the array.

```
JSONObject phoneFax = new JSONObject();
phoneFax.put("f",JSONObject.NULL);
```

To add null values to a JSON object, we use the static member variable JSONObject.NULL. To pretty-print the newly constructed JSONObject, we use the toString(int) method to make a formated, indented version of this JSONObject where the integer argument specifies the number of spaces to add to each level of indentation. The Ant target gen-json runs this program.

```
> ant gen-json
```

```
{
 "phone": [
    {"h": "212-555-1234"},
    {"m": "646-555-5678"},
    {"f": null}
  ],
  "nicknames": [
    "fiddy",
    "50¢"
  ],
  "name": "fifty-cent",
  "lucky_number": 2.99792458E8
}
```

5.5.3 Processing JSON Data Sent via HTTP

JSON is used primarily to transmit data between a server and web applications.

The example program GetJson accesses a JSON data feed and processes the response. The data feed used for this example is the US Geological Survey's real-time Earthquake Feed for the past hour, updated every minute.

```
http://earthquake.usgs.gov/earthquakes/feed/v0.1/summary/
all_hour.geojson
```

The feed format is GeoJSON, which encodes geographic data structures.[5]

GetJson sends an HTTP request, processes the response, and then prints a summary of the number of earthquakes in the past 60 minutes.

```
URL url
    = new URL("http://earthquake.usgs.gov/earthquakes/"
                + "feed/v0.1/summary/all_hour.geojson");
HttpURLConnection conn
    = (HttpURLConnection)url.openConnection();
conn.setRequestMethod("GET");
conn.setRequestProperty("Accept","application/json");
conn.connect();
```

As in the other demo programs EchoHttpHeader and EchoHttpBody, we use classes from the java.net package for networking. In GetJson we use an HttpURLConnection object, which extends URLConnection. We set the request header field Accept to application/json, the MIME media type for JSON text.

---

[5] See http://www.geojson.org/geojson-spec.html for details.

```
String charset = "UTF-8";
String contentType = conn.getContentType();
```

We need to know the character encoding in order to process the body of the
HTTP response. As in EchoHttpBody, we check the HTTP response header field
Content-Type to see whether or not it contains a charset parameter that
specifies the character encoding. If none is found, we use UTF-8, the default
encoding for JSON.

```
String content
    = readFromStream(conn.getInputStream(),charset);
JSONTokener tokener = new JSONTokener(content);
JSONObject quakes = new JSONObject(tokener);
```

To parse the HTTP response body into a JSON object, we assemble the
bytes in the body of the response into a string. To do this we create an
InputStreamReader using the specified character encoding and wrap this in
a BufferedReader from which we retrieve the response body. We create a
JSONTokener for this string and then pass it in to the JSONObject constructor,
which uses the JSONTokener to parse the data into a JSONObject.

```
String geoType = quakes.getString("type");
System.out.println("geoJSON object type: " + geoType);
JSONArray results = quakes.getJSONArray("features");
System.out.println("number of quakes in past hour: "
                   + results.length());
```

We know that our data feed format is GeoJSON. According to the GeoJSON
specification, a GeoJSON object must have a member with the name type,
whose value is a string. From inspecting the contents of this feed, we know
that the type is FeatureCollection. An object of type FeatureCollection
has a member named features whose value is an array. Each array element
is an earthquake. We use the method JSONObject.getJSONArray(String) to
retrieve this array and the method JSONArray.length() to report the number
of earthquakes. The Ant target get-json runs this program.

```
> ant get-json
geoJSON object type: FeatureCollection
number of quakes in past hour: 1
```

Chapter 6

Case Study: Ad Hoc Parsing

More often than not, the format of existing text data doesn't match the input format required by some application. This is especially common when using legacy data with general-purpose tools. In these situations it may be necessary to write a program to reformat the data before proceeding. In this chapter we develop a program that takes a file of semi-structured text data and splits it into a set of XML files using classes and methods from the Java libraries covered in the preceding chapters.

Writing programs that transform data from one format to another is both time-consuming and boring nonetheless, getting it right is critical. When creating one-off, single-use programs, correctness and code readability trump efficiency. These programs must faithfully extract the information from the texts and avoid data corruption. Transforming the text programmatically instead of processing it by hand pays off in the long run as the program guarantees reproducible results and provides a record of the changes made.

6.1   Dataset: *The Federalist Papers*

Our example dataset is *The Federalist Papers*, a collection of 85 essays written by James Madison, Alexander Hamilton, and John Jay. This is a small but real example of a collection of natural language texts. Altogether, these essays contain roughly 190,000 word instances over a vocabulary of about 8,000 words. The essays range in length from 1,000 to 5,000 words and the median length is 2,100 words.

The `javabook` examples distribution contains a copy of the Project Gutenberg Etext file in the directory:

```
javabook/data/federalist-papers
```

The program files for this chapter are in the example source code distribution subdirectory:

```
javabook/src/casestudy
```

This directory contains an Ant `build.xml` file with targets to compile and run the examples. The programs are in package `com.colloquial.casestudy`, and the Java source files are in the `src` subdirectory.

Our demo program is in the file `FederalistParser.java`. It splits the Project Gutenberg Etext into a series of XML files, one per essay. This requires setting up the correct I/O objects, identifying the constituent elements using both simple string matching and regular expressions, and generating well-formed XML using the Java XML libraries. In subsequent chapters we will use the Apache Lucene search engine and the Solr search server to index these essays so that we can do full-text search over *The Federalist Papers* to identify the most relevant essays given a set of words or phrases.

6.2   The Domain Model

The Federalist Papers consists of 85 essays. The essays are numbered from 1 through 85. Each essay has a title, publication journal, publication date, either a single author or a pair of authors, and the text of the essay.

We define a class `Paper` to model this information, also in package `com.colloquial.casestudy`. The line numbers in the left margin correspond to the line numbers in the source code file `Paper.java`. Following the recommendations in Joshua Bloch's *Effective Java*, we have designed the `Paper` object to be *immutable* by making all member variables `final` so that its state cannot be changed after construction.

```
/** Paper:  domain model of a single federalist paper */
public class Paper {
    private final int mNumber;
    private final String mTitle;
    private final String mPubName;
    private final Date mPubDate;
    private final String mAuthor1;
    private final String mAuthor2;
    private final List<String> mParagraphs;
```

Following the *Builder Pattern* we define a static inner class `Builder`. The `Builder` class does the work of assembling the field values using a series of setter methods that can be chained together. The only way to construct a `Paper` object is by calling the `Builder.build()` method. The `Builder.build()` method performs completeness and consistency checks on the field values and returns a new `Paper` object if they are valid or `null` if they aren't.

```java
public static class Builder {
    private int number;
    private String title;
    private String pubName;
    private Date pubDate;
    private String author1;
    private String author2;
    private List<String> paragraphs;

    public Builder(String str) {
        number = -1;
        try {
            number = Integer.parseInt(str);
        } catch (NumberFormatException e) {
            // do nothing
        }
        paragraphs = new ArrayList<String>();
    }

    public boolean isValid() {
        if (number < 1
            || title == null
            || pubName == null
            || pubDate == null
            || author1 == null
            || paragraphs == null)
            return false;
        return true;
    }
    public Builder title(String str) {
        title = str; return this;
    }
    public Builder pubName(String str) {
        pubName = str; return this;
    }
    public Builder pubDate(String str) {
        if (str == null) return this;
        String pattern = "MMMMM dd, yyyy";
        SimpleDateFormat format
            = new SimpleDateFormat(pattern,Locale.ENGLISH);
        Date date = format.parse(str, new ParsePosition(0));
        pubDate = date; return this;
```

```
        }
        public Builder author1(String str) {
            author1 = str; return this;
        }
        public Builder author2(String str) {
            author2 = str; return this;
        }
        public Builder paragraphs(List<String> list) {
            paragraphs.addAll(list); return this;
        }
        public Paper build() {
            if (isValid())
                return new Paper(this);
            return null;
        }
    }
```

To get the publication data, shown in bold text above, we use a
`java.text.SimpleDateFormat` object to parse the publication date from the
text file into a `java.util.Date` object. We supply the constructor with a date
pattern and a `Locale` (see section 2.14.4). The publication date as found in the
Etext is in the form *month day, year*, e.g., `December 11, 1787`. This is specified as the `SimpleDateFormat` pattern:

```
MMMMM dd, yyyy
```

The method `parse` takes two arguments: the text string to parse and the position at which to begin parsing. It returns a `java.util.Date` object if the text
matches the pattern or `null` if it cannot match the pattern. The `null` value
will be caught by the `isValid` method. 3 The `Paper` constructor is a private
constructor that takes a single `Builder` argument.

```
    private Paper(Builder builder) {
        mNumber = builder.number;
        mTitle = builder.title;
        mPubName = builder.pubName;
        mPubDate = builder.pubDate;
        mAuthor1 = builder.author1;
        mAuthor2 = builder.author2;
        mParagraphs = builder.paragraphs;
    }
```

6.3 Input File Format

Some Project Gutenberg texts were typed in manually by volunteers; later texts were scanned in. This by-hand processing sometimes introduces format errors or inconsistencies. In this text, blank lines are used to separate logical units of text such as titles, header information, and paragraphs. But these blank lines are sometimes missing or doubled. There irregularities are not critical for a human reader but do add to the challenge of writing a program to parse the data. The Project Gutenberg page for *The Federalist Papers* is:

```
http://www.gutenberg.org/ebooks/1404
```

This page provides bibliographic information and download links to get the book in various formats. We have chosen to use the plain-text UTF-8 version for this example. The link to download this file is:

```
http://www.gutenberg.org/ebooks/1404.txt.utf-8
```

The downloaded file name is `pg1404.txt`. This file is in the directory `javabook/data/federalist-papers`. In order to process this file programmatically, it was necessary to correct a few irregularities. There is a `README.txt` file that documents these changes, as well as the original Etext file: `pg1404.txt.as.downloaded`.

The plain-text version consists of a header section, the book itself, and a footer section. The header contains general information about the book and this Project Gutenberg version. A special separator line divides the header from the book, and a similar separator divides the book from the footer. The footer contains information about the text, Project Gutenberg, and the Project Gutenberg license.

Each essay starts with a header that gives the essay number, followed by the title, publication, and author or authors,[1] followed by the opening salutation: *To the People of the State of New York*. The publication information consists of the name of the journal in which the essay appeared and the date of publication. Blank lines set off each element, but as noted above, these are sometimes missing or doubled. Blank lines separate paragraphs. The maximum line length is 74 characters. All lines begin at position 0. The first word of the opening paragraph is always uppercase. All proper nouns are capitalized and uppercase is used for some words and phrases. The individual essays don't have an end marker, so we know that we have reached the end of the essay only when we find either the beginning of the next essay or the end of the book. Here is the header for Federalist Paper 20:

---

[1] These essays were all published under the pen name *PUBLIUS* and the true authors were revealed many years later. Authorship of a few of the essays is uncertain as both Madison and Hamilton claimed to have written them. The Etext doesn't indicate how authorship was determined. Much research has been done on this problem. See Mosteller and Wallace, 1964, *Applied Bayesian and Classical Inference: The Case of the Federalist Papers.*

```
FEDERALIST No. 20

The Same Subject Continued (The Insufficiency of the Present
Confederation to Preserve the Union)

From the New York Packet. Tuesday, December 11, 1787.

MADISON, with HAMILTON

To the People of the State of New York:

THE United Netherlands are a confederacy of republics, or rather of
aristocracies of a very remarkable texture, yet confirming all the
lessons derived from those which we have already reviewed.
```

6.4 XML Format

The output of this program will be indexed by Lucene or Solr. Lucene is a
search library written in Java that provides search over documents and is covered in chapter 7. A document is a collection of fields, where a field consists
of a name and a value or values. We model each essay as a document. Each
document has fields number, title, pubName, pubDate, author, and text. We
use the essay number as the unique identifier for each document.

Solr is a search server that uses Lucene for indexing and search and is covered in chapter 8. Solr accepts several different document formats, including
XML. A Solr XML document consists of a `<doc>` element that contains zero
or more `<field>` elements. Each field element takes an attribute `name` whose
value is the name of the Solr field. The element text is the field value. In the
XML documents, the `name` attribute of the `<field>` element takes the values
`number`, `title`, `pubName`, `pubDate`, `author`, and `text`.

6.5 Processing Strategy

The requirements for this program are to extract individual essays from the
Etext file for indexing with Lucene and Solr. We need to know the character
encoding of the input file and the character encoding required by Solr and
Lucene. Project Gutenberg texts are available in several different formats and
character encodings. Lucene and Solr use UTF-8 as the default character encoding. As stated earlier, the character encoding for the Project Gutenberg
plain-text file is also UTF-8.

We want to avoid losing information in the original data or corrupting the
text in any way, but this requires a precise definition of what we mean by original data, since the Project Gutenberg file is a compilation from one or more

public-domain editions of these essays. In the essay texts, we preserve capitalizations and paragraph information. We don't consider line breaks within paragraphs as significant, as these are an artifact of the Project Gutenberg files, not the original essays themselves.

As noted earlier, elements are separated by blank lines. We know the type and order of the header elements. Therefore, we can write a straightforward parser that collects the header elements in order, and then gets all of the paragraphs in the text of the essay. The parser throws an error if it can't find all header elements. This happens when the expected formatting and separator characters between two header elements are missing. This allows us to identify and correct problems in the Project Gutenberg file.

In this example we are dealing with a small fixed dataset in an idiosyncratic format. It is impossible to define a very general parser, but it is easy to define a very specific parser that can check that we have parsed the entire dataset and all essays are complete and correct. This is important since this dataset has been widely studied and in order to replicate previous results we need to make sure that all the data are present and accounted for. This same principle applies to closed corpora used for demos, bake-offs, or other evaluations.

6.6 `FederalistParser` Code Walkthrough

We present the demo program `FederalistParser` method by method. The program is in the file `FederalistParser.java` under the source directory `javabook/src/casestudy`, package `com.colloquial.casestudy`. The line numbers in the left margin correspond to the line numbers in the source code file.

The `FederalistParser` program takes two command-line arguments: the name of the input file and the name of the output directory for the XML files. The `main` method gets the arguments, does a little error-checking, and then calls the method `parsePapers`, which parses the Etext file into individual essays. We know that there are 85 essays total. If the number of essays found doesn't match this number, the program will print an error message and exit otherwise, it calls the method `paperToXml` on each essay, which transforms the essay into an XML document and writes it to an output file.

```
public static final int TOTAL_PAPERS = 85;

public static void main(String[] args)
    throws IOException, FileNotFoundException {
    if (args.length < 2) {
        System.err.println("usage: FederalistParser "
                        + "<etext> <outdir>");
        System.exit(-1);
```

```
        }
        File etextFile = new File(args[0]);
        File outputDir = new File(args[1]);

        FederalistParser parser = new FederalistParser();
        List<Paper> papers = parser.parsePapers(etextFile);
        if (papers.size() != TOTAL_PAPERS) {
            System.err.println("\nerror(s) found, "
                                   + " no files generated");
        } else {
            for (Paper paper : papers)
                parser.paperToXml(paper, outputDir);
            System.out.println("All papers processed.");
        }
    }
}
```

String constants are used for the name of the input and output encoding.

```
public static final String INPUT_ENCODING = "UTF-8";
public static final String OUTPUT_ENCODING = "UTF-8";
```

The method parsePapers breaks the Etext into individual essays.

```
public static final String START_PAPER
    = "FEDERALIST No.";
public static final String END_OF_BOOK
    = "End of the Project Gutenberg";

public List<Paper> parsePapers(File inFile)
    throws IOException, FileNotFoundException {
    ArrayList<Paper> papers = new ArrayList<Paper>();

    FileInputStream inStream = null;
    InputStreamReader inReader = null;
    BufferedReader bufReader = null;
    try {
        inStream = new FileInputStream(inFile);
        inReader = new InputStreamReader(inStream,INPUT_ENCODING);
        bufReader = new BufferedReader(inReader);

        // read from beginning of file to start of paper #1
        String line = null;
        while ((line = bufReader.readLine()) != null) {
            if (line.startsWith(START_PAPER)) break;
        }
        if (line == null)
            throw new IOException("unexpected EOF");
```

```
StringBuilder paragraph = new StringBuilder();
ArrayList<String> parsList = new ArrayList<String>();

int ct = 0;
// process all papers
while (!(line.startsWith(END_OF_BOOK))) {
    // process previous paper, if any
    if (parsList.size() > 0) {
        if (paragraph.length() > 0) {
            parsList.add(paragraph.toString());
        }
        Paper paper = parsePaper(parsList);
        if (paper != null) {
            papers.add(paper);
        } else {
            System.err.println("\nparse error paper: "
                                + ct);
        }
        parsList.clear();
        paragraph.setLength(0);
    }
    // get this paper
    ct++;
    parsList.add(line);  // header line
    while ((line = bufReader.readLine()) != null) {
        if (line.startsWith(START_PAPER)) break;
        if (line.startsWith(END_OF_BOOK)) break;
        if ("".equals(line)) {
            if (paragraph.length() > 0) {
                parsList.add(paragraph.toString());
                paragraph.setLength(0);
            }
        } else {
            paragraph.append(line + " ");
        }
    }
}
// process final paper in book
if (parsList.size() > 0) {
    if (paragraph.length() > 0)
        parsList.add(paragraph.toString());
    Paper paper = parsePaper(parsList);
    if (paper != null) {
```

```
                    papers.add(paper);
                } else {
                    System.err.println("\nparse error paper: "
                                            + ct);
                }
            }
        } finally {
            close(bufReader);
            close(inReader);
            close(inStream);
        }
        return papers;
    }
```

The first and last several lines of `parsePapers` handle the I/O on the input file. These are shown in bold. First we open the input file and create the chain of `java.io` objects which read the bytes from the input file and map them to characters using the specified `INPUT_ENCODING`. We embed these calls in a `try` block so that we can use a `finally` block (also in bold) to close the reader and stream objects again. The `close` method closes the reader and stream objects without raising an I/O exception.

```
void close(Closeable c) {
    if (c == null) return;
    try {
        c.close();
    } catch (IOException e) {
        // ignore
    }
```

Once we have a `Reader` object open on the input file, we read through the file line by line. We detect the beginning of the first paper and the end of the book by comparing the input to the string constants `START_PAPER` and `END_OF_BOOK`.

The two data structures used to assemble an individual essay are shown in bold. These are a `StringBuilder` object called `paragraph` that collects consecutive non-empty lines of text into a paragraph and a `java.util.ArrayList<String>` object called `parsList` that stores the paragraphs in order.

The `while` loop does the work of assembling each paper from the Etext file. First we process the paper found on the previous iteration. We check that all paragraphs have been added to the paper, and then we call the method `parsePaper`, which transforms the list of paragraphs into a structured object of type `Paper` or returns `null` if a formatting error was encountered. Finally we clear the contents of the `parsList` and continue parsing the next paper. When we read the last line of the book, we exit the `while` loop and process the final paper.

In the inner `while` loop (in bold) we read through all lines in the current essay. The `BufferedReader.readline()` method removes the end-of-line marker. Inspection of the Etext file shows that there are no trailing spaces at the end of a line of text, nor are any words split across two lines with hyphenation therefore, we append a space to the line in order to avoid running together the last word on this line and the first word on the next line (append method call shown in bold).

The method `parsePaper` transforms the list of paragraphs into a structured object of type `Paper`. We use `Pattern` and `Matcher` objects from the `java.util.regex` package to process the headers. We use regexes to extract the paper number from the opening header, to break the publication information apart into publication name and date, and to parse out the author or author names (see chapter 4, section 4.12).

```
static final String regexPaper
    = "FEDERALIST No. (\\d+).*";
static final Pattern patternPaper = Pattern.compile(regexPaper);

static final String regexPub
    = "\\w+ ([^\\.]+)\\. \\w+, ([^\\.]+).*";
static final Pattern patternPub = Pattern.compile(regexPub);

static final String regexAuthor
    = "(\\w+)(?:, with (\\w+))?.*";
static final Pattern patternAuthor = Pattern.compile(regexAuthor);
```

The regex string `regexPaper` contains a single capturing group that matches one or more digits. It is used to extract the number from the header line of the paper. For example, given a `Matcher` object over the `Pattern` object `patternPaper` and the header line:

```
FEDERALIST No. 20
```

the call to the method `matcher.group(1)` returns 20.

The regex string `regexPub` handles the publication information. The publication information consists of the name of the journal in which the essay appeared and the date of publication together on the same line, separated by a period.

```
From the New York Packet. Tuesday, December 11, 1787.
```

The publication name is preceded by the word *for* or *from*. We write a regex that skips the first word and following space, then captures all text up until the period separator. It matches the period, a space, a sequence of word characters, a comma, and another space. This effectively skips the day of the week, which is redundant information given the month, day, and year. A second capturing group captures the text following the comma up until the second period or end of line.

```
\\w+ ([^\\.]+)\\. \\w+, ([^\\.]+).*
```

We need to escape the period, else it will be treated as the wildcard character. We use brackets to define the character class that matches anything except a period. Getting this regex right took some trial and error, and we used the program RegexGroup (section 4.12) to check our work.

The author line always contains a first author name and in a few cases may contain a second author name. The regex string regexAuthor handles this.

```
(\\w+)(?:, with (\\w+))?.*
```

We need a group around this optional part, but since we want to extract only the second author name and not the entire optional phrase, we use a noncapturing group (see section 4.13).

We extract the header information from the opening paragraphs in the list, removing each header as we process it until the paragraph list contains just the paragraphs that make up the text of the essay. When we have processed the header information, we call the Paper.Builder.build() method in the return statement.

```
// process list of paragraphs
// first 5 list entries contain header information, rest are body
public Paper parsePaper(List<String> pars) {
    String header = pars.remove(0);
    String number = null;
    Matcher matcher = patternPaper.matcher(header);
    if (matcher.matches()) {
        number = matcher.group(1);
    }
    String title = pars.remove(0);
    String publication = pars.remove(0);
    String pubName = null;
    String pubDate = null;
    matcher = patternPub.matcher(publication);
    if (matcher.matches()) {
        pubName = matcher.group(1);
        pubDate = matcher.group(2);
    }
    String author = pars.remove(0);
    String author1 = null;
    String author2 = null;
    matcher = patternAuthor.matcher(author);
```

```
    if (matcher.matches()) {
        author1 = matcher.group(1);
        author2 = matcher.group(2);
    }
    pars.remove(0);              // skip salutation
    return new Paper.Builder(number).title(title)
        .pubName(pubName).pubDate(pubDate)
        .author1(author1).author2(author2)
        .paragraphs(pars).build();
}
```

The parsePaper method returns either a complete Paper object or null if
any fields are null, which happens when any of the regexes fail to match
header elements. The calling method must check the value of returned by the
parsePaper method and handle errors accordingly.

The method paperToXml transforms a Paper object into the XML representation of a Lucene document used by Solr and writes it out to disk.

```
public void paperToXml(Paper paper, File outDir)
    throws IOException {

    // pad paper number so that files sort nicely
    String numPaper
        = String.format("%02d",paper.getNumber());
    String filename = "paper_" + numPaper + ".xml";
    File outFile = new File(outDir,filename);

    FileOutputStream outStream = null;
    OutputStreamWriter outWriter = null;
    BufferedWriter bufWriter = null;
    try {
        outStream = new FileOutputStream(outFile);
        outWriter = new OutputStreamWriter(outStream,
                                        OUTPUT_ENCODING);
        bufWriter = new BufferedWriter(outWriter);

        Format format = Format.getPrettyFormat();
        format.setEncoding(OUTPUT_ENCODING);
        XMLOutputter outputter
            = new XMLOutputter(format);
        Element root = new Element("add");
        Document document = new Document(root);
        root.addContent(paper.toXml());
        outputter.output(document,bufWriter);
    } finally {
        close(bufWriter);
```

```
        close(outWriter);
        close(outStream);
    }
}
```

This method constructs the name of the output file programmatically. To make sure that the file sort order matches the file number, we use the `String.format` method (shown in bold) to pad the leading digit with zeros as needed. We construct the chain of I/O objects inside of a `try` block and close them in the corresponding `finally` block.

A `org.jdom2.output.Format` object is used to convert an XML document to a byte stream on lines. `Format.getPrettyFormat()` returns a new Format object that performs whitespace beautification with 2-space indents, uses the UTF-8 encoding, doesn't expand empty elements, includes the declaration and encoding, and uses the default entity escape strategy. The `org.jdom2.output.XMLOutputter` is used to write an XML document out to disk. See section 5.3.4 for details. The XML document that we create will be used in chapter 8. For that application, we need to create an XML document whose top-level element is <add>, so we create this element and then add the <doc> element to it.

The `Paper` class has method `toXml()`, which converts the structured Java object to an `org.jdom2.Element` object with a top-level element tag <doc>.

```
public Element toXml() {
    Element root = new Element("doc");

    Element fNumber = new Element("field");
    fNumber.setAttribute("name","number");
    String number = Integer.toString(mNumber);
    fNumber.addContent(new Text(number));
    root.addContent(fNumber);

    Element fTitle = new Element("field");
    fTitle.setAttribute("name","title");
    fTitle.addContent(new Text(mTitle));
    root.addContent(fTitle);

    Element fPubName = new Element("field");
    fPubName.setAttribute("name","pubName");
    fPubName.addContent(new Text(mPubName));
    root.addContent(fPubName);
    Element fPubDate = new Element("field");
    fPubDate.setAttribute("name","pubDate");

    DateFormat df
        = new SimpleDateFormat("yyyy-MM-dd'T'HH:mm:ss'Z'");
```

```
        String date = df.format(mPubDate);
        fPubDate.addContent(new Text(date));
        root.addContent(fPubDate);

        Element fAuthor1 = new Element("field");
        fAuthor1.setAttribute("name","author");
        fAuthor1.addContent(new Text(mAuthor1));
        root.addContent(fAuthor1);
        if (mAuthor2 != null) {
            Element fAuthor2 = new Element("field");
            fAuthor2.setAttribute("name","author");
            fAuthor2.addContent(new Text(mAuthor2));
            root.addContent(fAuthor2);
        }
        for (String par : mParagraphs) {
            Element fText = new Element("field");
            fText.setAttribute("name","text");
            fText.addContent(new Text(par));
            root.addContent(fText);
        }
        return root;
    }
```

We construct the XML element in a top-down fashion by first creating the root <doc> element and then creating a series of <field> elements with the appropriate attributes and contents and adding these to the top-level <doc> element (see section 5.3.4 for details). We use a SimpleDateFormat object to format the date using the ISO 8601 date and time formats. See http://www.w3.org/TR/NOTE-datetime.

6.7 Running the Program

The Ant target parse-papers runs the program. Command-line arguments are passed into the program via the Ant properties etext and xml.dir. The file javabook/src/casestudy/build.xml defines default values for these properties:

```
<property name="etext"
          value="../../data/federalist-papers/pg1404.txt"/>
<property name="xml.dir"
          value="../../data/federalist-papers/xml"/>
```

If all papers can be parsed and converted to XML, the program prints a status message to stdout, else the program prints error messages to stderr for papers that fail to parse. The file pg1404.txt has been regularized, so when

we run the program via Ant using the defaults, the status message indicates
success.

```
> ant parse-papers
All papers processed.
```

6.7.1 Finding, Correcting Etext Errors

As mentioned in section 6.3, in order to process the Project Gutenberg Etext
file pg1404.txt, we had to first correct some irregularities. Here is the Ant
output from running the FederalistParser program over the original Etext
file pg1404.txt.as.downloaded:

```
> ant parse-papers\
>  -Detext="../../data/federalist-papers/pg1404.txt.as.downloaded"
parse error paper: 18

parse error paper: 40

parse error paper: 58

error(s) found,  no files generated
```

6.7.2 XML Output

Here is the beginning of the XML file paper_01.xml, in output directory
javabook/data/federalist-papers/xml:

```
<doc>
  <field name="number">1</field>
  <field name="title">General Introduction</field>
  <field name="pubName">the Independent Journal</field>
  <field name="pubDate">October 27, 1787</field>
  <field name="author">HAMILTON</field>
  <field name="text">AFTER an unequivocal experience
    of the inefficacy of the subsisting federal government, you
    are called upon to deliberate on a new Constitution for the
    United States of America. The subject speaks its own importance;
    ...
  </field>
```

6.8 Discussion

Why bother to write a program to process one particular text or dataset? The
benefits are a processed dataset that contains every item in the original dataset
plus a clear and repeatable process. Although *The Federalist Papers* dataset is

small, it is just large enough that by-hand processing is too onerous, as is developing a set of macros for a text editor.

Considerable effort went into developing a good parsing strategy for this text. The program presented here underwent several revisions, and the total development time was several times greater than initially anticipated. Our initial attempt, based on a quick look at the data, was to write a long parse method that would read the file line by line, processing the essay at once. We looked at the header of the first essay and proceeded to write a method that expected to find: a header line; a blank line; a title on a single line; a blank line; publication information; a blank line; author; a blank line; salutation; a blank line; followed by one or more paragraphs of text. This method was too brittle to handle the actual text data. It bombed on the first essay, which contains an extra blank line between the header and the title.

Once we refined our parsing strategy, we realized that we needed to define a proper domain object, not only for clarity and convenience but also in order to be able to use this dataset in developing examples for Lucene and Solr in subsequent chapters. Lucene is a Java API, and therefore we need to operate on a `Paper` object directly. Solr is a webservice that operates on XML documents, so we use the method `Paper.toXml()` to generate inputs to Solr.

When writing the class `Paper`, it was easier to follow best practices and make our object immutable and use the Builder pattern than it was to explain why we didn't. We did, however, cut corners in error reporting. The diagnostic messages are minimal. The program reports only which essays are incomplete or don't conform to the expected format. We check that the program has inputs, but we don't bother to check whether or not the input files and output directory actually exist and have the correct file permissions.

Chapter 7

Text Search with Lucene

Apache Lucene is a search library written in Java. It's very popular in both academic and commercial settings due to its performance, configurability, and generous licensing terms. The Lucene home page is

```
http://lucene.apache.org/
```

Lucene is distributed under the Apache license version 2.0. Links to download the current version are prominently featured on the home page.

The Lucene API is composed of many packages. The top-level package is `org.apache.lucene`. Throughout this chapter we abbreviate this top-level path to `oal` when giving package and class names. For example, we write `oal.index` instead of `org.apache.lucene.index`.

In this chapter, we continue to use the classes from chapter 6 in order to index the 85 essays that make up *The Federalist Papers*. The program that indexes *The Federalist Papers* is included in the package for chapter 6, `javabook/src/casestudy`. All other example programs for this chapter are in the directory:

```
javabook/src/applucene
```

This directory contains an Ant `build.xml` file with targets to compile and run the examples. The programs belong to package `com.colloquial.applucene`, and the Java source files are in the `src` subdirectory. The Lucene jar files needed for these example are included in the `lib` subdirectory, and the `build.xml` file includes these jars in classpath specification.

7.1 Lucene Overview

Lucene provides search over documents. It manages an index over a dynamic collection of documents and provides very rapid updates to the index as documents are added to and deleted from the collection. Lucene has a highly

187

expressive search API that takes a search query and returns a set of documents ranked by relevancy with documents most similar to the query having the highest score.

A document is essentially a collection of fields. A field consists of a field name that is a string and one or more field values. Lucene does not in any way constrain document structures. An index may store a heterogeneous set of documents, with any number of different fields that may vary by document in arbitrary ways. Fields are constrained to store only one kind of data, either binary, numeric, or text data. There are two ways to store text data: string fields store the entire item as one string; text fields store the data as a series of tokens. Lucene provides many ways to break a piece of text into tokens as well as hooks that allow you to write custom tokenizers.

Lucene indexes *terms*, which means that Lucene search is search over terms. A term combines a field name with a token. The terms created from the non-text fields in the document are pairs consisting of the field name and field value. The terms created from text fields are pairs of field name and token.

The Lucene index provides a mapping from terms to documents. This is called an *inverted index* because it reverses the usual mapping of a document to the terms it contains. The inverted index provides the mechanism for scoring search results: if a number of search terms all map to the same document, then that document is likely to be relevant. Here is an example from the index over *The Federalist Papers*. The text of each paper is in a field called `text`, which has been tokenized into words, all lowercase, no punctuation. The inverted index for the terms consisting of field name `text` and tokens *abilities*, *able*, and *abolish* looks like:

term	*document*
abilities	2, 17, 21, 22, 35, 64, 76
able	1, 3, 4, 7, 8, 9, 10, 11, 12, 15, 16, 21, 23, 24, 25, 27, 29, 30, 33, 34, 35, 36, 37, 38, 41, 43, 46, 49, 51, 52, 58, 62, 63, 64, 67, 68, 70, 71, 75, 78, 85
abolish	10, 14, 26, 31, 39, 49, 45, 70, 71, 78, 81

Fig. 7.1: *Entries in an inverted index.*

A Lucene search is fielded. A search request carries out a search over a field given a query string. The query string is processed into a term or terms consisting of the field name and the tokenized query string. The tokenization applied to the query string is the same as the tokenization applied to the document values for that field.

Lucene's default search scoring algorithm weights results using TF–IDF, term frequency—inverse document frequency. *Term frequency* means that high-frequency terms within a document have higher weight than do low-frequency terms. *Inverse document frequency* means that terms that occur frequently across many documents in a collection of documents are less likely to be meaningful descriptors of any given document in a corpus and are therefore down-weighted. As of Lucene 4, the API provides alternative scoring algorithms and a pluggable architecture that allows developers to build their own custom scoring models.

It is possible to build an inverted index over just one document. This is called a *term vector*. A term vector is a vector over all the terms in the index where for each term, the value of the vector element is the number of times that term occurs in the document. For indexes over a large and diverse set of documents, this is likely to be a sparse vector. Representing a document as a term vector allows Lucene to compute document similarity and is the basis for many advanced search capabilities.

Lucene can also be used as a data store for documents by specifying fields as stored fields. They are not part of the index, per se, rather they are returned as part of a search result. Both stored fields and term vectors add to the size of the index. To address this problem, compressed formats have been introduced for both.

7.1.1 Lucene Versions

The behavior of many Lucene components has changed over time. To address this, the class `oal.util.Version` was introduced in Lucene 3. A `Version` object contains a `String` constant, which identifies the major and minor versions of Lucene for example, `LUCENE_45` identifies version 4.5. The Lucene version constant is supplied to the constructor of each of the components in an application. There's no requirement that all components in an application be of the same version however, for components used for both search and indexing, it is critical that the Lucene version is the same in the code that is called at indexing time and the code that is called at search time.

7.2 Tokenizing Text

The two components of a Lucene term are the field name and the token. A token is derived from segmenting the input text and possibly transforming the segments. Lucene offers a rich set of tokenizers that can be combined and extended.

The way that text is tokenized directly affects the way that an index can be searched. In order to build effective search applications for any data set, we need to understand the behavior of the data. For search applications over natural language data, we need to understand how language behaves.

In the following sections we cover tokenization strategies. We start with simple text processing techniques and then discuss more sophisticated natural language concepts, techniques, and considerations.

7.2.1   Whitespace Tokenization

We can break the text into a series of tokens by choosing to tokenize on whitespace. This strategy treats punctuation characters like any other non-whitespace character, so tokens may contain punctuation. For example, the input string *To the people:* can be tokenized as |*To*| |*the*| |*people:*| where | indicates token boundaries.

7.2.2   Case Normalization

We can transform the input string by applying case normalization to transform all characters to either uppercase or lowercase. Case normalization is often applied in contexts where the case of words doesn't matter or provides more noise than information.

7.2.3   Stop Lists

Removing very common words is known as *stop-listing*, and the set of words to remove is called a *stop list*. For example, a stop list for English often includes the words *be*, *of*, and *the*. These words are very common and typically convey very little information themselves, although they can convey more information in context.

7.2.4   *N*-Grams

A simple and general tokenization strategy is to process an input string into all substrings of the input string within a specified size bounds. Substrings of an input string of length n are typically called n-grams. The input string *To the people* can be tokenized into 5-grams starting with: |*To th*| |*o the*| through |*peopl*| |*eople*| where | indicates token boundaries.

7.2.5   Morphological Analysis

Tokenization strategies for natural language break text into linguistically meaningful units such as individual words or into even smaller units. Tokenizing a word into its constituent subparts improves search by allowing different forms of a word to count toward document relevancy.

In linguistics, *morphology* is the study of how words are formed. Morphology overlaps with the study of several other phenomena, including syntax (parts of speech and how words combine), phonology (how words are pronounced), orthography (how a language is written, including how words are spelled), and semantics (what a word means). A morpheme is the minimal meaningful unit of language. A morpheme doesn't need to be a word itself. Often the term morpheme is extended to include syntactic markers, though these almost always have some semantic or semantic-like effect, such as marking gender.

Languages are not all the same. Some code up lots of information in their morphological systems (e.g., Russian) and some not much at all (e.g., Chinese). Some languages allow very long words consisting of lots of independent morphemes (e.g., Turkish, Hungarian, and Finnish), whereas most allow only inflection and derivation.

We provide a brief overview of natural language morphology, and then consider the processes of stemming and lemmatization and how they relate to tokenization.

Inflectional Morphology

Inflectional morphology is concerned with how the basic paradigmatic variants of a word are realized. For instance, in English, the two nouns *computer* and *computers* differ in number, the first being singular, the second plural. These show up in different syntactic contexts—we say *one computer* and *two computers* but not *one computers* and *two computer*.[1] This is an instance of agreement—the grammatical number of the noun must agree with the number of the determiner. In English, there are only two numbers, singular and plural, but other languages, such as Icelandic and Sanskrit, have duals (for two things), and some languages go even further, defining numbers for three objects, or distinguishing many from a few.

In English, the forms *code*, *codes*, *coded*, and *coding* are all inflectional variants of the same underlying verb, differing in person, number, tense, and aspect. We get agreement between verbs and subject nouns in English for these features. For instance, a person might say *I code* in referring to himself or herself, but *she codes* when referring to his or her friend writing code. Other languages, such as French or Russian, also have agreement for gender, which can be natural (male person versus female person versus non-person) or grammatical (as in French). Natural gender is based on what is being talked about. That's the distinction we get in English between the relative pronouns *who*, which is used for people and other animate objects, and *what*, which is used for inanimate objects. For instance, we say *who did you meet?* if we expect the answer to be a person and *what did you see?* if we expect it to be a thing.

---

[1] These ungrammatical forms like *one computers* will appear in text. You'll find just about everything in free text and even in fairly tightly edited text such as newswire if you look at enough of it.

Most languages have fairly straightforward inflectional morphology, defining a few variants of the basic nouns and verbs. The actual morphological operations may be as simple as adding an affix, but even this is complicated by boundary effects. Examples of these are English present participle verbs such as *race/racing*, *eat/eating*, and *run/running*. In the first case, we delete the final *e* before adding the suffix *-ing* in the second case, we just append the suffix, and in the third case, we insert an extra *n* before adding the suffix. The same thing happens with number for nouns, as with *boy/boys* versus *box/boxes*, in which the first case appends the suffix *s* whereas the second adds an *e* before the suffix (the result of which, *boxes*, is two syllables).

It is also common to see internal vowel changes, as in the English alternation *run/ran*. Languages such as Arabic and Hebrew take this to the extreme with their templatic morphology systems in which a base form consists of a sequence of consonants and an inflected form mixes in vowels.

In many situations, the differences between morphological variants of the same base word are not particularly informative. For instance, should the query [new car][2] provide a different search result from the query [new cars]? The difference is that one query uses the singular form *car* and the other the plural *cars*.

Derivational Morphology

Derivational morphology, in contrast to inflectional morphology, involves modifying a word to create a new word, typically with a different function. For instance, from the verb *run* we can derive the noun *runner* and from the adjective *quick* we can derive the adverb *quickly*. After we've derived a new form, we can inflect it, with singular form *runner* and plural form *runners*.

Inflectional morphology is almost always bounded to a finite set of possible inflected forms for each base word and category. Derivational morphology, on the other hand, is unbounded. We can take the noun *fortune*, derive the adjective *fortunate*, the adjective *unfortunate*, and then the adverb *unfortunately*.

Sometimes there's zero derivational morphology, meaning that the category of a word changes but the form of the word remains the same. For instance, we can turn most nouns in English into verbs, especially in the business world, and most verbs into nouns (where they are called gerunds). In the phrase *the running of the race* the verb *running* is used as a noun, and in the phrase *Bill will leverage that deal* the noun *leverage* (itself an inflected form of *lever*) is used as a verb. In American English, we're also losing the adjective/adverb distinction, with many speakers not even bothering to use an adverbial form of an adjective, saying things such as *John runs fast*.

---

[2]We display queries as [*Q*] where the brackets indicate the scope of the search and are not part of the search itself.

Context Sensitivity of Morphology

Words are ambiguous in many different ways, including morphologically. Depending on the context, the same token may be interpreted differently. For instance, the plural noun *runs* is the same word as the present tense verb *runs*. For nouns, only *run* and *runs* are appropriate, both of which are also verbal forms. Additional verbal forms include *running* and *ran*. A word such as *hyper* might be used as the short-form adjective meaning the same thing as *hyperactive*, or it could be a noun derived from the the verb *hype*, meaning someone who hypes something (in the publicity sense).

Compounding

Some languages, such as German, allow two words to be combined into a single word, written with no spaces, as in combining *schnell* (fast) and *Zug* (train) into the compound *Schnellzug*.[3] An example of a longer compound is *Donaudampfschiffahrtsgesellschaft*, which translates to Danube Steamboat Shipping Company (note that in English, *steamboat* is itself a compound). Compounding may require insertion or deletion of phonological material at word boundaries, similar to insertions or deletions that occur with inflectional affixes.

Compounds may themselves be inflected. For instance, in English, we may combine *foot* and *ball* to produce the compound noun *football*, which may then be inflected in the plural to get *footballs*. They may also be modified derivationally, to get *footballer*, and then inflected, to get *footballers*.

7.2.6 Stemming and Lemmatization

Lemmatization is the process of mapping a word to its root form(s). It may also involve determining which affixes, vowel changes, wrappers, infixes, or templates are involved, but typically not for most applications.

Stemming is the process of mapping a word to a canonical representation. The main difference from a linguistic point of view is that the output of a stemmer isn't necessarily a word (or morpheme) itself.

Example: stem *author*

It is very hard to know where to draw the line in stemming. Some systems take a strictly inflectional point of view, stripping off only inflectional affixes or templatic fillers. Others allow full derivational morphology. Even so, the line is unclear.

---

[3] All nouns in German are capitalized whereas other parts of speech are not, therefore the nouns *Zug* and *Schnellzug* are capitalized but not the adjective *schnell*.

Consider the stem *author*. In the English Gigaword corpus,[4] which consists of slightly more than a billion words of English newswire text, which is relatively well behaved, the following variants are observed

> antiauthoritarian, antiauthoritarianism, antiauthority, author, authoratative, authoratatively, authordom, authored, authoress, authoresses, authorhood, authorial, authoring, authorisation, authorised, authorises, authoritarian, authoritarianism, authoritarians, authoritative, authoritatively, authoritativeness, authorities, authoritory, authority, authorization, authorizations, authorize, authorized, authorizer, authorizers, authorizes, authorizing, authorless, authorly, authors, authorship, authorships, coauthor, coauthored, coauthoring, coauthors, cyberauthor, deauthorized, multiauthored, nonauthor, nonauthoritarian, nonauthorized, preauthorization, preauthorizations, preauthorized, quasiauthoritarian, reauthorization, reauthorizations, reauthorize, reauthorized, reauthorizes, reauthorizing, semiauthoritarian, semiauthorized, superauthoritarian, unauthorised, unauthoritative, unauthorized

We're not just looking for the substring *author*. Because of the complexity of morphological affixing in English, this is neither necessary nor sufficient. To see that it's not sufficient, note that *urn* and *turn* are not related, nor are *knot* and *not*. To see that it's not necessary, consider *pace* and *pacing* or *take* and *took*.

Each of the words in the list above is etymologically derived from the word *author*. The problem is that over time, meanings drift. This makes it very hard to draw a line for which words to consider equivalent for a given task. Not only is the shared root of *author* and *authorize* lost to most native speakers but also the words are only weakly semantically related, despite the latter form being derived from the former using the regular suffix *-ize*. The meaning has drifted.

In contrast, the relation between *notary* and *notarize* is regular, and the meaning of the latter is fairly predictable from the meaning of the former. Moving down a derivational level, the relation between *note* and *notary* feels more opaque.

Suppose we search for [authoritarian], perhaps researching organizational behavior. We probably don't want to see documents about coauthoring papers. We probably don't want to see documents containing *unauthoritative*, because that's usually used in a different context, but we might want to see documents containing the word *antiauthority* and would probably want to see documents containing *antiauthoritarianism*. As you can see, it's rather difficult to draw a line here.

---

[4]Graff, David and Christopher Cieri. 2003. *English Gigaword*. Linguistic Data Consortium (LDC). University of Pennsylvania. Catalog number LDC2003T05.

David A. Hull provides a range of interesting examples of the performance of a range of stemmers from a very simple stemmer that removes
only word-final *s*, through the mainstream medium-complex systems (the
Porter stemmer,which removes suffixes and can handle vowel change and
word-final character normalization), to the very complex (Xerox's finite-state-
transducer based stemmer).[5] For example, one of Hull's queries contained
the word *superconductivity*, but matching documents contained only the word
superconductor. This clearly requires derivational morphology to find the right
documents. A similar problem occurs for the terms *surrogate mother* versus
surrogate motherhood and *genetic engineering* versus *genetically engineered*
in another. Another example where stemming helped was *failure* versus *fail*
in the context of bank failures.

An example where stemming hurt was in the compound term *client server*
matching documents containing the words *serve* and *client*, leading to numer-
ous false positive matches. This is really a frequency argument, as servers in
the computer sense do serve data, but so many other people and organizations
serve things to clients that it provides more noise than utility. Another example that caused problems was reducing *fishing* to *fish*; even though this looks
like a simple inflectional change, the nominal use of *fish* is so prevalent that
documents about cooking and eating show up rather than documents about
catching fish. Similar problems arise in lemmatizing *privatization* to *private*;
the latter term just shows up in too many contexts not related to privatization.

These uncertainties in derivational stem equivalence are why many people
want to restrict stemming to inflectional morphology. The problem with restricting to inflectional morphology is that it's not the right cut at the problem.
Sometimes derivational stemming helps, and sometimes inflectional stemming
hurts.

One approach to stemming that is surprisingly effective for English (and
other mostly suffixing languages) given its simplicity is to just map every word
down to its first k characters. Typical values for k would be 5 or 6.

7.3 Token Streams and Analyzers

The package `oal.analysis` contains the base classes for tokenizing and indexing text. The input text may undergo several transformations, e.g., whitespace tokenization, case normalization, stop-listing, and stemming.

The abstract class `TokenStream` breaks the incoming text into a sequence
of tokens that are retrieved using an iterator-like pattern. `TokenStream` has
two subclasses: `Tokenizer` and `TokenFilter`. A `Tokenizer` takes a `Reader`

---

[5] Hull, David A. 1996. Stemming algorithms: a case study for detailed evaluation. *Journal of the
American Society for Information Science* **47**(1).

as input whereas a `TokenFilter` takes another `TokenStream` as input. This allows us to chain together tokenizers such that the initial tokenizer gets its input from a reader and the others operate on tokens from the preceding `TokenStream` in the chain.

An `Analyzer` supplies the indexing and searching processes with `TokenStreams` on a per-field basis. It maps field names to tokenizers and may also supply a default analyzer for unknown field names. Lucene includes many analysis modules that provide a rich set of analyzers including a large number of language-specific ones.

The abstract class `Analyzer` contains methods used to extract `terms` from input text. Concrete subclasses of `Analyzer` must override the method `createComponents`, which returns an object of the nested class `TokenStreamComponents` that defines the tokenization process and provides access to initial and file components of the processing pipeline. The initial component is a `Tokenizer` that handles the input source. The final component is an instance of `TokenFilter` and it is the `TokenStream` returned by the method `Analyzer.tokenStream(String, Reader)`. Here is an example of a custom `Analyzer` that tokenizes its inputs into individual words with all letters lowercase.

```
Analyzer analyzer = new Analyzer() {
    @Override protected TokenStreamComponents
    createComponents(String fieldName, Reader reader) {
        Tokenizer source =
            new StandardTokenizer(VERSION,reader);
        TokenStream filter =
            new LowerCaseFilter(VERSION,source);
        return new TokenStreamComponents(source, filter);
```

Note that the constructors for the `StandardTokenizer` and `LowerCaseFilter` objects require a `oal.util.Version` argument, which is a constant specifying the Lucene version.

7.3.1 Analyzer and Tokenizer Implementations

Lucene includes many analysis modules that provide concrete implementations of different kinds of analyzers. As of Lucene 4, these modules are bundled into separate jarfiles.

There are several dozen language-specific analysis packages, from `oal.analysis.ar` for Arabic to `oal.analysis.tr` for Turkish. The package `oal.analysis.core` provides several general-purpose analyzers, tokenizers, and tokenizer factory classes.

Whitespace Tokenization

The class `WhitespaceTokenizer` in package `oal.analysis.core` divides text at whitespace and treats adjacent sequences of non-whitespace characters as tokens. The method `Character.isWhitespace(int)` determines whether or not a code point is a Java whitespace character.[6] The package also contains corresponding analyzer and tokenizer factory classes.

Case Normalization

The package `oal.analysis.core` contains the class `LoweraseFilter`, which normalizes token text to lowercase using the Java method `Character.toLowerCase()`. There is also a corresponding filter factory class.

The package also contains the class `LowerCaseTokenizer` and its corresponding factory class. This class tokenizes the input into maximal strings of adjacent letters using a `LetterTokenizer`, also in package `oal.analysis.core`. Applying a `LowerCaseTokenizer` to the text *The 49 Steps* yields the tokens *the* and *steps*. This is not appropriate for languages such as Chinese that don't use whitespace, especially since these languages don't have the notion of upper- and lowercase.

Stop Lists

The package `oal.analysis.core` contains the class `StopFilter`, which removes stop words from a token stream and its corresponding filter factory class. The `StopFilter` constructor takes three arguments. The first two are the usual Lucene `Version` and `TokenStream`. The third argument is the stop words list in the form of a `CharArraySet` object from package `oal.analysis.util`.

The package also contains the class `StopAnalyzer`. This analyzer applies a `LetterTokenizer` and `LowerCaseFilter` to the input text before applying a `StopFilter`. A `StopAnalyzer` with a stop list that includes the word *the* would tokenize the text *The 49 Steps* as the single token *steps*.

N-Grams

The package `oal.analysis.ngram` contains several tokenizers and filters and corresponding factory classes that operate over character *n*-grams. An *n*-gram tokenizer uses a specified pair of integers for the minimum and maximum length of *n*-grams to produce. The `NGramTokenizer` has two `int` fields

---

[6]The Java definition of a whitespace character includes all of the Unicode characters with property WSpace=Y (see section 2.7.3) and several additional control characters such as form feed and line feed.

DEFAULT_MIN_NGRAM, and DEFAULT_MAX_NGRAM which are used if the minimum and maximum lengths are not specified overtly. In Lucene 4.5, the defaults are 1 and 2 respectively, meaning that the n-gram tokenizer produces unigrams and bi-grams over the input.

In addition to n-gram tokenizers, Lucene contains *edge n-gram* tokenizers and filters and corresponding factory classes. An EdgeNGramTokenizer tokenizer tokenizes its input from either edge into n-grams between the minimum and maximum n-gram length. The edge is specified using the enumeration Side, which has constants FRONT and BACK. For example, given a minimum and maximum of (2,5) and with Side.FRONT specified, an EdgeNGramTokenizer will tokenize the input *I, Robot* into tokens |*I,* | |*I,* | |*I, R* | |*I, Ro* |.

Word-level n-grams are called *shingles*. Package oal.analysis.shingle has filters that produce shingles. A shingle filter takes a specified pair of integers for the minimum and maximum length of word n-grams to produce, fields DEFAULT_MIN_SHINGLE_SIZE and DEFAULT_MAX_SHINGLE_SIZE. The value of both of these constants is 2, so that this filter produces word bi-grams by default. It is also necessary to specify the string used when joining adjacent tokens to form a shingle. The default is specified by static field TOKEN_SEPARATOR. The default is the string consisting of a single space. Given an input of tokens *I sing the body electric* and default setting, a ShingleFilter produces |*I sing* | |*sing the* | |*the body* | |*body electric* |.

Language-Specific Morphological Analysis

There are several dozen language-specific analysis packages, from oal.analysis.ar for Arabic to oal.analysis.tr for Turkish. These packages are lightly documented. To understand the exact behavior of a particular analyzer class, we recommend using the javadoc for the createTokenStreamComponents. For example, in class ArabicAnalyzer the javadoc tells us that the analyzer uses a StandardTokenizer to break text into a stream of words, discarding punctuation and whitespace, then a LowerCaseFilter, then a StopFilter, next an ArabicNormalizationFilter, then a KeywordMarkerFilter is used to mark words that should not be stemmed, and finally an ArabicStemFilter is used for stemming.

The package oal.analysis.en includes two different stemmers for English. The Porter stemmer removes suffixes and can handle vowel change and word-final character normalization. The class KStemmer is more conservative than the Porter stemmer. This package provides both token filters and token filter factories for each.

7.3.2 Token Stream Attributes

Lucene now uses the interface `Attribute` to hold information about token streams and other basic objects. This is a very general design pattern that is less convenient than a direct implementation of data attributes, but it gives developers enormous flexibility to add new features without breaking backward compatibility. Subinterfaces of `Attribute` that are relevant for tokenization are `CharTermAttribute`, which holds a token's text, `OffsetAttribute`, which holds the token's start and end character offset in the input text, `FlagsAttribute`, which can be used to pass information from one token filter to another, `KeywordAttribute`, which can be used as a flag to indicate that a token should not be modified by stemmers and other morphological analyzers, `TypeAttribute`, which gives a token's lexical type (the default type is *word*), and `PositionIncrementAttribute`, which stores the position of the token relative to the previous tokens in the token stream. Lucene uses these values for phrase-based search (i.e., searching for a fixed sequence of tokens in the given order without intervening material).

7.3.3 Tokenization Demo

To see the workflow of the `TokenStream` API, we provide an example class `LuceneTokenize`, which splits an input string into a series of tokens and retrieves information stored in the token attributes.

The file `LuceneTokenize.java` is under the source directory of `javabook/src/applucene`, in package `com.colloquial.applucene`. All the work is done in the `main()` method. The text to be tokenized is passed in on the command line and stored in the variable `text`.

```
Reader textReader = new StringReader(text);
StandardTokenizer standardTokenizer
    = new StandardTokenizer(VERSION,textReader);
LowerCaseFilter lowercaseFilter
    = new LowerCaseFilter(VERSION,standardTokenizer);
StopFilter stopFilter
    = new StopFilter(VERSION,lowercaseFilter,STOPWORDS);
PorterStemFilter stemFilter
    = new PorterStemFilter(stopFilter);
```

First we must create a `Reader`, which we do by wrapping the input text string in a `StringReader` (from `java.io`).[7] We use a `Tokenizer` and a series of `TokenFilters` to process the input text. Lucene's `StandardTokenizer`, in

---

[7]Unlike the case for documents, there is no alternative to using readers for analysis. It is common to use string readers because they do not maintain handles on resources other than their string reference.

package oal.analysis.standard, splits text into words and discards whitespace and punctuation.[8] Then we apply Lucene's LowerCaseFilter and a
StopFilter, both of which are in package oal.analysis.core. Then we apply a stemmer. The package oal.analysis.en includes an implementation of
the Porter stemmer, PorterStemFilter. This class requires that its inputs be
in lowercase. Since this filter follows the LowerCaseFilter, this should always
be the case.

For this example we create a very short stop list called STOPWORDS, which
contains exactly four lowercase words.

```
public static ArrayList<String> STOPLIST;
static {
    STOPLIST = new ArrayList<String>();
    STOPLIST.add("a");
    STOPLIST.add("of");
    STOPLIST.add("the");
    STOPLIST.add("to");
}
public static CharArraySet STOPWORDS
        = new CharArraySet(VERSION,STOPLIST,true);
```

The last filter in this chain of filters is the PorterStemFilter. If this were
part of a custom Analyzer, then the TokenStream returned by the analyzer's
tokenStream method would be the object stemFilter. In this demo we use it
directly to get the tokens from the input.

```
stemFilter.reset();
CharTermAttribute terms =
    stemFilter.addAttribute(CharTermAttribute.class);
OffsetAttribute offsets
    = stemFilter.addAttribute(OffsetAttribute.class);
PositionIncrementAttribute positions
    = stemFilter
    .addAttribute(PositionIncrementAttribute.class);
int position = 0;
while (stemFilter.incrementToken()) {
    String term = terms.toString();
    position += positions.getPositionIncrement();
    int start = offsets.startOffset();
    int end = offsets.endOffset();
    System.out.printf("%s \t%d (%2d, %2d)\n",
                        term,position,start,end);
```

---

[8]Segmentation is based on Unicode Text Segmentation Guidelines, Technical Report 29. See:
http://unicode.org/reports/tr29/.

```
}
stemFilter.end();
```

In Lucene 4, once a `TokenStream` object has been instantiated, the `reset()` method must be called before it can be used. After calling `reset()` we attach attributes of interest to the token stream. We use a `CharTermAttribute` to retrieve the token text, an `OffsetAttribute` to get the start and end character offset in the input text, and a `PositionIncrementAttribute` to get the token position.

The while loop continually calls `incrementToken()` on the token stream, which advances to the next token, returning `true` if there are more tokens. This pattern of increment-then-get is particularly popular for tokenizers. The body of the loop just pulls out the increment, start and end positions, and term for the token. We call end() so that any end-of-stream operations can be performed. This code sits inside a `try` block. In the corresponding `finally`, not shown, we call close() on the token stream to release any resources.

The Ant target `lucene-tokenize` uses the property `inputs` to pass in the text to be tokenized.

```
> ant -Dinputs="The Molecular Biology of the Cell, 9th Edition."\
> lucene-tokenize
The Molecular Biology of the Cell, 9th Edition.
01234567890123456789012345678901234567890123456
0         1         2         3         4

TERM POSITION (START, END)
molecular  2 ( 4, 13)
biologi    3 (14, 21)
cell    6 (29, 33)
9th     7 (35, 38)
edit    8 (39, 46)
```

The token, word position, and character start (inclusive) and end (exclusive) are shown. The tokens have been lowercased, and non-word-internal punctuation has been removed. The Porter stemmer has changed the final *y* of *biology* to *i* and it has reduced *edition* to *edit*.[9]

The `StandardTokenizer` breaks the text into a stream of words, discarding whitespace and punctuation. The stop words *the* and *of* have been removed from the output. Because the lowercase filter was applied before the stop filter, the capitalized instance of *The* at position 1 was removed as well as the lowercase instance at position 5. When a stop word is removed, it causes the increment between terms to be larger. For instance, the first term position is 2 because the first word was stop-listed and similarly, we see the position jump from 3 to 6 because both *of* and *the* were stop-listed.

---

[9]The same stemmer reduces *biological* to *biolog*, *biologists* to *biologist*.

7.4 Fields

A document is a collection of fields. Each field has three parts: name, type, and value. At search time, the supplied field name restricts the search to particular fields. The field type is an object that implements `IndexableFieldType`. Values may be text, binary, or numeric.

For example, a MEDLINE citation can be represented as a series of fields: one field for the name of the article, another field for name of the journal in which it was published, another field for the authors of the article, a pub-date field for the date of publication, a field for the text of the article's abstract, and another field for the list of topic keywords drawn from Medical Subject Headings (MeSH). Each of these fields is given a different name, and at search time, the client could specify that it was searching for authors or titles or both, potentially restricting to a date range and set of journals by constructing search terms for the appropriate fields and values.

The value of a field can be indexed for search or stored for retrieval or both. The value of an indexed field is processed into terms that are stored in the inverted index. The raw value of a stored field is stored in the index in a non-inverted manner. Storing the raw values allows you to retrieve them at search time but may consume substantial space.

7.4.1 Class `FieldType` Specifies Indexing Details

The package `oal.document` contains classes and interfaces for fields. The Lucene API for fields has changed across the major versions of Lucene as the functionality and organization of the underlying Lucene index have evolved. Lucene 4 introduces a new interface `IndexableField`, which is implemented by class `Field`. Lucene 4 also introduces datatype-specific subclasses of `Field` that encapsulate indexing and storage details for common use cases. For example, to index integer values, use class `IntField`, and to index simple unanalyzed strings (keywords), use `StringField`. These so-called *sugar subclasses* are all final subclasses.

The class `FieldType`, introduced in Lucene 4, holds information about how a field is indexed and stored. In Lucene 3 this functionality was implemented by a number of flags passed in to the `Field` constructor. Class `FieldType` implements the new interface `IndexableFieldType`. The `Fieldable` interface is now deprecated, and most of its functionality has been moved into `IndexableFieldType`.

In Lucene 4 indexing and storage options are specified via setter methods on `FieldType`. These include the method `setIndexed(boolean)`, which specifies whether or not to index a field, and the method `setTokenized(boolean)`, which specifies whether or not the value should be tokenized. The method `setOmitNorms(boolean)` controls how Lucene computes term frequency.

Lucene's default behavior is to represent term frequency as a proportion by computing the ratio of the number of times a term occurs to the total number of terms in the document, instead of storing a simple term frequency count. To do this calculation it stores a normalizing factor for each field that is indexed. Calling method `setOmitNorms` with value `true` turns this off and the raw term frequency is used instead. `FieldType` contains getter methods corresponding to these setter methods. The names of the getter methods omit the word *set* with the corresponding camel case conventions. The method `indexed` is the getter corresponding to `setIndexed`, `stored` corresponds to `setStored`, and so forth.

Some indexing choices are interdependent. Lucene checks the values on a `FieldType` object at `Field` construction time and throws an `IllegalArgumentException` if the `FieldType` has inconsistent values. For example, a field must be either indexed or stored or both, so `indexed` and/or `stored` must be `true`. If `indexed` is false, then `stored` must be true and all other indexing options should be set to false.

The source code of the subclasses of `Field` provides good examples of how to define a `FieldType`. The following code fragment defines a custom `FieldType` and then creates a `Field` of this type:

```
FieldType myFieldType = new FieldType();
myFieldType.setIndexed(true);
myFieldType.setOmitNorms(true);
myFieldType.setIndexOptions(IndexOptions.DOCS_AND_FREQS);
myFieldType.setStored(false);
myFieldType.setTokenized(true);
myFieldType.freeze();
Field myField = new Field("field name",
                          "field value",
                          myFieldType);
```

The argument to the method `setIndexOptions` is an enum constant of type `FieldInfo.IndexOptions` in package `oal.index`. It controls how much information is stored in the inverted index. The default value is `DOCS_AND_FREQS_AND_POSITIONS_AND_OFFSETS`. Positions and offsets correspond to the term attributes that we examined in the demo class `LuceneTokenize` (see section 7.3.3).

The field type is mutable, although changes should not be made after the field has been instantiated. The method `freeze()` is used to prevent further changes to the field type. Any `FieldType` setter method will throw an `IllegalStateException` if it is called after `freeze()` has been called.

7.4.2 Constructing Fields

Lucene 4 provides the class `Field` in package `oal.document`, which implements the interface `IndexibleField` and subclasses of `Field` for common data types: `IntField`, `LongField`, `FloatField`, `DoubleField`, `BinaryDocValuesField`, `NumericDocValuesField`, `SortedDocValuesField`, `StringField`, `TextField`, and `StoredField`. The class `StoredField` is used for fields that are stored but not indexed.

A field requires all of its components to be specified in the constructor. Even so, fields are defined to be mutable so that their values, but not their field names, may be reset after construction.

The `Field.Store` Enum

The enum `Field.Store` is used to mark whether or not to store the value of a field. Its two instances, `Store.YES` and `Store.NO`, have the obvious interpretations.

The `Field` subclass `StoredField` is automatically stored. The `StoredField` constructor takes arguments field name and value. All other constructors for a `Field` object take arguments field name, value, and an instance of enum `Field.Store`.

Specifying the Value Argument

Each constructor for a field requires a value for the field, which may be supplied as a Java `String`, Lucene `TokenStream`, `Reader`,[10] or a `byte` array or reference to a byte array. Lucene doesn't copy the byte array values, so these cannot be changed as long as the `Field` is being used. If the field is a stored field, the value must be supplied as a `String`.

The getter method for the field value must match the type used in the constructor. There are three getter methods: `stringValue`, `binaryValue`, and `readerValue()`. If the field value is a `String`, the method `stringValue()` will return the field value and the other two methods will return `null`.

7.4.3 Date Fields

Lucene doesn't support a primitive date field type, so we must either use a `LongField` or a `StringField` to index a `java.util.Date` object. The class

---

[10] We recommend against using a `Reader`, because the policy on closing such readers is confusing. It's up to the client to close, but the close can be done only after the document has been added to an index. Making fields stateful in this way introduces a lifecycle management problem that's easily avoided. Very rarely will documents be such that a file or network-based reader may be used as is in a field; usually such streams are parsed into fields before indexing, eliminating any performance advantage readers might have.

oal.document.DateTools has a set of static methods that provide support for manipulating date and time information for both numeric and string fields.

A java.util.Date object holds a long, which stores the date as number of milliseconds from January 1, 1970. The method getTime returns this value. Here is a time value of a Date object, printed as a decimal:

    1372601887935

The toString method prints out a formatted version of the Date. This format depends on the default platform Locale and other settings. Here is the result of the toString method for the same Date object, using the default settings on a MacBook Air configured for the North American Eastern Time Zone.

    Sun Jun 30 10:18:07 EDT 2013

Given a set of dates, the sort order of the formatted date string won't necessarily match the chronological sort order. In order to get a string representation where the lexicographic sort order matches chronological order, the date and time values must be organized from the most to the least significant: year, month (or week), day, hour, minute, second, millisecond, and ordinal values, not names, are used for months. The date string representation used by Lucene is a compact format:

    yyyyMMddHHmmssSSS

The format string yyyy is 4 digit year, MM is 2-digit month (01 for January through 12 for December), dd is 2-digit day padded with zero, HH is hour, (where noon is 12 and midnight is 00), mm are minutes, ss are seconds and SSS are milliseconds.

It is important to index dates and times at the appropriate level of granularity and no finer. For example, an application that indexes information about films may care about only the calendar year in which a film was released when it comes to search and indexing and therefore may need date resolution only at the year level. An application that indexes journal articles may need date resolution down to the day (i.e., day, month, year) level, while an application that indexes real-time data may need date resolution down to the millisecond.

The DateTools class contains an enum type Resolution , which is used to specify time granularity. The set of constants are {MILLISECOND SECOND MINUTE HOUR DAY MONTH YEAR}.

Indexing dates at too fine a level of resolution can increase the size of the index unnecessarily. A Lucene index is an index over terms. If one document contains the date *June 25, 2013, 07:00.0000* and another document contains the date *June 25, 2013, 07:01.0000*, then each date is a different index term. If the application requires resolution only at the year level, indexing the raw dates at full resolution may waste a large amount of space.

Indexing dates at too fine a level of resolution can also be problematic for sorting. If the primary sort order is by date and a secondary sort order is specified as well, the secondary sort order will not be applied unless the dates are equal. If the dates differ at some finer resolution than is actually significant, the secondary sort order won't be applied.

The sample class `DateDemo` transforms a `java.util.Date` object into string and numeric objects at various levels of granularity.

```
Date now = new Date();
String strMilli
    = DateTools.dateToString(now,
                            Resolution.MILLISECOND);
String strDay
    = DateTools.dateToString(now,
                            Resolution.DAY);
long numDay =
    DateTools.round(now.getTime(),
                    Resolution.DAY);
```

We create a new `java.util.Date` object using the zero-arg constructor, which returns a `Date` that represents the time at which it was allocated, measured to the nearest millisecond. The static method `DateTools.dateToString` method takes a `Date` object and a `DateTools.Resolution` as arguments and returns a formatted string at the specified resolution. Specifying `Resolution.MILLI` returns a string in the format yyyyMMddHHmmssSSS, while specifying DAY returns a string in the format yyyyMMdd. The static method `DateTools.round` takes the time value from a `Date` object (i.e., the `long` returned by the `getTime` method) and a resolution and returns a `long` where all values above the specified resolution have been set to 0 or 1. The Ant target `date-demo` runs the demo.

```
> ant date-demo
now: Sun Jun 30 19:42:07 EDT 2013
strMilli: 20130630234207109
strDay: 20130630
time now: 1372635727109
time rounded: 1372550400000
```

7.5 Documents

In Lucene, documents are represented as instances of the final class `Document`, in package `oal.document`.

7.5.1 Constructing and Populating Documents

Documents are constructed using a zero-arg constructor `Document()`. Once a document is constructed, the method `add(IndexableField)` is used to add fields to the document.

Lucene does not in any way constrain document structures. An index can store a heterogeneous set of documents. These documents can have any number of different fields that vary by document in arbitrary ways.

A document may have more than one field with the same name added to it. All of the fields with a given name will be searchable under that name (if the field is indexed, of course). The behavior is conceptually similar to what you'd get from concatenating all the field values; the main difference is that phrase searches don't work across the concatenated items.

7.5.2 Accessing Fields in Documents

The `Document` class provides methods to get a field by name. The method `getField(String)` returns the value of the field with the specified name. If no such field exists, it returns `null` rather than raising an exception. If there are multiple values for that field, `getField` returns the first one added to the document. The method `getFields(String)` returns an array of all fields in a document with the given name. It's costly to construct arrays at run time (in both space and time for allocation and garbage collection), so if there is only a single value, the simpler method is preferable. The method `get(String)` returns the string value of the field. It is equivalent to `getField(String).toString()`.

The `getField` and `getFields` methods return an object or array of objects of type `IndexableField`. This is an interface type that defines getter methods on a field's name, type, and value but no setter method for the field value. To set the value of a field it is necessary to cast it to a concrete class.

7.5.3 Document Demo

We provide a simple demo class, `DocDemo`, which shows how to construct and populate a document and how to access its constituent fields.

```
Document doc = new Document();

doc.add(new TextField("title", "The Federalist Papers",
                    Store.YES));
doc.add(new IntField("etextId",1404,
                    Store.NO));
doc.add(new StoredField("downloadUrl",
                "www.gutenberg.org/ebooks/1404.txt.utf-8"));
doc.add(new StringField("releaseDate","198807",
                    Store.YES));
```

```
for (IndexableField f : doc.getFields()) {
    String name = f.name();
    String value = f.stringValue();
    IndexableFieldType fieldType = f.fieldType();
    boolean isIndexed = fieldType.indexed();
    boolean isStored = fieldType.stored();
    boolean isTokenized = fieldType.tokenized();
```

We instantiate an empty document and add fields to it. After constructing the document, we loop over the fields and inspect them. Note that the access is through the `IndexableField` interface. We include the calls to the relevant methods, but omit the actual print statements The Ant target `doc-demo` runs the demo.

```
> ant doc-demo
name=title
  value=The Federalist Papers
  indexed, tokenized, stored,
name=etextId
  value=1404
  indexed, tokenized,
name=downloadUrl
  value=www.gutenberg.org/ebooks/1404.txt.utf-8
  tokenized, stored,
name=releaseDate
  value=198807
  indexed, stored,
```

7.6 Indexing

A Lucene index consists of an inverted index from terms to documents as well as the contents of stored fields. The key classes involved in indexing are `IndexWriter` in package `oal.index`, which is responsible for adding documents to an index, and `Directory` in package `oal.store`, which is the storage abstraction used for the index itself.

Directories provide an interface that's similar to an operating system's file system. A `Directory` contains any number of sub-indexes called *segments*. Maintaining the index as a set of segments allows Lucene to rapidly update and delete documents from the index.

The index file format is subject to change from release to release as different methods of indexing and compressing the data are implemented. A Lucene index knows what version of Lucene was used to create it (by using the

Lucene Version enum constant). Lucene is backward compatible with respect to searching and maintaining old index versions because it includes classes that can read and write all versions of the index up through the current release.

7.6.1 Types of Directories

The FSDirectory abstract base class extends Directory to support implementations based on a file system. This is the most common way to create a directory in Lucene. The implementation RAMDirectory supports in-memory directories, which are efficient but less scalable than file-system directories. The package oal.store contains additional specialized implementations.

7.6.2 Constructing File-System Directories

An instance of a file-system directory may be created using the factory method FSDirectory.open(File), which returns an implementation of FSDirectory. As of Lucene 3.6, this method returns a specific FSDirectory implementation, based on your environment and the known limitations of each implementation.

At construction, all FSDirectory implementations are supplied with a File and a LockFactory object, which specifies how the files on the file system will be locked. The LockFactory class is an abstract class. Several implementations are provided in the package oal.store. Convenience constructors supply a default LockFactory. As of Lucene 3.6, this is a NativeFSLockFactory.

7.6.3 Constructing an IndexWriter

An IndexWriter is constructed from a lucene.store.Directory and a IndexWriterConfig object. The IndexWriterConfig specifies the Lucene version of the index, the default Analyzer, and how the IndexWriter uses memory and processing resources during indexing. The IndexWriterConfig constructor takes the Lucene version and the default analyzer as arguments and sets its properties to default values accordingly. Getter and setter methods are used to query and update these properties.

The Analyzer Used for Indexing

When a document is added to the index, the default Analyzer is invoked on each indexed field in the document. We follow the Lucene documentation in calling the analyzer passed in to the IndexWriterConfig's constructor the default analyzer although it is the only analyzer used by the IndexWriter.

If the different fields of a document require different tokenization strategies, then a `PerFieldAnalyzerWrapper` is used to map fields to analyzers. A `PerFieldAnalyzerWrapper` maintains a map from field names to analyzers and also specifies an analyzer to be used for fields whose name is not in the map from fields to analyzers. It is in package `oal.analysis.miscellaneous`. The following code fragment defines an analyzer that tokenizes all fields in the document, excepting the field named `id`, which is treated as a single token:

```
Map<String,Analyzer> fieldAnalyzerMap
    = new HashMap<String,Analyzer>();
fieldAnalyzerMap.put("id", new KeywordAnalyzer());
PerFieldAnalyzerWrapper perFieldAnalyzer =
    new PerFieldAnalyzerWrapper(new StandardAnalyzer(VERSION),
                                fieldAnalyzerMap);
```

Segments and Merges

Indexing maintains a small buffer of documents in memory, periodically writing the data in that batch of documents out to disk as a segment file. After enough such batches have been written to disk, Lucene automatically merges smaller segments into larger segments and as these accumulate, they too are merged. Being able to merge indexes makes it easy to split the indexing job into multiple independent jobs.

You can observe this behavior in your file browser if you're using a disk directory for indexing a large batch of documents. As more documents are added, small index segments are continually added. Then, at various points, these smaller segments are merged into larger segments.

The `IndexWriterConfig` object has controls for the size of the in-memory buffer, how often it's flushed, and how often and how aggressively segments are merged. Getting the merge policy right is an important part of Lucene performance tuning.

7.6.4 Indexing Demo

The demo class `IndexPapers` shows how basic text indexing works. This class indexes the 85 essays that make up *The Federalist Papers*, the dataset used for the case study in chapter 6. We've made this class part of the package `com.colloquial.casestudy` since it uses the `FederalistParser` class to parse the Project Gutenberg Etext file into a list of `Paper` objects.

The class `IndexPapers` consists of a `main()` method that takes two command-line arguments corresponding to the location of the Project Gutenberg Etext file and the location of the Lucene index.

```
public static void main(String[] args)
    throws CorruptIndexException, LockObtainFailedException,
        IOException {

    if (args.length < 2) {
        System.err.println("usage: IndexPapers "
                            + "<etext> <index>");
        System.exit(-1);
    }
    File etextFile = new File(args[0]);
    File indexDir = new File(args[1]);

    Directory fsDir = FSDirectory.open(indexDir);

    Analyzer stdAn
        = new StandardAnalyzer(Version.LUCENE_45);
    IndexWriterConfig iwConf
        = new IndexWriterConfig(Version.LUCENE_45,stdAn);

    iwConf.setOpenMode(IndexWriterConfig.OpenMode.CREATE);
    IndexWriter indexWriter
        = new IndexWriter(fsDir,iwConf);
```

First we get and check the command-line arguments, then we construct the index writer. We create a file-system-based directory and instantiate a StandardAnalyzer (in package oal.analysis.standard). This analyzer chains together a StandardTokenizer, which breaks the text into a stream of words, discarding whitespace and punctuation, followed by a StandardFilter, a LowerCaseFilter, and then a StopFilter, which uses a list of English stop words. Next we specify the config for the index writer. We call the setOpenMode method with the enum constant IndexWriterConfig.OpenMode.CREATE, which causes the index writer to create a new index or overwrite an existing one. The other two possible open-mode enums are IndexWriterConfig.OpenMode.CREATE_OR_APPEND, which creates a new index if one does not exist, else opens an existing index and appends documents, and IndexWriterConfig.OpenMode.APPEND, which opens an existing index or throws an error if it doesn't exist.

For both the standard analyzer and the index writer config, we pass in a Lucene version constant. Finally, we create an index writer from the directory and the index writer config.

Constructing the index may throw all three exceptions listed on the main() method. The first two exceptions are Lucene's, and both extend IOException. You may wish to catch them separately in some cases, as they clearly indicate what went wrong. A CorruptIndexException will be thrown if we attempt to open an index that is not well formed. A LockObtainFailedException will be thrown if the index writer could not obtain a file lock on the index directory. A

plain-old Java IOException will be thrown if there is an underlying I/O error
reading or writing from the files in the directory.

The second half of the main() method parses the Project Gutenberg Etext
file into a list of Paper objects and then loops over the items in the list. It
converts each Paper into a Lucene Document and adds it to the index.

```
FederalistParser parser = new FederalistParser();
List<Paper> papers = parser.parsePapers(etextFile);
for (Paper paper : papers) {
    Document d = new Document();
    d.add(new IntField("number",
                        paper.getNumber(),Store.YES));
    d.add(new TextField("title",
                        paper.getTitle(),Store.YES));
    d.add(new StringField("author",
                        paper.getAuthor1(),Store.YES));
    if (paper.getAuthor2() != null) {
        d.add(new StringField("author",
                        paper.getAuthor2(),Store.YES));
    }
    d.add(new StringField("pubName",
                        paper.getPubName(),Store.YES));
    Date date = paper.getPubDate();
    long roundDate = DateTools.round(date.getTime(),
                                    Resolution.DAY);
    d.add(new LongField("pubDate",
                        roundDate,Store.YES));
    d.add(new TextField("text",
                        paper.getTitle(),Store.YES));
    for (String paragraph : paper.getParagraphs()) {
        d.add(new TextField("text",
                        paragraph,Store.YES));
    }
    indexWriter.addDocument(d);
}
int numDocs = indexWriter.numDocs();
indexWriter.commit();
indexWriter.close();
```

We populate the document using a series of addField calls. All documents have fields number, title, author, pubName, pubDate, and text.
The author and text fields have multiple values. The title and text
fields are analyzed while the pubName and author fields aren't. We
use the oal.document.DateTools to insure that the pubDate values are

rounded to the `Resolution.DAY`. After creating the document, we call the `addDocument(Document)` method of the index writer to add it to the index.

After we've finished indexing all papers, we call the index writer's `commit` method. This commits all pending changes on the index and syncs all referenced index files so that the changes are visible to index readers. Lucene now implements a two-phase commit so that if the commit succeeds, the changes to the index will survive a crash or power loss. A commit may be expensive, and part of performance tuning is determining when to commit as well as how often and how aggressively to merge the segments of the index.

We close the index writer using the `close()` method, which may throw an `IOException`. Finally, we get the number of documents that are in the current index using the method `numDocs()`; if documents were in the index when it was opened, these are included in the count. We also print out other counts, such as the number of characters (print statements omitted from above code listing).

Since this program is part of package `com.colloquial.casestudy`, we use the Ant `build.xml` file in `javabook/src/casestudy`. The Ant target `index-papers` runs the indexing demo. Command-line arguments are passed into the program via the Ant properties `etext` and `lucene.dir`. The `build.xml` files defines default values for these properties:

```
<property name="etext"
          value="../../data/federalist-papers/pg1404.txt"/>
<property name="lucene.dir"
          value="../../data/federalist-papers/lucene"/>
```

We run the program using the default property values:

```
> cd javabook/src/casestudy
> ant index-papers
index=lucene
num docs=85
```

The run indexed 85 documents consisting of approximately 1.1 million words total. Lucene's very fast. On a workstation, it takes less than a second to run the demo, including forking a new JVM. On a modest notebook computer it takes three seconds.

The Lucene index directory (as specified specified by the `lucene.dir` property) contains a set of binary files that constitute the index.

The package `oal.codecs` defines the API for the encoding and organization of the index and for each version of Lucene there is a corresponding codec package. The package javadoc describes the file naming conventions. In this demo, the version constant used to instantiate the `IndexWriterConfig` was `LUCENE_45` and so the package `oal.codecs.lucene45` was used to generate these file.

After indexing, we can look at the contents of the index directory, showing file size in kilobytes. The size of the Project Gutenberg plain-text version of *The Federalist Papers* is 1.16 MB. The size of the Lucene index is a little smaller, 1.06 MB, even though it comprises both the inverted index over the text and the stored text of the 85 papers themselves.

```
> export BLOCKSIZE=1024; ls -sl ../../data/federalist-papers/lucene/
   4 _0.cfe
1060 _0.cfs
   4 _0.si
   4 segments.gen
   4 segments_1
```

These files were generated by the codec for version Lucene45. The javadoc for the oal.lucene.codex.lucene45 describes the file contents and naming conventions (see: http://lucene.apache.org/core/4_5_1/core/org/apache/lucene/codecs/lucene45/package-summary.html).

7.6.5 Duplicate Documents

The IndexWriter is opened with mode OpenMode.CREATE_OR_OVERWRITE in this demo. If we configure it using OpenMode.CREATE_OR_APPEND and run the demo program for a second time using the existing index, the 85 papers will be added to the index again, resulting in an index that contains 170 documents altogether. Although a Lucene index provides identifiers for documents that are unique (though not necessarily stable over optimizations), nothing in the index enforces uniqueness of document contents. Lucene can and will happily create a document that has exactly the same fields and values as another document, giving the new document a unique internal identifier.

7.7 Queries and Query Parsing

Lucene provides a highly configurable hybrid form of search that combines exact boolean searches with softer, more relevance-ranking-oriented vector-space search methods. All searches are field specific, because Lucene indexes terms and a term is composed of a field name and a token.[11]

---

[11]Given that search is carried out over terms, there's no way to easily have a query search over all fields. Instead, field-specific queries must be disjoined to achieve this effect. Scoring for this approach may be problematic because hits on a shorter field will have a higher score than hits on a longer field. Another approach is to denormalize the documents by creating synthetic fields that concatenate the value of other fields.

7.7.1 Constructing Queries Programmatically

Queries may be constructed programmatically using the dozen or so built-in implementations of the `Query` abstract base class from the package `oal.search`.

The most basic kind of query is a search for a single token on a single field, i.e., a single term. This query is implemented in Lucene's `TermQuery` class, also in the `search` package. A term query is constructed from a `Term`, which is found in package `oal.index`. A term is constructed from a field name and text for the term, both specified as strings.

The `BooleanQuery` class is very misleadingly named; it supports both hard boolean queries and relevance-ranked vector-space queries, as well as allowing them to be mixed. A boolean query may be constructed with the no-argument constructor `BooleanQuery()`. Other queries may then be added to the boolean query using the method `add(Query,BooleanClause.Occur)`. The second argument, an instance of the nested enum `BooleanClause.Occur` in package `search`, indicates whether the added query is to be treated as a hard boolean constraint or contribute to the relevance ranking of vector queries. Possible values are `BooleanClause.MUST`, `BooleanClause.MUST_NOT`, and `BooleanClause.SHOULD`. The first two are used for hard boolean queries, requiring the term to appear or not appear in any result. The last value, `SHOULD`, is used for vector-space queries. With this occurrence value, Lucene will prefer results that match the query but may return results that do not match the query.

The recursive nature of the API and the overloading of queries to act as both hard boolean and vector-type relevance queries leads to the situation where queries may mix hard and soft constraints. It appears that clauses constrained by hard boolean occurrence constraints, `MUST` or `MUST_NOT`, do not contribute to scoring. It's less clear what happens when one of these hybrid queries is nested inside another boolean query with its own occurrence specification. For instance, it's not clear what happens when we nest a query with must-occur and should-occur clauses as a must-occur clause in a larger query.

```
BooleanQuery bq1 = new BooleanQuery();
bq1.add(new TermQuery(new Term("text","red")), Occur.MUST);
bq1.add(new TermQuery(new Term("text","blue")), Occur.SHOULD);

BooleanQuery bq2 = new BooleanQuery();
bq2.add(new TermQuery(new Term("text","green")), Occur.SHOULD);
bq2.add(bq1,Occur.MUST);
```

7.7.2   Query Parsing

Lucene specifies a language in which queries may be expressed. For instance, [computer NOT java][12] produces a query that specifies the term *computer* must appear in the default field and the term *java* must not appear. Queries may specify fields, as in *text:java*, which requires the term *java* to appear in the text field of a document.

The full syntax specification is in the package level javadoc for package oal.queryparser.classic. The query syntax includes basic term and field specifications, modifiers for wildcard, fuzzy, proximity, or range searches, and boolean operators for requiring a term to be present, absent, or for combining queries with logical operators. Finally, sub-queries may be boosted by providing numeric values to raise or lower their prominence relative to other parts of the query.

The query language in Lucene suffers from a confusion between queries over tokens and queries over terms. Complete queries must be over terms. But parts of queries are naturally constrained to be over tokens in the sense of not mentioning any field values. For instance, if *Q* is a well-formed query, then so is foo:*Q*. In proper usage, the query *Q* should be constrained to not mention any fields. In other words, *Q* should be a query over tokens, not a general query.

Query Language Syntax

In Figure 7.2, we provide an overview of the full syntax available through Lucene's query parser. The following characters must be escaped by preceding them with a backslash:

+   -   & | !   (   )   {   }   [   ]   ^   "   ~   *   ?   :   \

For example, [foo:a\(c] searches for the three-character token *a(c* in the field foo. Of course, if the queries are specified as Java string literals, further escaping is required (see section 2.6).

7.7.3   Default Fields, Token Queries, and Term Queries

When we set up a query parser, we will be supplying a default field. Unmarked token queries will then be interpreted as if constrained to that field. For instance, if title is the default query field, then query [cell] is the same as the query [title:cell].

Like the programmatic queries, Lucene's query language does not clearly separate the role of token-level queries, which match tokens or sequences of tokens, and term-level queries, which match tokens within a field. Thus,

---

[12]We display queries *Q* as [*Q*] to indicate the scope of the search without using quotes, which are often part of the search itself.

Type	Syntax	Description
Token	t	Match token t
Phrase	`"cs"`	Match tokens in cs in exact order without gaps
Field	`f:Q`	Match query Q in field f
Wildcard, Char	`cs1?cs2`	Match tokens starting with $cs1$, ending with $cs2$, with any char between
Wildcard, Seq	`cs1*cs2`	Match tokens starting with $cs1$, ending with $cs2$, with any char sequence between
Fuzzy	`t~`	Match token t approximately
Fuzzy, Weighted	`t~d`	Match token t within minimum similarity d
Proximity	`P~n`	Match tokens in phrase P within distance n
Range, Inclusive	`f:[t1 TO t2]`	Match tokens lexicographically between tokens $t1$ and $t2$ inclusive
Range, Exclusive	`f:(t1 TO t2)`	Match tokens lexicographically between tokens $t1$ and $t2$ exclusive
Boosting	`P^d`	Match phrase P, boosting score by d
Disjunction	`Q1 OR Q2`	Match query $Q1$ or query $Q2$ (or both)
Conjunction	`Q1 AND Q2`	Match query $Q1$ and match query $Q2$
Difference	`Q1 NOT Q2`	Match query $Q1$ but not query $Q2$
Must	`+P`	Token or phrase P must appear
Mustn't	`-P`	Token or phrase P must not appear
Grouping	`(Q)`	Match query Q (disambiguates parsing)

Fig. 7.2: Lucene's Query Syntax. *In the table, t is a token made up of a sequence of characters, f is a field name made up of a sequence of characters, $cs1$ is a non-empty sequence of characters, $cs2$ is any sequence of characters, d is a decimal number, n is a natural number, Q is an arbitrary well-formed query, and P is a well-formed phrase query.*

it's possible to write out queries with rather unclear structure, such as
[text:(money AND author:JAY)]; this query will actually match (as you can
try with the demo in the next section) because the embedded field author
takes precedence over the top-level field text.

7.7.4   Range Queries over Terms

The classes TermRangeQuery and NumericRangeQuery in package
oal.search provide search for a range of values on a field. The class
NumericRangeQuery<T extends Number> is used to search numeric fields
(subclasses IntField, LongField, FloatField, DoubleField) and the class
TermRangeQuery is used to search string and text fields. Range searches
require five parameters: the name of the field to search, two values giving
the lower and upper bounds of the search, and two booleans that indicate
whether or not these bounds are inclusive or exclusive.

The following code fragment shows how to construct range queries over
the example index created by IndexPapers in section 7.6.4:

```
BytesRef brI = new BytesRef("I");
BytesRef brJ = new BytesRef("J");
Query termRangeQuery
    = new TermRangeQuery("author",brI,brJ,true,true);

Query numericRangeQuery
    = NumericRangeQuery.newIntRange("number",1,5,true,true);
```

As of Lucene 4, the oal.util.BytesRef object is used for terms in the
index, which are encoded as UTF-8 bytes. Many methods that previously
took Java String objects now require a BytesRef instead, including the
TermRangeQuery constructor. The author field in the example index is a
StringField. There are three author names: HAMILTON, JAY, and MADISON.
In order to search for authors whose names begin with the letters *I* to *J* inclusive, first we construct a BytesRef for each letter (brI and brJ). We pass
these into the TermRangeConstructor and specify true for both the parameters includeLower and includeUpper.

The NumericRangeQuery class provides static factory methods used to create queries. The number field in our example is an IntField so we call the
static factory method newIntRange accordingly.

7.7.5   The QueryParser Class

Lucene's QueryParser class, in package oal.queryparser, converts string-
based queries that are well-formed according to Lucene's query syntax into
Query objects. A query parser is constructed using an analyzer, default field,
and Lucene version. The default field is used for queries that do not otherwise

specify the field they search over. It may then be used to convert string-based queries into query objects for searching.

The constructor `QueryParser(Version,String,Analyzer)` requires a Lucene version, a string picking out a default field for unmarked tokens, and an analyzer with which to break phrasal queries down into token sequences.

Query parsing is accomplished through the method `parse(String)`, which returns a `Query`. The parse method will throw a Lucene `ParseException`, also in package `queryparser`, if the query is not well formed. The `Query.toString` method returns an explicit representation of the query using the syntax described in Figure 7.2.

7.8 Search

Lucene uses instances of the aptly named `IndexReader` to read data from an index. Lucene supplies an `IndexSearcher` class that performs the actual search. Every index searcher wraps an index reader to get a handle on the indexed data. Once we have an index searcher, we can supply queries to it and enumerate results in order of their score.

There is really nothing to configure in an index searcher other than its reader, so we'll jump straight to the demo code. All of our search demo programs are part of package `com.colloquial.applucene`. Ant targets are defined in the `build.xml` file in `javabook/src/applucene`.

7.8.1 Search Demo

We provide a demo class `LuceneSearch` that we use to run searches over the index created by class `IndexPapers` in section 7.6.4. The code is in the `main()` method of the demo class `LuceneSearch`. The method starts off by reading in command-line arguments.

```
public static void main(String[] args)
    throws ParseException, CorruptIndexException,
          IOException {

    File indexDir = new File(args[0]);
    String query = args[1];
    int maxHits = Integer.parseInt(args[2]);
```

We need the directory for the index, a string representing the query in Lucene's query language, and a specification of the maximum number of hits to return. The method is declared to throw a Lucene corrupt index exception if the index isn't well formed, a Lucene parse exception if the query isn't well formed, and a general Java I/O exception if there is a problem reading from or writing to the index directory.

After setting the command-line arguments, the next step is to create a Lucene directory, index reader, index searcher, and query parser and use the query parser to parse the query.

```
Directory fsDir = FSDirectory.open(indexDir);
DirectoryReader reader = DirectoryReader.open(fsDir);
IndexSearcher searcher = new IndexSearcher(reader);
Analyzer stdAn
    = new StandardAnalyzer(Version.LUCENE_45);
QueryParser parser
    = new QueryParser(Version.LUCENE_45,"text",stdAn);
Query q= parser.parse(query);
System.out.println("parsed query=" + q.toString());
```

Since class `IndexPapers` uses a `StandardAnalyzer`, we also use one here.

It is important to use the same analyzer in the query parser as is used in the creation of the index. If they don't match, queries that should succeed will fail should the different analyzers produce differing tokenizations given the same input. For instance, if we apply stemming to the contents of text field `foo` during indexing and reduce the word *codes* to *code*, but we don't apply stemming to the query, then a search for the word *codes* in field `foo` will fail. The search term is `foo:codes` but the index contains only the term `foo:code`.

The `QueryParser.parse` method returns a `Query` object if the query string is well formed and throws a `ParseException` if it is not. It recognizes the Lucene query syntax language. All tokens are analyzed using the specified `Analyzer`. We call the `toString` method on the resulting query to inspect the parsed query. Finally we search the index and report the results.

```
TopDocs hits = searcher.search(q,maxHits);
ScoreDoc[] scoreDocs = hits.scoreDocs;
System.out.println("hits=" + scoreDocs.length);
System.out.println("Hits (rank,score,paper)");
for (int n = 0; n < scoreDocs.length; ++n) {
    ScoreDoc sd = scoreDocs[n];
    float score = sd.score;
    int docId = sd.doc;
    Document d = searcher.doc(docId);
    String number = d.get("number");
```

The searcher's `search` method takes two arguments: the query and an upper bound on the number of hits to return. It returns an instance of the Lucene class `TopDocs` (package `oal.search`). The `TopDocs` result provides access to an array of search results. Each result is an instance of the Lucene class `ScoreDoc`, also in the `oal.search` package, which encapsulates a document reference with a floating point score.

The array of search results is sorted in decreasing order of score, with higher scores representing better matches. We enumerate over the results array. For each ScoreDoc object, we get the score from the public member variable score. We get the document reference number (Lucene's internal identifier for the doc) from the public member variable doc. We use the Lucene document identifier to retrieve the document from the searcher. Finally, with the document in hand, we retrieve the paper number via the get() method. We use get() here rather than getValues(), which returns an array, because we know there is only one number per document.

The Ant target lucene-search runs the search demo. Command-line arguments are passed into the program via the Ant properties lucene.dir, query, and max.hits. The build.xml file defines the following default values for these properties:

```
<property name="lucene.dir"
          value="../../data/federalist-papers/lucene"/>
<property name="query"
          value="Powers of the Judiciary"/>
<property name="max.hits"
          value="10"/>
```

We run the program via Ant using the default arguments specified in the build.xml file in the in javabook/src/applucene directory.

```
> ant lucene-search
index=lucene
query=Powers of the Judiciary
max hits=10
parsed query=text:powers text:judiciary
hits=10
Hits (rank,score,paper)
  0 0.29  47
  1 0.23  48
  2 0.19  78
  3 0.17  80
  4 0.14  44
  5 0.14  45
  6 0.14  49
  7 0.14  71
  8 0.11  66
  9 0.11  38
```

The query parser treats the query string as a stream of tokens and uses the default field to create a query consisting of one or more terms. In the case of multiple terms, Lucene uses a BooleanQuery where each term is added as a `BooleanClause.SHOULD`. The analyzer stop-lists the words *of* and *the*, reducing this query to a boolean search for the terms [`text:powers`] and/or [`text:judiciary`]. Lucene returns 10 results numbered 0 to 9. Paper 47 is the best match. This paper contains 18 instances of the term *powers* and 24 instances of *judiciary*. This document matches all tokens in the query, yet the score is only 0.30. The reason for this is that these documents are relatively long, median length 2,100 words, over a vocabulary of roughly 8,000 words, so the percentage of tokens in the document matching the query tokens is relatively low.

The token *food* does not show up in any documents, so the query [`text:food`] returns no hits.

```
> ant lucene-search -Dquery=food
index=lucene
query=food
max hits=10
parsed query=text:food
hits=0
```

The query *powers of the judiciary food* returns exactly the same hits as the query *powers of the judiciary*, in exactly the same order but with lower scores.

```
> ant lucene-search -Dquery="Powers of the Judiciary food"
index=lucene
query=Powers of the Judiciary food
max hits=10
parsed query=text:powers text:judiciary text:food
hits=10
Hits (rank,score,paper)
  0 0.08   47
  1 0.07   48
  ...
  9 0.03   38
```

The query parser recognizes the Lucene query language. To run this search on the `title` field instead of the `text` field, we specify the field name overtly and use parentheses around the search tokens:

```
> ant lucene-search -Dquery="title:(Powers of the Judiciary)"
index=lucene
query=title:(Powers of the Judiciary)
max hits=10
parsed query=title:powers title:judiciary
hits=10
Hits (rank,score,paper)
```

```
    0 2.86  80
    1 0.83  78
    ...
    9 0.42  42
```

The Lucene search syntax uses double quotes (") to enclose a phrase.

```
> ant lucene-search -Dquery="\\\"Powers of the Judiciary\\\""
index=lucene
query="Powers of the Judiciary"
max hits=10
parsed query=text:"powers ? ? judiciary"
hits=1
Hits (rank,score,paper)
  0 0.08  80
```

Question marks indicate stop-listed words. This exact phrase occurs in only one document in the index.

The double quote character is syntactically significant for both the Unix shell and Ant therefore, it must be escaped twice. The Unix shell strips off one set of backslash characters, taking the sequence \\\" to \". Ant strips off the remaining backslash leaving the double quotes in the string passed in as the argument to the Java program.

Because the LuceneSearch program applies the QueryParser.parse method to the command-line query string, all tokens are analyzed using a StandardAnalyzer. This is exactly what we need in order to search the text and title fields of the example index. Searches over the other fields in the index using this program will fail because the terms created by the query parser won't match the terms stored in the index.

7.8.2 Ranking

For scoring documents against queries, Lucene uses the complex and highly configurable abstract base class Similarity in the package in oal.search.similarities. Similarity deals with how Lucene weights query terms. When no Similarity class is specified, as in the demos here, the concrete subclass DefaultSimilarity is used.

The basic idea is that the more instances of query terms in a document, the better the score. Terms are not weighted equally. A term is weighted based on its inverse document frequency (IDF), so that terms that occur in fewer documents receive higher weights. Weights may also be boosted or lowered in the query syntax or programmatically with a query object. There is also a component of scoring based on the percentage of the query terms that appear in the document. All else being equal, the more terms in the query covered by the document, the higher the score.

When two documents contain the same number of instances of the query term or terms, the shorter document will have the higher score if Lucene is computing term frequency as a proportion rather than as a raw frequency count (see discussion of document normalization in section 7.4.1). The proportional term frequency is the number of times the query term occurs over the total number of terms in the document. The proportional term frequency may also be higher for a short document that contains only a few instances of a query term compared to a very long document that contains many instances of the query term. This scoring metric can be problematic when a document collection contains both very short and very long documents.

Lucene scoring can be explored programmatically. Lucene provides the class `Explanation` in package `oal.search`. Given an `IndexSearcher` `searcher`, a `Query` `query`, and a `Document` with internal document id `docId`, the call to method `searcher.explain(query,docId)` returns an `Explanation` object, which can be rendered either as plain text or as HTML.

7.9   Deleting and Updating Documents

The `IndexWriter` class supports methods to delete documents from an index based on a term or query. There is also a `deleteAll()` method to completely clear the index. This class also supports methods to update a document or documents that contain a term. The update operation consists of first deleting the existing document(s) that contain a given term and then adding new one(s). This operation is atomic with respect to any index readers open on the index. In earlier versions of Lucene, document deletion was handled by an `IndexReader`.[13] This was deprecated in Lucene 3.6 and removed completely in Lucene 4.

7.9.1   Visibility of Deletes

When a writer's delete method is called, whether based on a term or document identifier, the documents are not immediately physically deleted from the index. Instead, their identifiers are buffered and they are treated as if virtually deleted. The storage space for a deleted document in the index directory is reclaimed only during a merge step.

This approach to document deletion was made for the same efficiency reasons and faces many of the same issues as concurrent sets of variables in Java's memory model. Even when deletes are called on one index, not every

---

[13] Because the `IndexWriter` was originally designed just to append documents to an existing index, it didn't need to keep track of documents already in the index. But in order to delete a document, first it must be found. Since this couldn't be done with an `IndexWriter`, the `deleteDocument` methods were added to the `IndexReader` class.

reader with a handle on that index will be able to see the delete, but any new reader opened on the index after the delete will see the deletion.

7.9.2 Lucene Deletion Demo

We provide a demo class `LuceneDelete` to delete documents from the index created by class `IndexPapers` in section 7.6.4. The `main` method takes three command-line arguments: the name of the Lucene index, a field name, and a token. The field name and token are used to construct the term to delete.

We open the index directory and create a default analyzer just as we did in the demo class `IndexPapers`.

```
Directory fsDir = FSDirectory.open(indexDir);
Analyzer stdAn
    = new StandardAnalyzer(Version.LUCENE_45);
IndexWriterConfig iwConf
    = new IndexWriterConfig(Version.LUCENE_45,stdAn);
iwConf.setOpenMode(IndexWriterConfig.OpenMode.APPEND);

IndexWriter indexWriter
    = new IndexWriter(fsDir,iwConf);
int numDocsBefore = indexWriter.numDocs();
```

We create an `IndexWriterConfig` object that will be passed in to the `IndexWriter` constructor. We set the open mode to `IndexWriterConfig.OpenMode.APPEND` in order to perform deletions on the index. Since class `IndexPapers` uses a `StandardAnalyzer`, we also use one here.

We then construct a term out of the field and token and pass it to the index writer's delete method.

```
Term term = new Term(field,token);
indexWriter.deleteDocuments(term);
```

Finally we call the `commit` method and close the index. We report the number of docs before and after the call to the `commit()` method.

```
int numDocsAfterDeleteBeforeCommit = indexWriter.numDocs();
indexWriter.commit();
indexWriter.close();

IndexWriterConfig iwConf2
    = new IndexWriterConfig(Version.LUCENE_45,stdAn);
iwConf2.setOpenMode(IndexWriterConfig.OpenMode.APPEND);
IndexWriter indexWriter2
    = new IndexWriter(fsDir,iwConf2);
```

```
int numDocsAfter = indexWriter2.numDocs();
indexWriter2.close();
```

The Ant target `lucene-delete` invokes the class, supplying the value of properties `index.dir`, `field`, and `token` as command-line arguments. The `build.xml` file defines the following default values for these properties:

```
<property name="lucene.dir"
          value="../../data/federalist-papers/lucene"/>
<property name="field"
          value="text"/>
<property name="token"
          value="zebra"/>
```

Because deletion is a destructive operation, we supply a default search token that is not in the index so that running this command will have no effect on the index. To regenerate or create an index that matches the index created in section 7.6.4, first delete all files in the Lucene index dir, then rerun the commands in section 7.6.4. In this example we're operating over a small, unchanging document set, so deleting and rebuilding the index is trivial.

We run the delete demo program using the Ant target `lucene-delete` using the default arguments in the `build.xml` file:

```
> ant lucene-delete
index=lucene
field=text
token=zebra
num docs before delete=85
num docs after delete before commit=85
num docs after commit=85
```

To delete all documents whose author is John Jay, we supply the following command-line arguments:

```
> ant lucene-delete -Dfield=author -Dtoken=JAY
index=lucene
field=author
token=JAY
num docs before delete=85
num docs after delete before commit=85
num docs after commit=80
```

The command-line argument `token` is passed to the `Term` constructor without any intervening analysis. In the index, the field `author` is a string field, so the author name is stored as an unanalyzed whole. In the Project Gutenberg Etext file, author names are all uppercase therefore, the query uses uppercase too.

We can use the LuceneSearch program to see how many documents contain a specific word in the title or text field before deleting these documents.

```
> ant lucene-search -Dquery="title:Constitution"
index=lucene
query=title:Constitution
max hits=10
parsed query=title:constitution
hits=5
...
```

When calling the LuceneDelete program, the term constructed from the field and token arguments must match existing terms in the index. The StandardAnalyzer removes punctuation, then removes stop-listed items, and then lowercases tokens. If we want to delete documents based on the contents of the title or author fields, the value of the token argument must be lowercase. Passing in a capitalized word as argument token fails:

```
> ant lucene-delete -Dfield=title -Dtoken=Constitution
index=lucene
field=title
token=Constitution
num docs before delete=80
num docs after delete before commit=80
num docs after commit=80
```

Lowercasing the word succeeds:

```
> ant lucene-delete -Dfield=title -Dtoken=constitution
index=lucene
field=title
token=constitution
num docs before delete=80
num docs after delete before commit=80
num docs after commit=75
```

After document deletion, we relist the files in the index directory:
```
> export BLOCKSIZE=1024; ls -s1 ../../data/federalist-papers/lucene/
total 1080
   4 _0.cfe
1060 _0.cfs
   4 _0.si
   4 _0_2.del
   4 segments.gen
   4 segments_3
```

There is now an extra file with suffix .del that holds information about which items have been deleted. These deletes will now be visible to index readers that open (or re-open) their indices.

7.10   Lucene and Databases

Lucene is like a database in its storage and indexing of data in a disk-like abstraction as well as its ability to handle very large amounts of data.

7.10.1   Key Differences

The first difference between Lucene and a database is in the type of objects they store. Databases store rows of small data objects in multiple type-able tables. Lucene deals with exactly one kind of object: documents. Documents contain fields, and each field is indexed and searched separately. Lucene can also store the contents of (the fields of) a document. These are stored separately from the index and can be returned as part of the search result.

Lucene stores information in an inverted index that provides a mapping from terms to documents, where a term is a pairing of field names and field values (see section 7.1, Figure 7.1). The term index can be used to compute term frequency across all documents. This aggregated information provides information about the document collection as a whole and provides the basis for general text processing functions such as spell checking.

A second difference is the kinds of searches and search results that Lucene and databases provide. Lucene was designed to carry out relevance-ranked search over text data. The result of a Lucene search is a scored list of documents where the score indicates how well the document matches the query. The Lucene query language provides a rich set of expressions for search over text data, as well as exact match and range searches over numerical data.

The Structured Query Language (SQL) is used to retrieve results from a database. SQL queries often require complex joins and filters across multiple tables. Results are returned in the form of a table of zero or more rows that meet the query criteria. Text search is limited to simple pattern matching via the LIKE statement, although some database management systems have added more advanced search functions.

In addition to the term index and stored document fields, Lucene can store document summary information in the form of term vectors, which are a per-document inverted index that give the frequency counts for that document of all terms in the index. For indexes over a large and diverse set of documents, this is likely to be a sparse vector. This representation allows Lucene to compute document similarity, which can be used as the basis for both clustering and classification. Term vectors can also store term position and offsets which can be used to re-create the contents of the document.

The size of the inverted index depends on the number and size of the documents being indexed, the amount of common language and vocabulary used, and the kinds of tokenization strategies employed. An inverted index over a collection of texts that are all written in the same language and use a relatively homogeneous vocabulary will take up less storage than the documents themselves, providing that the number of fields is small and tokenization is done at the word level. Using more elaborate tokenization strategies, term vectors, and stored fields will increase the size of the index. Stored fields are stored in a compressed format; how well the data compress is yet another factor in index size.

Lucene is an API, not a server. The Lucene API only provides mechanisms for operating over a local index. Lucene uses a simple locking mechanism that allows multiple readers and at most one writer to access an index simultaneously. In order to access Lucene remotely, it is necessary to use Solr, which wraps Lucene indexes in a web server and is covered in the following chapter. Using Solr, it is possible to create very large distributed indexes and to replicate indexes across servers, providing for highly scalable, high-throughput performance.

7.10.2 Transactional Support

In enterprise settings, maintaining data integrity is very important. In addition to backups, we want to ensure that our indexes don't get corrupted as they are being processed.

A *transaction*, in both the database and Java 2 Enterprise Edition (J2EE) contexts, is a way of grouping a sequence of complex operations, such as committing changes to an index, such that they all happen or none of them happen. Transactions make complex operations look as if they were atomic in the concurrency sense.

Unlike databases, earlier versions of Lucene didn't have any kind of transactional support. More recently, Lucene introduced configurable commit operations for indexes. These commit operations are transactional in the sense that if they fail, they roll back any changes they were in the middle of. This allows standard database-type two-phase commits to be implemented directly with fine-grained control over preparing and rolling back.

7.11 Document Classification with Lucene

A *classifier* takes some input, which could be just about anything, and returns a *classification* of the input over a finite number of discrete categories. For text classification, the input is some kind of text. Given a set of texts that contain discrete category labels, we can use Lucene's ranked search results and document store to build a simple classifier that can assign these labels to new documents based on the similarity of the new documents to labeled documents in the index.

The texts we use are taken from the 20 Newsgroups corpus, a set of roughly 20,000 messages posted to 20 different newsgroups. The names of the newsgroups in this corpus are:

comp.graphics	rec.autos	sci.crypt
comp.os.ms-windows.misc	rec.motorcycles	sci.electronics
comp.sys.ibm.pc.hardware	rec.sport.baseball	sci.med
comp.sys.mac.hardware	rec.sport.hockey	sci.space
comp.windows.x		
misc.forsale	talk.politics.misc	talk.religion.misc
	talk.politics.guns	alt.atheism
	talk.politics.mideast	soc.religion.christian

We treat these names as the category labels. The classification task is to assign each message to a newsgroup. Since all the messages in the corpus are already labeled, we can use one set of newsgroup posts to train our classifier and use the other set to test the classifier. To test the system, we compare the newsgroup name generated by the classifier against the name of the newsgroup that the message was posted to.

This dataset is maintained by Jason Rennie. There are no licensing terms listed and the data may be downloaded directly from: `http://people.csail.mit.edu/jrennie/20Newsgroups/`. The corpus is distributed in three versions, each as a `tar.gz` bundle. The bundle `20news-bydate.tar.gz` is divided into two sets of posts, a training set comprising roughly 60% of the posts to each group and a test set containing the remaining 40% of the posts. This version of the corpus doesn't include cross-posts (messages posted to more than one newsgroup) and the newsgroup-identifying header lines have been removed. We use this version for testing and training. It unpacks into two top-level directories: `20news-bydate-train` and `20news-bydate-test`. Both of these contain 20 subdirectories of newsgroup data, where the directory name is the same as the newsgroup name, and each of these contains a set of newsgroup messages, roughly 400-600 posts for the training sets and roughly 250-400 posts for the test sets.

The program `ClassifyNewsgroups.java` constructs the Lucene index from the training data and then uses this index to do a first-best classification of the test data. The classification results are presented as a confusion matrix that shows the full response profile of the classifiers. This is a 20-by-

20 matrix where both the rows and columns are newsgroup names. Each row represents the performance of the classifier on posts from a given newsgroup, and each column represents the classifier response, so that reading across a row, we can see the number of posts given a particular category label. The classifier also reports the percentage of posts in the test set that were correctly labeled.

7.11.1 Code Walkthrough

The method buildIndex walks over the training data directory and parses the newsgroup messages into a NewsPost object, which is a simple domain model of a newsgroup post, consisting of the newsgroup name, subject, body, and filename (a string of numbers). We treat each post as a Lucene document consisting of two fields: a StringField named category for the newsgroup name and a TextField named text that holds the message subject and message body.

```
NewsPost post = parse(postFile, groupName, number);
Document d = new Document();
d.add(new StringField("category",
                      post.group(),Store.YES));
d.add(new TextField("text",
                    post.subject(),Store.NO));
d.add(new TextField("text",
                    post.body(),Store.NO));
indexWriter.addDocument(d);
```

The method testIndex iterates over the posts in the test set and tabulates the results in a 20-by-20 confusion matrix. To index the rows and columns of the matrix by newsgroup name, we define a String array of newsgroup names called NEWSGROUPS:

```
public static final String[] NEWSGROUPS
    = { "alt.atheism",
        "comp.graphics",
        "comp.os.ms-windows.misc",
```

As we process each newsgroup we fill in the confusion matrix, one row at a time.

```
void testIndex(File indexDir, File testDir)
    throws IOException, FileNotFoundException {
    Directory fsDir = FSDirectory.open(indexDir);
    DirectoryReader reader = DirectoryReader.open(fsDir);
    IndexSearcher searcher = new IndexSearcher(reader);
```

```
int[][] confusionMatrix
    = new int[NEWSGROUPS.length][NEWSGROUPS.length];
File[] groupsDir = testDir.listFiles();
for (File group : groupsDir) {
    int postCt = 0;
    String groupName = group.getName();
    int rowIdx = Arrays.binarySearch(NEWSGROUPS,groupName);

    File[] posts = group.listFiles();
    for (File postFile : posts) {
        postCt++;
        String number = postFile.getName();
        NewsPost post = parse(postFile, groupName, number);
        BooleanQuery termsQuery
            = buildQuery(post.subject()
                            + " " + post.body());
        // only get first-best result
        TopDocs hits = searcher.search(termsQuery,1);
        ScoreDoc[] scoreDocs = hits.scoreDocs;
        for (int n = 0; n < scoreDocs.length; ++n) {
            ScoreDoc sd = scoreDocs[n];
            int docId = sd.doc;
            Document d = searcher.doc(docId);
            String category = d.get("category");
            // record result in confusion matrix
            int colIdx
                = Arrays.binarySearch(NEWSGROUPS,category);
            confusionMatrix[rowIdx][colIdx]++;
        }
    }
```

The method `buildQuery` creates a Lucene query from the subject and body
text of the test message by tokenizing the message subject and body (see section 7.3.3). The Lucene query ORs together all terms (up to a maximum of
1,024) into a `BooleanQuery` using the SHOULD (see section 7.7.1).

```
BooleanQuery buildQuery(String text) throws IOException {
    BooleanQuery termsQuery = new BooleanQuery();
    Reader textReader = new StringReader(text);
    TokenStream tokStream
        = mAnalyzer.tokenStream("text",textReader);
    try {
        tokStream.reset();
        CharTermAttribute terms =
            tokStream.addAttribute(CharTermAttribute.class);
```

```
      int ct = 0;
      while (tokStream.incrementToken()
            && ct++ < 1024) {
         termsQuery.
            add(new TermQuery(new Term("text",
                                        terms.toString())),
               Occur.SHOULD);
      }
      tokStream.end();
   } finally {
      tokStream.close();
      textReader.close();
   }
   return termsQuery;
```

In order to ensure that the tokenization applied to the query matches the tokenization used to build the index, we use the member variable mAnalyzer to hold the reference to a LuceneAnalyzer so that is it available to both the buildIndex and buildQuery methods.

The ClassifyNewsgroups program allows the user to specify the analyzer used. This allows us to see how different tokenization strategies affect classification. The three analyzers available are: the Lucene StandardAnalyzer, which chains together a StandardTokenizer that breaks the text into a stream of words, discarding whitespace and punctuation, followed by a StandardFilter, a LowerCaseFilter, and then a StopFilter, which uses a list of English stop words; an analyzer that chains together just a StandardTokenizer and a LowerCaseFilter; and an Analyzer that uses only a Lucene NGramTokenizer (from package oal.analysis.ngram) to index the data using 4-grams.

A command-line argument is used to specify the choice of analyzer. If the value of this argument is std, then the Lucene StandardAnalyzer is used. If the value of this argument is lc, then the analyzer consisting of the StandardTokenizer and LowerCaseFilter is used. If the value of this argument is ngram, then the NGramTokenizer is used. The ClassifyNewsgroups constructor checks the value of this argument and instantiates the mAnalyzer accordingly.

```
if ("std".equals(aType)) {
   mAnalyzer
      = new StandardAnalyzer(VERSION);
} else if ("lc".equals(aType)) {
   mAnalyzer = new Analyzer() {
         @Override protected TokenStreamComponents
            createComponents(String fieldName,
```

```
                              Reader reader) {
            Tokenizer source =
                new StandardTokenizer(VERSION,reader);
            TokenStream filter =
                new LowerCaseFilter(VERSION,source);
            return new TokenStreamComponents(source,
                                                filter);
        }
    };
} else if ("ngram".equals(aType)) {
    mAnalyzer = new Analyzer() {
            @Override protected TokenStreamComponents
            createComponents(String fieldName,
                              Reader reader) {
            Tokenizer source =
                new NGramTokenizer(VERSION,reader,4,4);
            return new TokenStreamComponents(source);
        }
    };
```

The `build.xml` in the directory `javabook/src/applucene` contains the Ant target `classify` that runs the classifier over the 20 Newsgroups dataset. The Ant properties `train.dir` and `test.dir` specify the location of the training and test datasets. The Ant properties `newsgroups.index` and `analyzer` specify the name of the Lucene index and the choice of analyzer. We adopt the convention of appending the analyzer choice to the name of the Lucene index in order to compare tokenization strategies.

```
<property name="train.dir"
          value="../../data/20news-bydate-train"/>
<property name="test.dir"
          value="../../data/20news-bydate-test"/>
<property name="newsgroups.index"
          value="../../data/20news-bydate-lucene-lc"/>
<property name="analyzer"
          value="lc"/>
```

Figure 7.3 shows the top-left quadrant of the confusion matrix, with the results for the first 10 newsgroups of running the classifier using the Lucene `StandardAnalyzer`. The cells on the diagonal show that in general, this classifier performs well on the data. Posts to alt.atheism are correctly classified in 247 out of 319 cases, at a rate of roughly 75 percent, whereas a classifier which always guessed at random, choosing uniformly among the newsgroups, would be correct only 5 percent of the time. In comparing the classification rates for the posts to the different computer newsgroups, we see a certain amount of

	ath	grphx	oswin	ibm	mac	win-x	sale	auto	cycle	bb
ath	247	1	0	2	0	1	0	1	2	0
grphx	1	301	14	4	4	28	2	1	2	1
oswin	3	54	182	28	43	42	3	0	1	1
ibm	1	25	27	249	36	9	9	1	3	0
mac	0	31	10	25	257	6	7	3	3	0
win-x	0	43	7	1	7	313	1	2	4	3
sale	0	17	5	24	40	9	230	12	13	1
auto	1	7	5	0	1	0	6	324	9	0
cycle	1	0	1	0	0	3	0	13	341	3
bb	0	3	1	0	0	1	0	2	2	336

Fig. 7.3: *Confusion matrix for first 10 newsgroups.*

confusion between the different kinds of computers and operating systems, as well as confusion with the listings in the misc.forsale newsgroup however, there is little confusion between the posts to the computer newsgroup and alt.atheism or with rec.sports.baseball.

7.11.2 Evaluating the Classifier

To evaluate how well this program is able to identify the newsgroup to which a post belongs, we did several runs over the 20 Newsgroups dataset using different tokenization strategies and tabulated the results.

When interpreting the program results, it is useful to know exactly how much training and testing data are available for each newsgroup. Figure 7.4 shows the number of training and testing posts available for each newsgroup. Almost all newsgroups have close to 600 training posts and 400 test posts. The three newsgroups with the least amount of data are talk.religion.misc (377 training, 251 test), talk.politics.misc (465, 251), and alt.atheism (480, 319).

Figure 7.5 compares the correct classification rates for the three different analyzers for all newsgroups. All classifiers work pretty well. No one classifier works best for all categories, reflecting the difference in the kinds of vocabulary and writing styles used across the different newsgroups. *N*-Grams can be very effective for both regular search and classification, however the storage requirements for *n*-grams are considerably greater than for word-based tokenization. The size of index over the 20 Newsgroups training data is 7 MB when the Lucene `StandardAnalyzer` is used, 8 MB when the lowercase only analyzer is used, and 24 MB for the length-4 *n*-grams.

Newsgroup name	Training data	Test data
alt.atheism	480	319
comp.graphics	584	389
comp.os.mswindows.misc	591	394
comp.sys.ibm.pc.hardware	590	392
comp.sys.mac.hardware	578	385
comp.windows.x	593	395
misc.forsale	585	390
rec.autos	594	396
rec.motorcycles	598	398
rec.sport.baseball	597	397
rec.sport.hockey	600	399
sci.crypt	595	396
sci.electronics	591	393
sci.med	594	396
sci.space	593	394
soc.religion.christian	599	398
talk.politics.guns	546	364
talk.politics.mideast	564	376
talk.politics.misc	465	310
talk.religion.misc	377	251

Fig. 7.4: *Training and testing posts per newsgroup.*

Newsgroup name	Standard Analyzer	Lowercase Only	N-Grams length 4
alt.atheism	0.77	**0.80**	0.74
comp.graphics	**0.77**	**0.77**	0.62
comp.os.ms-windows.misc	0.46	0.52	**0.60**
comp.sys.ibm.pc.hardware	0.63	**0.66**	0.59
comp.sys.mac.hardware	**0.67**	0.66	0.57
comp.windows.x	**0.79**	**0.79**	0.57
misc.forsale	0.59	**0.60**	0.58
rec.autos	**0.82**	**0.82**	0.70
rec.motorcycles	**0.86**	**0.86**	0.83
rec.sport.baseball	0.85	**0.86**	0.78
rec.sport.hockey	0.91	**0.92**	0.86
sci.crypt	**0.91**	0.89	0.85
sci.electronics	0.61	**0.64**	0.61
sci.med	0.67	**0.70**	0.66
sci.space	0.79	**0.81**	0.74
soc.religion.christian	0.64	0.65	**0.78**
talk.politics.guns	0.74	0.75	**0.76**
talk.politics.mideast	0.79	**0.81**	0.74
talk.politics.misc	0.56	0.55	**0.62**
talk.religion.misc	0.59	0.59	**0.66**

Fig. 7.5: *Classification rates by analyzer.*

Chapter 8

Solr

Apache Solr is a search server that uses Lucene for indexing and search. It is highly scalable and enables the distribution and replication of extremely large indexes across multiple machines in a network or in the cloud. Solr powers search and navigation for many popular websites including several of the largest retail websites. The Solr home page is

```
http://lucene.apache.org/solr/
```

Solr is distributed under the Apache license version 2.0. Both the Lucene and Solr home pages contain links to download the latest version.

Solr has an impressive set of features already, and it continues to evolve rapidly, thanks to its active developer community. With each major release the core libraries are modified to improve performance and scalability. With each minor release new features are added. This makes Solr very difficult to document, and all except the most general documentation is necessarily version specific. The official documentation for each version of Solr is available from the URL `http://lucene.apache.org/solr/VERSION` where VERSION is of the form MAJOR_MINOR_REV e.g., for Solr 4.5.1 the official documentation page is:

```
http://lucene.apache.org/solr/4_5_1
```

The Solr wiki contains general and version-specific documentation:

```
http://wiki.apache.org/solr/Solr.xml
```

There is also a reference guide for Solr 4 from LucidWorks.com, home of several core Solr developers. Throughout this chapter we abbreviate this top-level Solr path to `oas` when giving package and class names. For example, we write `oas.schema` instead of `org.apache.solr.schema`.

In this chapter we focus on using Solr as a search server for natural language text data. Solr uses Lucene to do this therefore, this chapter assumes that you have already read chapter 7 on Lucene. As in the Lucene chapter, we create a Solr index over the 85 essays that make up *The Federalist Papers*. The program that indexes *The Federalist Papers* is included in the package for chapter 6, `javabook/src/casestudy`. The directory `javabook/src/appsolr/` contains the Solr configuration files used to create and query this index.

8.1   Solr Overview

Solr is written in Java. It runs in a servlet container and handles HTTP requests. Unlike Lucene, which places no constraints on the structure or contents of a document, Solr uses XML configuration files to specify what kind of fields are in a document and how they are stored, indexed, and searched.

To add or update a document in the index, you send an HTTP request to the Solr server. The body of the request contains the document, and the `content-type` field of the header specifies the document format. Allowable document formats are JSON, XML, CSV, or binary. Search is also carried out via HTTP. Parameters on the search request specify both the query and the `content-type` used for the Solr response. The Solr query language augments Lucene's query language. The default Solr response format is XML. Solr has a rich set of plug-ins that can generate documents in many different formats. HTTP requests are used for document deletion, commits to the index, and index optimization as well.

A Solr index is called a *core*. A core is a logical collection of documents that all have the same structure. The document fields and types are defined in the core's `schema.xml` file. A single Solr server instance can manage multiple cores from within a servlet container, eliminating the need to stop and restart the Solr webapp in order to create, merge, or swap out indexes.

Solr manages the files that make up each core according to configuration information in the core's `solrconfig.xml` file. Solr provides distributed search capabilities to split indexes across multiple machines (*sharding*), allowing for very large indexes, and to replicate indexes across machines, allowing for higher search throughput. As of Solr 4, the `SolrCloud` facility is used to manage clusters of Solr servers. Distributed search can also be set up across multiple machines in a master/slave configuration.

8.2   Getting Started

The components of a Solr installation are a servlet container such as Tomcat, Jetty, or JBoss, the Solr webapp itself as a `.war` file, and a directory containing configuration and data subdirectories, which is known as the *Solr Home* directory.

To leapfrog the complicated process of installing a web server and servlet container and deploying the Solr webapp, the Solr binary release contains an example of a Solr installation consisting of a pre-built Solr server and one example application. This example uses the Jetty web server and servlet container from the Eclipse project. Jetty is dual licensed under the Apache 2 license and the Eclipse Public License (EPL). The Jetty home page is:

```
http://www.eclipse.org/jetty
```

The Solr download page contains links to both binary and source releases. Solr binary releases are named `solr-VERSION.zip` (or `.tgz`) where VERSION is the version number of the release e.g., 4.5.1. Solr source releases are named `solr-VERSION-src.zip` (or `.tgz`). Both binary and source bundles unpack into a top-level directory `solr-VERSION`, henceforth `$SOLR`.

8.2.1 Running the Example from the Solr Binary Release

The directory `$SOLR/example` is included with the Solr binary release. This directory contains the Jetty-based Solr server and an example application. The `README.txt` file contains the commands used to start the Solr server and load a set of example XML documents into the index and links to a short tutorial that covers key Solr features.

The example Solr home directory `$SOLR/example/solr` contains configuration files for a Solr index. This example is based on the CNET Reviews website, which was the first website to use Solr. The directory also contains a set of sample documents and a script that loads them into the index.

Step 1: Start the Solr Server

The file `start.jar` in `$SOLR/example` directory contains an instance of the Jetty Servlet container. Running the `java` command with `start.jar` as the jarfile starts the server. The `java` command must be executed from within the `$SOLR/example` directory in order to correctly resolve the relative path names in the application configuration files. The subdirectory `etc` contains the Jetty configuration file `jetty.xml`. By default, Jetty is configured to accept connections on port 8983. To use another port, edit `jetty.xml` and change all occurrences of 8983 to the port that you wish to use instead.

Following the `README.txt` instructions, first we move into the example directory, and then start the Jetty instance.

```
> cd $SOLR/example
> java -jar start.jar
```

Jetty is configured to send logging information both to the terminal display and to the `solr.log` file in the `logs` subdirectory.

Once the Solr server is running, we can access the Solr browser-based admin page via the URL `http://localhost:8983/solr/`. The Solr server will continue to run and send log messages to the terminal window in which is was started. Sending `CTRL-c` from the terminal initiates the shutdown process.

Step 2: Populate the Solr Index

A Solr index is called a *core*. The Solr core used in this example is `collection1` which is located in the example Solr home directory `$SOLR/example`. The `collection1` directory contains a subdirectory called `data` that wraps a Lucene index.

On initial startup, the Solr server creates the `data` directory as well as a subdirectory called `index` that contains the new Lucene index. After the Solr server has been started but before any documents have been uploaded, this index contains general Lucene information but no data files.

```
> export BLOCKSIZE=1024; ls -s1 solr/collection1/data/index
4 segments.gen
4 segments_1
```

The `$SOLR/example` directory contains a subdirectory called `exampledocs` that contains a set of XML files along with a script that loads these documents into the Solr index. Each XML file contains one or more documents to be indexed. Some documents contain product information and others contain information needed for the e-commerce features on the example website.

The `$SOLR/example` directory also contains the script `post.sh`, which is used to populate the example index. This script takes a list of filenames and submits each file to the Solr server as an update request. We run this script over all the XML files in the `exampledocs` directory:

```
> cd $SOLR/example/exampledocs
> ./post.sh *.xml
```

```
Posting file gb18030-example.xml
  to http://localhost:8983/solr/update
<?xml version="1.0" encoding="UTF-8"?>
<response>
  <lst name="responseHeader">
    <int name="status">0</int>
    <int name="QTime">118</int>
  </lst>
</response>
```

The script echoes the response from the Solr server to the command line. Line breaks have been added for readability. The `status` code of 0 indicates a successful request. The `QTime` gives the query time in milliseconds.

After running this script, we see that the Lucene index now contains a set of data files.

```
> ls solr/collection1/data/index
_0.fdt    _0.nvm    _0_Lucene41_0.doc    _0_Lucene41_0.tip
_0.fdx    _0.si     _0_Lucene41_0.pay    segments.gen
_0.fnm    _0.tvd    _0_Lucene41_0.pos    segments_2
_0.nvd    _0.tvx    _0_Lucene41_0.tim    write.lock
```

Because the Solr server is running, there is a file called `write.lock` listed as well. This lockfile is released after a successful shutdown.

Step 3: Run Queries from the Solr Tutorial over the Index

The Solr tutorial is an HTML document linked to from the Solr home page.

```
http://lucene.apache.org/solr/tutorial.html
```

Every version of Solr has its own tutorial. For example, the URL of the tutorial for Solr version 4.5.1 is

```
http://lucene.apache.org/solr/4_5_1/tutorial.html
```

The Solr tutorial contains examples of different kinds of search queries and different ways of grouping and displaying search results. The example search queries are coded up as links in the HTML file, using the address of the default Jetty installation as the base URL. Thus, once the example Solr server is running and the sample documents have been loaded, you can work through the examples in the tutorial link by link.

8.3   The Solr Admin User Interface

The Solr browser-based admin interface provides tools for development, tuning, and testing, as well as for monitoring and managing Solr applications. The Solr example is configured to allow access to this tool. If you're using the Solr example Jetty server, then the actual URL is:

```
http://localhost:8983/solr
```

Solr 4 introduced a new version of the admin tool. The LucidWorks Solr version 4 reference guide documents the layout and features of the Solr 4 Admin UI.

Figure 8.1 is a screenshot of the Solr admin UI showing the overview of core `collection1`. The Apache Solr logo is in the top left corner of the screen. The space to the right of the logo is used to display error messages. Below this there is a tools menu on the left side and a main content screen to the right. The tools on the top half of the left column are for managing the Solr instance

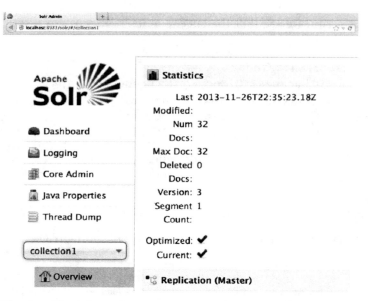

Fig. 8.1: *The Solr 4 Admin UI, overview of core* `collection1`.

itself. Below these is a pull-down menu that lists all available cores. Once a core
has been selected, a second menu appears in the bottom half of the left column
showing the core-specific tools used for browsing, configuring, and testing the
selected core. Selecting a core automatically selects the Overview tool, which
displays information about the core in the main panel of the Admin UI. The
main center panel of the Admin UI shows the overview of this core. Because we
worked through the Solr tutorial (section 8.2.1) and used the script `post.sh`
to load all the example docs, there are now 32 documents in the index.

Of the core-specific tools, the Query tool and the Analysis tool are particularly useful to the application developer. The Query tool displays a query
screen in the main panel. The left side of the query screen contains controls for
constructing the Solr query. The right side of the screen displays the query request at the top and the query response below it. The Analysis tool shows how
data will be handled by Solr during search and indexing. We include screen-
shots of both later in this chapter.

8.4   The Solr Home Directory `solr.solr.home`

The Solr home directory contains a config file called `solr.xml` and one directory per Solr core. By default, each Solr core directory contains the index
data in a subdirectory called `data`, as we saw in section 8.2 step 2. Each Solr
core directory also contains a subdirectory called `conf` that contains all the
configuration information needed for search and indexing.

Solr configuration is done through a set of XML files. With each major release these may undergo major changes and with each minor release any number of elements and attributes may be added or deprecated. There is documentation for these files in the Solr wiki (`http://wiki.apache.org/solr/Solr.xml`) and there is some documentation in the comments in the XML schema files.

In addition to the example home directory `$SOLR/example/solr`, which contains the configuration for the CNET application and uses the full range of Solr features for search and indexing, the Solr example contains the example home directories `multicore` and `example-DIH`. The `multicore` directory is a minimal example that is designed to show how to configure a Solr server to manage multiple indexes. In the `multicore` example, the two cores are toy indexes. Each core contains a `conf` directory that contains only the required configuration files for a Solr index. The directory `example-DIH` shows how to create a Solr index from the contents of a relational database.

8.4.1 Server Configuration: `solr.xml`

The Solr server needs to know the name and location of the cores that it manages. This information is specified in an XML config file called `solr.xml`, which must be located in the Solr home directory.[1] The file `$SOLR/example/solr/solr.xml` in the Solr example is documented via comments and the Solr wiki contains a good description of the contents of this file as well.

The top-level element is `solr`, which accepts two attributes. The attribute `persistent` allows runtime changes to be saved to this file, and the attribute `sharedLib` specifies the relative path (relative to the directory containing this `solr.xml` file) to directories or jar files that will be shared across all cores. If `persistant` is true, then this file will be overwritten and any comments will be lost, provided that the file permissions allow the file to be overwritten by the web server.

The `solr` element contains a single `cores` element. Attributes of the `cores` element are used to specify access to the cores. The attribute `adminPath` specifies the relative path used to manage cores. Setting this to `null` disables core administration via a request handler and therefore via the Solr Admin UI. The optional attribute `defaultCoreName` specifies the core used when no core name is specified in an access URL. For example, if the `defaultCoreName` is `baz`, then the request `localhost:8983/solr/select?q=foo` is treated as `localhost:8983/solr/baz/select?q=foo`. Here is the `cores` tag from the Solr example `solr.xml` file:

---

[1] This will be deprecated in Solr 5 and will be replaced by a new index discovery mechanism. See the Solr wiki for details.

```
<cores adminPath="/admin/cores" defaultCoreName="collection1"
       host="${host:}" hostPort="${jetty.port:8983}"
       hostContext="${hostContext:solr}"
       zkClientTimeout="${zkClientTimeout:15000}">
```

The attributes starting with host and zk apply only for SolrCloud mode. This config specifies that core collection1 is the default core, so the following requests are equivalent:

```
http://localhost:8983/solr/collection1/select
http://localhost:8983/solr/select
```

The cores element must contain at least one core element. Here is the core element from the Solr example solr.xml file:

```
<core name="collection1" instanceDir="collection1" />
```

The solr.xml config file in the Solr example directory multicore specifies two cores:

```
<core name="core0" instanceDir="core0" />
<core name="core1" instanceDir="core1" />
```

8.4.2   Index Configuration: the conf Directory

Each Solr core directory contains a subdirectory conf of configuration information. At a minimum, this directory contains two XML files: solrconfig.xml and schema.xml. The solr example index collection1/conf directory contains files that are referenced by the schema.xml file, such as general lists of stop words as well as language-specific files and subdirectories.

8.4.3   The solrconfig.xml File

The solrconfig.xml file defines the set of Solr functions available and the way in which the index is managed. Configuration information is specified during application development and modified as needed during performance tuning. The Solr wiki contains documentation for the XML statements used in this file for both Solr 4 and legacy releases, and the LucidWorks Solr Reference Guide provides good documentation for Solr 4.

   Under the hood, Solr uses Lucene for indexing and search, and therefore, Lucene configuration information is specified here, including the location and type of the Lucene index directory and the way in which changes to the index are managed by the Lucene index writers. Declarations for the Solr instance include: the plug-in library and jarfile locations; how to cache and commit update requests; how search queries over the index are processed and cached; and the behavior of the Solr Admin UI. Finally, the `solrconfig.xml` file provides the mechanism for specifying complex search functions built up out of combinations of search queries, query filters, and plug-ins, including spell-checking and clustering. This is a lot of configuration information to bundle into a single file, and the `solrconfig.xml` included with the Solr example runs to 1,800 lines, most of which are either comments or commented out examples of configuration options not applicable to the Solr CNET example. In this section we cover the basic configuration.

The top-level element `luceneMatchVersion` (see section 7.1.1) is required. For a new application, the latest Lucene version should be used e.g., for Solr version 4.5, this element will be:

```
<luceneMatchVersion>4.5</luceneMatchVersion>
```

The default location of the index data is a subdirectory called `data`. This location can be overridden via the `dataDir` element.

The low-level behavior of the Lucene index is controlled by settings in the `indexConfig` element. These include the number of threads used for indexing documents and the merge policy. The `updateHandler` element contains settings controlling how Solr caches and commits update requests. The `query` element contains settings controlling caching and processing of search queries. The `requestDispatcher` element contains settings for specific details of the HTTP protocol, e.g., file upload size, file streaming, and HTTP caching.

The `requestHandler` elements define the HTTP requests allowed on the index. They map request names to Solr classes and specify default parameters for the request. A `solrconfig.xml` file can contain multiple `requestHandler` elements that map different names to the same Solr class using different parameter specifications.

The class `solr.SearchHandler` handles search requests. Here is how the `select` request is defined for the Solr example:

```
<requestHandler name="/select" class="solr.SearchHandler">
   <lst name="defaults">
     <str name="echoParams">explicit</str>
     <int name="rows">10</int>
     <str name="df">text</str>
   </lst>
</requestHandler>
```

The name specifies the path appended to the URL of the Solr instance. This corresponds to the URL used in the Solr tutorial:

```
http://localhost:8983/solr/collection1/select
```

The `lst` element with attribute `name`, value `defaults` specifies the default set of parameters used for this request handler. Each parameter is a `str` element with attribute name that specifies the parameter name, and the str element contents specify the parameter value.

Complex search functions require chaining together a series of search queries, query filters, and plug-ins. The searchComponent element defines the logic used by the search handler. Request handlers that use a search component specify the order in which these components are used. Here is an example of the Solr QueryElevationComponent, which can be used to override Lucene scoring.

```
<searchComponent name="elevator"
                 class="solr.QueryElevationComponent" >
  <!-- pick a fieldType to analyze queries -->
  <str name="queryFieldType">string</str>
  <str name="config-file">elevate.xml</str>
</searchComponent>

<requestHandler name="/elevate"
                class="solr.SearchHandler"
                startup="lazy">
  <lst name="defaults">
    <str name="echoParams">explicit</str>
  </lst>
  <arr name="last-components">
    <str>elevator</str>
  </arr>
</requestHandler>
```

For the Solr Admin UI, the class solr.admin.AdminHandlers registers all admin handlers.

```
<requestHandler name="/admin/"
                class="solr.admin.AdminHandlers"/>
```

8.4.4   The schema.xml File

The schema file specifies the contents of an index. It provides definitions of the types and names of the fields in a document and how they are stored, indexed, and searched. The default location of this file is conf/schema.xml.

The comments in the schema.xml file for the example index solr/collection1 serve as documentation of the elements and attributes allowed in any schema.xml file. The information on the Solr wiki page is not version specific. For Solr 4, the Lucidworks Apache Solr Reference Guide provides a good discussion of documents, fields, and schema design.

The top-level `schema` element has attributes `name` and `version`. The `version` attribute defines the schema syntax and semantics. As of Solr 4.5, the latest version number is 1.5.

Specifying Field Types: The `fieldType` Element

The top-level element `types` contains one or more `fieldType` elements. A `fieldType` element has attributes `name` and `class`. For example, the first `fieldType` element defined in the `schema.xml` file for the example index `collection1` is:

```
<fieldType name="string" class="solr.StrField"
        sortMissingLast="true" />
```

Class names starting with `solr`, such as `solr.StrField` in the above example, refer to Java classes in one of several standard packages directly under the top-level Solr package `org.apache.solr`, which we abbreviate to `oas`. These are: `oas.analysis`, `oas.core`, `oas.request`, `oas.update`, `oas.search`, and `oas.schema`. The URL for the javadoc for the core Solr packages is:

```
http://lucene.apache.org/solr/4_5_1/solr-core
```

The class `StrField`, in package `oas.schema`, is a subclass of the abstract class `oas.schema.PrimitiveType`. Primitive types are used for non-analyzed fields such as int, float, and string. The attribute `sortMissingLast` is appropriate for primitive types that are stored as strings or numeric values. When this attribute is set to true and documents are sorted on a field of this type, documents without the field will always come after documents with the field, regardless of whether the specified sort order is ascending or descending.

The class `solr.TextField`, also in package `oas.schema`, is the basic type for fields that contain text data. Text is processed into one or more terms by an analyzer. The analyzer used for fields of this type is defined by an `analyzer` element within the `fieldType` declaration. The `analyzer` element specifies the tokenizer or chain of tokenizers used to process the contents of the field. If no analyzer is defined, then the field will not be analyzed thus, it will be indexed like a field of class `StrField`.

The available tokenizers include the Lucene tokenizer factory classes from the Lucene packages in `oal.analysis`, including `oal.analysis.core` and `oal.analysis.standard` (see section 7.3.1). The Lucene javadoc for the tokenizer factory classes contains examples of the Solr schema XML declarations showing all required elements and attributes for each.

Here is an example of an analyzer definition:

```
<fieldType name="text_lcstem" class="solr.TextField"
        positionIncrementGap="100">
```

```
    <analyzer>
      <tokenizer class="solr.WhitespaceTokenizerFactory"/>
      <filter class="solr.LowerCaseFilterFactory"/>
      <filter class="solr.StopFilterFactory"
              ignoreCase="true"
              words="stopwords.txt"
              enablePositionIncrements="true"/>
      <filter class="solr.PorterStemFilterFactory"/>
    </analyzer>
  </fieldType>
```

We chain together one tokenizer and three filters to define an analyzer that first tokenizes on whitespace, then converts the tokens to lowercase, then removes stop words, and finally applies an implementation of the Porter stemmer. This analyzer behaves like the chain of tokenizers and filters used for the Lucene example in section 7.3.3.

The `fieldType` attribute `positionIncrementGap` is used for text field types that may contain multiple values. Setting this attribute to a large number prevents phrase searches from matching across the boundary of two distinct values of a multi-valued field.

The `solr.StopFilterFactory` uses a text file that contains a list of stop-words, one per line. The value attribute `words` is the name of this text file. The file path is interpreted relative to the location of the `schema.xml` file. In this example, Solr expects to find this file in the `conf` directory itself.

The `analyzer` element has an optional attribute `type` that takes the values `index` and `query`. This makes it possible to define a pair of custom analyzers for index and query time so that additional processing can be done as the situation warrants it. In the CNET example `schema.xml` file there are several field types that have different index and query time analyzer definitions. The field type `text_en` is a text field type for English:

```
<fieldType name="text_en" class="solr.TextField"
           positionIncrementGap="100">
  <analyzer type="index">
    <tokenizer class="solr.StandardTokenizerFactory"/>
    <filter class="solr.StopFilterFactory"
            ignoreCase="true"
            words="lang/stopwords_en.txt"
            enablePositionIncrements="true"
            />
    <filter class="solr.LowerCaseFilterFactory"/>
    <filter class="solr.EnglishPossessiveFilterFactory"/>
    <filter class="solr.KeywordMarkerFilterFactory"
            protected="protwords.txt"/>
```

```
    <filter class="solr.PorterStemFilterFactory"/>
  </analyzer>
  <analyzer type="query">
    <tokenizer class="solr.StandardTokenizerFactory"/>
    <filter class="solr.SynonymFilterFactory"
            synonyms="synonyms.txt"
            ignoreCase="true" expand="true"/>
    <filter class="solr.StopFilterFactory"
            ignoreCase="true"
            words="lang/stopwords_en.txt"
            enablePositionIncrements="true"
            />
    <filter class="solr.LowerCaseFilterFactory"/>
    <filter class="solr.EnglishPossessiveFilterFactory"/>
    <filter class="solr.KeywordMarkerFilterFactory"
            protected="protwords.txt"/>
    <filter class="solr.PorterStemFilterFactory"/>
  </analyzer>
</fieldType>
```

Both analyzers tokenize with StandardTokenizer, remove English stop words, convert to lowercase, protect tokens that match the set of words in protwords.txt from further filters, and apply the Porter stemmer to the unprotected tokens. The query time analyzer also applies a SynonymFilterFactory. Search queries that contain a word that has a known set of synonyms will be expanded to include the synonyms.

Figure 8.2 is a screenshot of using the Analysis tool in the Solr Admin UI. The Solr server is running over the example core collection1. We've selected the field text_en and enter the same text for both the index and query analysis. The (non-verbose) output of the analysis is given below for each. There are six successive operations shown for the index analyzer and seven operations shown for the query analyzer.

Specifying Fields: the field Element

The top-level element fields contains one or more field elements. Valid field attributes are documented at the beginning of the fields section in the example schema.xml file and in the Solr wiki.

A field element has mandatory attributes name and type. The field name should consist of alphanumeric or underscore characters only and not start with a digit. Names with both leading and trailing underscores, e.g., _version_, are reserved. The value of the type attribute is the name of a fieldType defined in the types section.

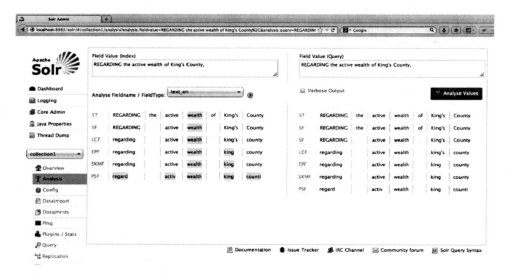

Fig. 8.2: *The Solr 4 Admin UI, Analysis tool for field type* `text_en`.

The attributes `indexed` and `stored` take boolean values `true` and `false` according to whether or not the field should be indexed and stored, respectively. It is good practice to always specify these attributes overtly.

The attribute `multiValued` is `true` if the field may contain multiple values per document. The `positionIncrementGap` attribute should be set to a reasonably large number if the field is multi-valued, in order to prevent phrase-level searches from returning spurious matches across the boundaries of different values of this field. If the attribute `required` is `true`, then Solr will throw an error if this field is not found when adding the document to the index.

Given the definition of field type `text_lcstem` in the previous section, we can define a text field that will be analyzed accordingly with the following declaration:

```
<field name="text" type="text_lcstem"
       indexed="true" stored="true"
       multiValued="true"/>
```

Mandatory Fields and FieldTypes

Solr automatically adds a `_version_` field to all documents. This field contains a long value that is used internally by some of the update, logging, and Solr-Cloud processes. Since all documents contain this field, both the `_version_` field and field type `long` must be declared in the `schema.xml` file.

```
<fields>
  <field name="_version_" type="long"
         indexed="true"  stored="true"/>
</fields>
<types>
  <fieldType name="long" class="solr.TrieLongField"
             precisionStep="0" positionIncrementGap="0"/>
</types>
```

The uniqueKey Element

The element uniqueKey contains the name of the field used to enforce document uniqueness.

```
<uniqueKey>id</uniqueKey>
```

For example, if the id field is declared unique and the index contains a document with field value pairs id=1 and name="foo", adding another document that has field value pairs id=1 and name="bar" will cause the document with name foo to be replaced by the document with name bar. Adding the same document to the index multiple times will have no effect; the index will contain only one copy of the document. This avoids the problem of document duplication that we saw in section 7.6.5, where adding multiple copies of a document to a Lucene index results in duplicate documents in the index.

8.4.5 Specifying the Solr Home Directory for the Solr Server

The location of the Solr home directory is specified by the Java environment variable solr.solr.home.[2] When starting the Jetty Solr server we can specify this environment variable from the command line:

```
> java -jar start.jar -Dsolr.solr.home=your/pathname/here
```

If this variable isn't set, Solr looks for a directory called solr in the current working directory. This is why the $SOLR/example directory is organized as it is. We can start the Jetty Solr server from that directory without needing to set the Java environment variable solr.solr.home since Solr uses the local directory $SOLR/example/solr as the home directory.

8.5 MultiCore Solr

A core is a logical collection of documents that all have the same structure. *MultiCore Solr* is the term applied to a Solr server that manages more than

---

[2]This seemingly redundant name is due to the convention of prefixing all Java environment variables with solr to avoid name conflicts.

one core, allowing for unified administration of the different indexes. The `solr.xml` file contains the names of all cores managed by the Solr server.

Although a single Solr server can manage multiple cores, the server cannot handle a query across different cores. In section 8.4.1 we saw that requests to the Solr server always contain the name of the core as part of the URL, explicitly, or by specifying a `defaultCoreName` in the `solr.xml` config file. Given this, in order to use Solr for search across multiple document types, you must create an index that contains definitions for all fields in both documents (assuming that all fields with the same name have the same type), plus an additional field specifying the document type.

8.6   Case Study: Indexing *The Federalist Papers*

To show how to build a custom Solr application, we use the 85 essays that make up *The Federalist Papers*, the case study dataset from chapter 6, to build the Solr equivalent of the Lucene index that we created in section 7.6.4. The home directory for this example is:

    javabook/src/appsolr/home_fedpapers

8.6.1   Configuring the Index

The directory `home_fedpapers` contains the required Solr configuration files and subdirectories for the Solr core for this application.

```
home_fedpapers/
  solr.xml
  core_fedpapers/
    conf/
      lucene_english_stopwords.txt
      schema.xml
      solrconfig.xml
```

The `core_fedpapers` `solr.xml` file

The directory for the Solr index is called `core_fedpapers`. The `solr.xml` file declares this as the single core:

```
<core name="core_fedpapers"
      instanceDir="core_fedpapers"/>
```

The `core_fedpapers solrconfig.xml` file

The Solr config file `solrconfig.xml` defines the set of request handlers for this application. The default search handler is:

```
<requestHandler name="/select"
                class="solr.SearchHandler">
  <lst name="defaults">
    <str name="echoParams">explicit</str>
    <int name="rows">10</int>
    <str name="df">text</str>
  </lst>
</requestHandler>
```

The default values are overridden by parameters in the request. We include the admin handlers for the Solr Admin UI:

```
<requestHandler name="/admin/"
                class="solr.admin.AdminHandlers"/>
```

We also need a separate declaration for the Ping tool that is used to check the server for a specific core.

```
<requestHandler name="/admin/ping"
                class="solr.PingRequestHandler"/>
```

The `schema.xml` file

The program `IndexPapers` (see section 7.6.4) takes each essay from *The Federalist Papers* and creates a corresponding Lucene `Document` with fields: `number` for the essay number, an `IntField`; `title` for the essay title, a `TextField` analyzed by Lucene's `StandardAnalyzer`; `author` for the essay author(s), a `StringField`; `pubName` for the name of publication the essay appeared in, a `StringField`; `pubDate` for the date the essay was published, a `LongField` where the date is rounded to midnight of the day; and a field `text` that contains both the essay title and all paragraphs, a `TextField` analyzed by Lucene's `StandardAnalyzer`. The document will have two author fields if the essay has two authors. The document will have multiple text fields, one for the title and one for each paragraph of the essay.

The Solr `schema.xml` file defines the corresponding fields and field types. The field types are:

```
<types>
  <fieldType name="date" class="solr.TrieDateField"/>
  <fieldType name="int" class="solr.TrieIntField"/>
  <fieldType name="long" class="solr.TrieLongField"/>
```

```
<fieldType name="string" class="solr.StrField"/>
<fieldType name="text_std_analyzer" class="solr.TextField"
          positionIncrementGap="100">
  <analyzer>
    <tokenizer class="solr.StandardTokenizerFactory"/>
    <filter class="solr.StandardFilterFactory"/>
    <filter class="solr.LowerCaseFilterFactory"/>
    <filter class="solr.StopFilterFactory"
            ignoreCase="true"
            words="lucene_english_stopwords.txt"
            enablePositionIncrements="true"/>
  </analyzer>
</fieldType>
</types>
```

Unlike Lucene, Solr has a primitive type for dates, so we define a
field type `date` of class `solr.TrieDateField`. All of the Lucene numeric field subclasses have a corresponding Solr primitive type; a Lucene
`IntField` corresponds to a `solr.TrieIntField`, a Lucene `LongField` corresponds to a `solr.TrieLongField`, and so on.[3] The Lucene `StringField`
corresponds to a `solr.StrField` and a `TextField` corresponds to
a `solr.TextField`. For the `TextField` we want to use an analyzer that behaves exactly like Lucene's `StandardAnalyzer`. The Lucene
`StandardAnalyzer` takes a `StandardTokenizer` that breaks a piece of text
into a stream of words, discarding whitespace and punctuation. The tokens are filtered by Lucene's `StandardFilter`, a `LowerCaseFilter`, and a
`StopFilter`. We supply the `StopFilter` with a file of stop words called
`lucene_english_stopwords.txt`. This file contains the set of stop words
that correspond to the Lucene constant `ENGLISH_STOP_WORDS_SET`, which is
defined in the Lucene class `oal.analysis.core.StopAnalyzer`. These are
the `field` definitions:

```
<fields>
  <field name="number" type="int"
         indexed="true" stored="true"
         required="true" multiValued="false"/>
  <field name="title" type="text_std_analyzer"
         indexed="true" stored="true"
         required="true" multiValued="false"/>
  <field name="author" type="string"
         indexed="true" stored="true"
```

[3]Solr also has a set of legacy types `solr.IntField`, `solr.LongField`, etc. These types encode
the numeric value as a simple string. These fields sort in numeric order, but queries that use
numeric ranges will not work as expected.

```
                    required="true" multiValued="true"/>
    <field name="pubName" type="string"
           indexed="true" stored="true"
           required="true" multiValued="false"/>
    <field name="pubDate" type="date"
           indexed="true" stored="true"
           required="true" multiValued="false"/>
    <field name="text" type="text_std_analyzer"
           indexed="true" stored="true"
           required="true" multiValued="true"/>

    <field name="_version_" type="long"
           indexed="true" stored="true"/>
    </fields>
```

The `_version_` field of field type `long` is mandatory. The other fields correspond to the fields created by the `IndexPapers` program.

In the program `IndexPapers`, we indexed the title of the essay twice: both as a `title` field and also as a `text` field. In the Solr schema we use the `copyfield` directive:

```
<copyField source="title" dest="text"/>
```

The field `number` is declared to be unique (see section 8.4.4). When newer versions of the document are added to the index, they will replace the existing document, so the index won't contain multiple versions or duplicates of the document.

```
<uniqueKey>number</uniqueKey>
```

To check that this configuration is correct, we start the Jetty server and specify the directory `home_fedpapers` as the `solr.solr.home`.

```
> java -jar start.jar\
> -Dsolr.solr.home="javabook/src/appsolr/home_fedpapers"
```

The Jetty server logs messages to the terminal window. These report the parsing of the `schema.xml` file, index creation, and instantiation of the request handlers. If an error occurs during startup, the error messages will be logged to the terminal. In a successful startup, no errors are thrown and the final log messages is:

```
Started SocketConnector@0.0.0.0:8983
```

When starting the Jetty server over the `core_fedpapers` index for the very first time, the `core_fedpapers` directory contains a `data` directory that contains an empty Lucene index:

```
> ls javabook/src/appsolr/home_fedpapers/core_fedpapers/data
segments.gen    segments_1
```

8.6.2   Adding Documents to the Solr Index

In section 6.7 we used the program FederalistParser to split the Project
Gutenberg Etext into a series of XML files, one per essay. In this section we
upload these XML files to the core_fedpapers Solr index.

Updates to the Solr index (i.e., adding, deleting, and replacing documents) are handled by the Solr update request handler. The Solr update request handler accepts POSTed XML messages that Add/Replace, Delete, and
Delete documents by query. The message syntax is documented in the Solr
wiki, http://wiki.apache.org/solr/UpdateXmlMessages. The top-level element of the XML message specifies the operation, e.g., add or delete.

In section 8.2.1 we worked through the Solr binary release examples and
populated the Solr index collection1 with a set of XML files in the subdirectory $SOLR/example/exampledocs. Each of the XML files consists of a top-level
add element that contains one or more doc elements. The script post.sh uses
the curl command-line tool to send the XML files to the Solr server:

```
FILES=$*
URL=http://localhost:8983/solr/update

for f in $FILES; do
  echo Posting file $f to $URL
  curl $URL --data-binary @$f -H 'Content-type:application/xml'
  echo
done

#send the commit command to make sure
#all the changes are flushed and visible

curl "$URL?softCommit=true"
echo
```

The specified URL is the local Solr server and the default port for the
Jetty installation. The protocol specified by the URL is HTTP. The option
--data-binary sends the data as the body of a POST request to the HTTP
server. The @ symbol prefix causes curl to read in the data from the specified
file name. The -H option sends extra header information to the server, in this
case, specifying the content type as XML.

In section 6.7 we used the program FederalistParser to split
the Project Gutenberg Etext into a series of XML files, one per essay. The XML documents have a top-level element add that contains one doc element. Here is the beginning of the output file
javabook/data/federalist-papers/xml/paper_01.xml:

```
<?xml version="1.0" encoding="UTF-8"?>
```

```
<add>
  <doc>
    <field name="number">1</field>
    <field name="title">General Introduction</field>
    <field name="pubName">the Independent Journal</field>
    <field name="pubDate">1787-10-27T00:00:00Z</field>
    <field name="author">HAMILTON</field>
    <field name="text">AFTER an unequivocal experience ...
```

The Ant task `parse-papers` in the `build.xml` file in the directory `javabook/src/casestudy` runs this program. The command-line arguments are specified using Ant properties. The default arguments are input EText file `javabook/data/federalist-papers/pg1404.txt` and output XML directory `javabook/data/federalist-papers/xml`.

To add documents to the index, we use the `curl` command. The name of the Solr index is `core_fedpapers` therefore, the update URL is: `http://localhost:8983/solr/core_fedpapers/update`. We add `paper_01.xml` to the index using the following commands:

```
> cd javabook/data/federalist-papers/xml
> curl http://localhost:8983/solr/core_fedpapers/update\
>   --data-binary @paper_01.xml -H 'Content-type:application/xml'
```

The Solr server sends an XML response. The response header contains a `status` code of 0, which indicates a successful request and the query time in milliseconds.

```
<?xml version="1.0" encoding="UTF-8"?>
<response>
<lst name="responseHeader">
  <int name="status">0</int>
  <int name="QTime">6</int>
</lst>
</response>
```

We add all papers to the index using a `for` loop, as in `post.sh`. After we have added all 85 papers, we send a commit request.

```
> curl http://localhost:8983/solr/core_fedpapers/update?commit=true
```

The Solr server sends an XML response, as before.

```
<?xml version="1.0" encoding="UTF-8"?>
<response>
<lst name="responseHeader">
  <int name="status">0</int>
  <int name="QTime">621</int>
```

```
</lst>
</response>
```

The relatively long query time (`QTime` of 621 milliseconds) is the result of writing the index to disk.

Fig. 8.3: *The Solr 4 Admin UI, overview of* `core_fedpapers` *after adding all documents.*

Figure 8.3 shows the Solr Admin UI after the commit. There are now 85 files in the index. Once we have added these documents to the index, adding them again has no effect. Solr updates/overwrites the existing documents; the index contains 85 documents, as before.

8.7   SolrJ

SolrJ provides a Java interface to a Solr index. It is a client library included in the Solr binary distribution. The SolrJ API provides the abstract class `SolrServer` that handles the HTTP communications with the Solr server. The `SolrServer` class provides methods for adding documents, updating, and querying a Solr index.

SolrJ provides several concrete subclasses of `SolrServer`. The subclass `HttpSolrServer` uses the Apache commons HTTP Client to connect to a remote Solr instance. The subclass `CloudSolrServer` uses Apache ZooKeeper to communicate with a SolrCloud, which is a distributed cluster of Solr servers.

Both of these servers may be wrapped by a `LBHttpSolrServer`, a load-balancing Solr server. A `ConcurrentUpdateSolrServer` buffers all added documents and writes them into open HTTP connections, providing a means of doing high-speed bulk updates to the index. This class is thread safe.

In this section we use a `ConcurrentUpdateSolrServer` to add documents to the index. The demo class `SolrJPapers` is based on the demo class `IndexPapers` (section 7.6.4). This class is in the package `com.colloquial.casestudy`. It uses the `FederalistParser` class in that package to parse the Project Gutenberg Etext file into a list of `Paper` objects and a `ConcurrentUpdateSolrServer` to add these to a Solr index.

Code Walkthrough

The class `SolrJPapers` consists of a `main()` method that takes two command-line arguments corresponding to the location of Project Gutenberg Etext file and the URL of the Solr index.

```
File etextFile = new File(args[0]);
String solrUrl = args[1];
ConcurrentUpdateSolrServer solrServer
    = new ConcurrentUpdateSolrServer(solrUrl,10,3);
```

The `main()` method gets the command-line arguments. It uses the Solr index URL to instantiate a `ConcurrentUpdateSolrServer` by calling the 3-arg constructor that takes a `String` specifying the URL of the Solr server, an `int` specifying the number of documents to be buffered before sending a request to the server, and an `int` specifying the maximum number of threads used to empty the queue. This instance will use an internally managed `HttpClient` instance to communicate with the Solr server. The constructor throws a runtime exception if the URL is malformed. The remainder of the `main` does the indexing.

```
try {
    FederalistParser parser = new FederalistParser();
    List<Paper> papers = parser.parsePapers(etextFile);
    for (Paper paper : papers) {
        SolrInputDocument doc = new SolrInputDocument();
        doc.addField("number", paper.getNumber());
        doc.addField("title", paper.getTitle());
        doc.addField("author", paper.getAuthor1());
        if (paper.getAuthor2() != null) {
            doc.addField("author",paper.getAuthor2());
        }
        doc.addField("pubName", paper.getPubName());
        doc.addField("pubDate", paper.getPubDate());
```

```
            for (String paragraph : paper.getParagraphs()) {
                doc.addField("text", paragraph);
            }
            solrServer.add(doc);
        }
        UpdateResponse response = solrServer.commit();
        System.out.println(response.toString());
    } finally {
        solrServer.shutdown();
    }
```

We use a `try-finally` construct to ensure that the `shutdown` method is always called in order to release any allocated resources.

We parse the Project Gutenberg text into a list of **Paper** objects. Then we instantiate a `SolrInputDocument` (package `oas.solr.common`) for each paper, using the `addField(String,Object)` method to populate the document. The `ConcurrentUpdateSolrServer` queues up these requests as background processes. When all documents have been added to the index, we call the `commit()` method, which sends a commit request to the remote Solr server. Finally, we call the `shutdown()` method, which shuts down the `ConcurrentUpdateSolrServer` (not the remote Solr server) and releases all allocated resources.

The `ConcurrentUpdateSolrServer` sends batches of documents to the Solr server. The batch size is determined by the `queueSize` and `threadCount` parameters. If the Solr server encounters an ill-formed document, it throws an error and the remaining documents in that batch will not be processed. The response header from the Solr server includes an error code and error message. These errors are logged by the `ConcurrentUpdateSolrServer` as they occur. The enum class `SolrException.ErrorCode` in package `oas.common` defines the valid HTTP Status error codes that Solr returns. This processing happens in background threads; the `status` code returned by the call `solrServer.add(doc)` is always 0.

Compilation and Configuration

Both Solr and SolrJ use the SFL4J API (Simple Logging Facade for Java, see `http://slf4j.org`) for logging. SFL4J provides an abstraction for various logging frameworks allowing the end user to plug in the desired logging framework at deployment time. The Solr example Jetty server uses the Apache Log4J framework and we use both the jars and configuration files here. The Log4J manual provides a concise introduction to the Log4J framework.

```
http://logging.apache.org/log4j/1.2/manual.html
```

The set of jarfiles needed to build a SolrJ application are included with the Solr binary release in the `dist` directory. The SolrJ jarfile is named `solr-solrj-VERSION.jar` where VERSION is of the form MAJOR_MINOR_REV, e.g., `solr-solrj-4.5.1.jar`. The subdirectory `dist/solrj-lib` contains additional jarfiles that may be needed depending on the subclass of `SolrServer` and the logging used by the application. We have copied these jarfiles over to the `lib` subdirectory of the casestudy source code directory (`javabook/src/casestudy/lib`) and added them to the classpath used in the Ant buildfile:

```
<path id="classpath">
   ...
   <pathelement location="lib/solr-solrj-4.5.1.jar"/>
   <pathelement location="lib/httpclient-4.2.3.jar"/>
   <pathelement location="lib/httpcore-4.2.2.jar"/>
   <pathelement location="lib/httpmime-4.2.3.jar"/>
   <pathelement location="lib/jcl-over-slf4j-1.6.6.jar" />
   <pathelement location="lib/log4j-1.2.16.jar" />
   <pathelement location="lib/noggit-0.5.jar" />
   <pathelement location="lib/slf4j-api-1.6.6.jar"/>
   <pathelement location="lib/slf4j-log4j12-1.6.6.jar" />
</path>
```

The Apache Log4J framework is configured at runtime using configuration files and will send warning messages to the console if no configuration information can be found. We have copied the file `$SOLR/example/resources/log4j.configuration` to the source code directory for this chapter and changed the configuration so that all logging goes only to a file and not to the console as well:

```
log4j.rootLogger=INFO, file
```

The property: `log4j.appender.file.File` specifies the path for the logfile:

```
log4j.appender.file.File=logs/solrj.log
```

There are many ways to specify the location of this configuration file. We choose to do this by setting the Java environment variable `log4j.configuration`, which expects a value in the form of a URL for the location of the configuration file.

Running the Program

The `build.xml` file in the Ant target `javabook/src/casestudy` directory contains the target `solr-index-papers`, which runs the indexing demo.

Command-line arguments are passed into the program via the Ant properties `etext` and `solr.url`. The `build.xml` file defines default values for these
properties:

```
<property name="etext"
          value="../../data/federalist-papers/pg1404.txt"/>
<property name="solr.url"
          value="http://localhost:8983/solr/core_fedpapers/"/>
```

The Java environment variable `log4j.configuration` takes a URL as its
value. We create an Ant property that specifies the absolute path to the
`log4j.properties` properties file and then use this to construct the URL:

```
<property name="log4j.props"
          location="log4j.properties"/>
<target name="solr-index-papers"
        depends="jar">
  <java classname="com.colloquial.casestudy.SolrJPapers"
        classpathref="classpath"
        fork="true">
    <jvmarg value="-Dlog4j.configuration=FILE:///${log4j.props}"/>
    <arg value ="${etext}"/>
    <arg value="${solr.url}"/>
  </java>
</target>
```

We run the program via Ant using the defaults:

```
> cd javabook/src/casestudy
> ant solr-index-papers
{responseHeader={status=0,QTime=735}}
```

The Log4j logger has created the directory and file `logs/solr.log`. Examination of this file shows that the `ConcurrentUpdateSolrServer` instantiated
three threads that were used to add documents to the Solr index. Examination
of the Solr server console (or logfile) shows the server receiving and respond-
ing to these requests.

8.8   Indexing Database Content

The Solr `DataImportHandler` (DIH) is a contributed module that builds a Solr
core from the contents of a relational database, XML documents, or other
structured data source. Search over the resulting core proceeds just as search
over any other Solr core.

Cores built by the DIH module are registered in the `solr.xml` file just like a regular index and are configured via the usual `schema.xml` and `solrconfig.xml` configuration files. The `conf` directory also contains a `data-config.xml` file, which specifies how to get/map/transform the data from the data source into the fields of the Solr document.

The `DataImportHandler` is implemented as a `SolrRequestHandler` and must be registered in the `solrconfig.xml` file. The location of the `data-config.xml` file is specified here.

```
<requestHandler name="/dataimport"
  class="org.apache.solr.handler.dataimport.DataImportHandler">
  <lst name="defaults">
    <str name="config">solr-data-config.xml</str>
  </lst>
</requestHandler>
```

The data source may be defined within the `requestHandler` element in the `solrconfig.xml` file or it may be defined within the data config file.

Here is a short example of a `data-config.xml` file that extracts all rows from a database table `item` and creates a document corresponding to each row, mapping columns `ID` and `NAME` into fields `id` and `name`:

```
<dataConfig>
<dataSource driver="org.hsqldb.jdbcDriver"
  url="jdbc:hsqldb:/temp/example/ex" user="sa" />
  <document name="products">
    <entity name="item" query="select * from item">
      <field column="ID" name="id" />
      <field column="NAME" name="name" />
    </entity>
  </document>
</dataConfig>
```

The directory `$SOLR/example/example-DIH`, included with the Solr CNET example, provides an example of a Solr core that is created via the DIH module from a supplied RDBMS, together with configuration examples for importing data from RSS, mail, and using the Apache project TIKA tool. The Solr wiki page `http://wiki.apache.org/solr/DataImportHandler` provides good documentation for these examples.

8.9 Document Search

Document search is carried out by search request handlers on a per-index basis. The <solrconfig.xml> file contains the mapping from path names to handlers. Any number of search request handlers can be defined, allowing an application to provide many types of custom search via different URLs, each with its own default or invariant parameters.

Solr search is composed of a chain of search components. The conventional Solr search request handler is the `SearchHandler` class in package `oas.handler.components`. As of Solr 4, it chains together six search components. The first component is the `QueryComponent`, which performs the document search over the index, and the last is the `Debug` component, which provides diagnostics for all components in the processing chain. This processing chain provides the maximum amount of server-side processing for the minimum number of HTTP requests.

All parameters used by the components in the processing chain are sent to the request handler. This configurable, componentized architecture leads to a long list of possible query request parameters, which we discuss on a component-by-component basis.

Document search results are formatted by a `QueryResponseWriter`. The choice of response writer is also configurable and customizable. The request parameter `wt` (*writer type*) controls this choice. Solr provides a large number of response formats, including XML, JSON, and CSV. In our examples we use either the `XMLResponseWriter` (`wt=xml`), which is both reusable and general purpose or the `JSONResponseWriter` (`wt=json`).

Search requests are sent to the Solr server via HTTP and therefore must be URL encoded to escape any special characters in the request (see section 5.2.1 and `http://wiki.apache.org/solr/SolrQuerySyntax#urlescaping` for examples). When developing queries from a web browser, this URL encoding is usually done automatically by the browser. Applications that generate queries programmatically must be sure to properly URL encode them.

8.9.1 Search Queries

Document search over the index is carried out by a `QueryComponent`. This is the first component in the chain of components invoked by the Solr `SearchHandler`. It uses and expands on Lucene's search query syntax. Most of the parameters will be familiar to Lucene users.

In the example `core_fedpapers` index we define a request handler named `select` that handles document search over the index:

```
<requestHandler name="/select" class="solr.SearchHandler">
  <lst name="defaults">
    <str name="df">text</str>
    <str name="fl">score,number,title</str>
    <int name="rows">5</int>
```

```
    </lst>
  </requestHandler>
```

This definition includes three default parameter settings.

The `df` parameter specifies the name of the default field. This parameter must be specified, either implicitly in the request handler configuration, as above, or overtly as part of the query parameter. The query will return an error message if this parameter is missing.

The parameter `fl` (field list) limits the fields returned in a document to a comma-separated list of field names supplied as the parameter value. By specifying `score`, the document score is returned as well. If no field list is specified, all stored fields in the document are returned.

The `rows` parameter controls the number of search results. If unspecified, it defaults to 10.

The parameter `q` specifies the query string. The query string is parsed by a query parser. The default query parser is the Lucene query parser. The standard Solr query syntax is based on the Lucene query syntax. Details and a list of differences between the Solr and Lucene query languages are found on the Solr wiki page:

```
http://wiki.apache.org/solr/SolrQuerySyntax
```

To see the default behavior of the `/select` search handler, we search the `core_fedpapers` index for documents containing the word *union*:

```
http://localhost:8983/solr/core_fedpapers/select?q=union
```

The default response writer is the `XMLResponseWriter` therefore, the response is in XML format:

```xml
<response>
  <lst name="responseHeader">
    <int name="status">0</int>
    <int name="QTime">140</int>
  </lst>
  <result name="response" numFound="69"
          start="0" maxScore="0.1345497">
    <doc>
      <int name="number">32</int>
      <str name="title">The Same Subject Continued
        (Concerning the General Power of Taxation) </str>
      <float name="score">0.1345497</float>
    </doc>
    <doc>
      <int name="number">20</int>
      ...
```

```
    </doc>
    <doc>
      <int name="number">31</int>
      ...
    </doc>
    <doc>
      <int name="number">82</int>
      ...
    </doc>
    <doc>
      <int name="number">14</int>
      ...
    </doc>
  </result>
</response>
```

The top-level element is `response`. The 1st element named `responseHeader` provides information on the query status and the elapsed time in milliseconds for query completion by the request handler (not including response formatting time). The `result` element contains the results returned by the `QueryComponent`, that is, the result of the search over the index. Attributes of the `result` element contain summary information including the total number of hits (69), the maximum score (0.1345), and the starting point in the list for the docs returned (0). The `result` element contains the five top-scoring `doc` elements.

Additional `QueryComponent` parameters include the `start` and `rows` parameter, which together provide a mechanism for paging through a set of search results, and the `sort` parameter provides the mechanism for ordering documents based on field values or functions. The `fq` (filter query) parameter is used to improve search performance. Results of each `fq` query are cached individually. The `fq` (filter query) parameter restricts the Solr search (specified by the q parameter) to the documents in the `fq` cache, instead of searching the entire index. See the Solr wiki page `http://wiki.apache.org/solr/CommonQueryParameters` for further details.

8.9.2   Post-query `SearchHandler` Components

The default chain of search components for the Solr `SearchHandler` is: `QueryComponent`, `FacetComponent`, `MoreLikeThis`, `Highlighting`, `Statistics`, and `Debug`. The search request parameters determine which of these components are invoked. The query response contains a top-level element corresponding to each component.

The Debug Component

The Debug component is the final component invoked by the Solr SearchHandler. By setting the debugQuery parameter to true, the search response includes information about the query parsing and a detailed explanation for the scoring of every document returned in the result, as well as a breakdown of the time used to prepare and process each of the search components. This component is invaluable for query tuning.

We rerun our previous example query over the core_fedpapers index q=union and add the parameter debugQuery=true. The query response now includes the following lst named debug:

```
<lst name="debug">
  <str name="rawquerystring">union</str>
  <str name="querystring">union</str>
  <str name="parsedquery">text:union</str>
  <str name="parsedquery_toString">text:union</str>
  <lst name="explain">
    <str name="32">
      0.13454969 = (MATCH) weight(text:union in 12)
      [DefaultSimilarity],
      result of:
      0.13454969 = score(doc=12,freq=13.0 = termFreq=13.0),
      product of: 0.99999994 = queryWeight,
      product of: 1.194156 = idf(docFreq=69, maxDocs=85)
      0.83741146 = queryNorm 0.1345497 = fieldWeight in 12,
      product of: 3.6055512 = tf(freq=13.0),
      with freq of: 13.0 = termFreq=13.0
      1.194156 = idf(docFreq=69, maxDocs=85)
      0.03125 = fieldNorm(doc=12)
    </str>
...
  </lst>
  <str name="QParser">LuceneQParser</str>
  <lst name="timing">
    <double name="time">13.0</double>
    <lst name="prepare">
      <double name="time">1.0</double>
      <lst name="query">
        <double name="time">1.0</double>
      </lst>
...
    </lst>
    <lst name="process">
```

```
      <double name="time">11.0</double>
      <lst name="query">
        <double name="time">1.0</double>
      </lst>
      <lst name="facet">
        <double name="time">0.0</double>
      </lst>
      <lst name="mlt">
        <double name="time">0.0</double>
      </lst>
      <lst name="highlight">
        <double name="time">0.0</double>
      </lst>
      <lst name="stats">
        <double name="time">0.0</double>
      </lst>
      <lst name="debug">
        <double name="time">10.0</double>
      </lst>
    </lst>
  </lst>
</lst>
```

The final lst element named timing provides a breakdown of the preparation and processing time for each query component. We see that it took 1 millisecond to prepare the search query and 1 millisecond to process it and it took 10 milliseconds to process the debug information. (Note that this timing information doesn't include the time it takes for the ResponseWriter to format this information.) This query doesn't invoke any of the other search components therefore, they take time 0.0.

Faceted Search

Faceted search breaks up search results into multiple categories and returns a facet_counts section within a search response that provides a per-category breakdown of the search results. Faceting is done on a per-field basis. Faceting information comes from the Solr index therefore, only indexed fields can be used for faceting. The faceting component provides date range operations for date fields and generalized range operations for numeric fields.

Faceting is turned on by the request parameter facet=true. All parameters to the faceting component are prefixed by facet. The faceting component requires at least one of the following parameters to be overtly specified: facet.field, facet.date, or facet.range. As an example, we run a search over the `core_fedpapers` index, searching the text field for the token *union* and facet by author field. The HTTP request is:

```
http://localhost:8983/solr/core_fedpapers/select?
q=union&rows=0&wt=json&indent=true&
facet=true&facet.field=author&debugQuery=true
```

The query string parameter is `q=union`. In order to slim down the response, we request the first zero documents to be returned `rows=0` and we use JSON output format `wt=json`, setting `indent=true` for readability. To request faceting we set `facet=true` and specify faceting by field `facet.field=author`. The HTTP response is:

```
{
  "responseHeader":{
    "status":0,
    "QTime":3},
  "response":{"numFound":69,"start":0,
              "maxScore":0.1345497,"docs":[]
  },
  "facet_counts":{
    "facet_queries":{},
    "facet_fields":{
      "author":[
        "HAMILTON",47,
        "MADISON",21,
        "JAY",4]},
    "facet_dates":{},
    "facet_ranges":{}},
  "debug":{
...
    "timing":{
      "time":3.0,
      "prepare":{
        "time":1.0,
        "query":{
          "time":1.0},
        "facet":{
          "time":0.0},
...
        "debug":{
          "time":0.0}},
      "process":{
        "time":2.0,
        "query":{
```

```
        "time":1.0},
      "facet":{
        "time":1.0},
...
      "debug":{
        "time":0.0}}}}}
```

We have omitted most of the debug information, save for the timing on the query, facet, and debug components. The facet field contains only three terms altogether therefore, processing the facet request takes only 1 millisecond.

The Solr wiki provides a good overview of faceting and documentation and examples of the parameters available for faceted search. See wiki pages:

```
http://wiki.apache.org/solr/SolrFacetingOverview
```

```
http://wiki.apache.org/solr/SimpleFacetParameters
```

MLT: More Like This

More Like This (MLT) is the technique of finding other documents similar to a given document by constructing a search query from (some of) the terms in a document. MLT treats a document as a bag of (fielded) words. The intuition is that similar or related documents will contain roughly the same set of words in roughly the same proportion.

The Solr `MoreLikeThisComponent` performs a new search for each document in the result set. It returns a `1st` element named `moreLikeThis`, which contains a new set of results for each document in the query result. This component is expensive in terms of both processing time and the size of the Solr response.

The Solr documentation recommends using term vectors for the fields used to construct the query. This speeds up the MLT search, at the cost of increasing the size of the index. To see how this works using the *The Federalist Papers* case study dataset, we first change the schema and rebuild the index in order to store term vectors for the text fields `title` and `text`. We add the attribute `termVectors="true"` to the field definitions:

```
<fields>
...
  <field name="title" type="text_std_analyzer"
         indexed="true" stored="true"
         required="true" multiValued="false"
         termVectors="true" termPositions="true"
         termOffsets="true"/>
...
  <field name="text" type="text_std_analyzer"
```

```
           indexed="true" stored="true"
           required="true" multiValued="true"
           termVectors="true" termPositions="true"
           termOffsets="true"/>
  </fields>
```

With this change in place, we delete and rebuild the index using the Ant target `solr-index-papers` as we did before in section 8.7. The size of the resulting index increases from 1.1 MB to 1.8 MB.

MoreLikeThis is turned on by the request parameter `mlt=true`, and all parameters to this component are prefixed by `mlt`. The required parameter `mlt.fl` specifies the field or fields used for the terms in the new query. The parameter `mlt.count` specifies the maximum number of documents returned. There are several parameters used to tune the query performance by limiting the terms used in the search query to those that are most likely to be relevant and discriminative. Finding the optimum setting of these parameters depends on the contents of the index, the kind and number of desired search results, and performance constraints.

To see how this works, we choose to run a search for the word *law*, a term that occurs in roughly half of the documents in the index, and run an MLT query using the terms in the `text` field of each document in the query results. The HTTP request is:

```
http://localhost:8983/solr/core_fedpapers/select?
q=law&rows=3
&mlt=true&mlt.fl=text&mlt.count=5
&debugQuery=true
```

We restrict the maximum number of documents returns by the search query to three. For each document in the query results, we perform a MoreLikeThis query, using the default setting, and retrieve the top five documents.

Attributes of the `result` element contain summary information including the total number of hits (40), the maximum score (0.1621), and the starting point in the list for the docs returned (0). The top three documents returned for the query `law` are Federalist Papers 33, 81, and 42.

```
<result name="response" numFound="40"
        start="0" maxScore="0.16210118">
  <doc>
    <int name="number">33</int>
    <str name="title">The Same Subject Continued
    (Concerning the General Power of Taxation) </str>
    <float name="score">0.16210118</float>
  </doc>
  <doc>
```

```
    <int name="number">81</int>
    <str name="title">The Judiciary Continued, and
    the Distribution of the Judicial Authority. </str>
    <float name="score">0.1584004</float>
  </doc>
  <doc>
    <int name="number">42</int>
    <str name="title">The Powers Conferred by
    the Constitution Further Considered </str>
    <float name="score">0.1344072</float>
  </doc>
</result>
```

The top-level query `result` section is followed by the MLT section, enclosed in a `lst` element with `name moreLikeThis`. It contains a `result` element. Attributes of this `result` element contain summary information on how this new query that is composed of terms from Paper 33 matches the remaining documents in the index. The total number of hits is 84, showing that at least one of the terms in the query occurs at least once in every other document in the index. The starting point in this list is 0. The top five documents like Federalist Paper 33, *Concerning the General Power of Taxation*, are Papers 32, 36, 31, 83, and 21:

```
<lst name="moreLikeThis">
  <result name="33" numFound="84"
  start="0" maxScore="0.36850253">
    <doc>
      <int name="number">32</int>
      <str name="title">The Same Subject Continued
      (Concerning the General Power of Taxation) </str>
      <float name="score">0.36850253</float>
    </doc>
    <doc>
      <int name="number">36</int>
      <str name="title">The Same Subject Continued
      (Concerning the General Power of Taxation) </str>
      <float name="score">0.2803799</float>
    </doc>
    <doc>
      <int name="number">31</int>
      <str name="title">The Same Subject Continued
      (Concerning the General Power of Taxation) </str>
      <float name="score">0.2662683</float>
    </doc>
```

```
  <doc>
    <int name="number">83</int>
    <str name="title">The Judiciary Continued
    in Relation to Trial by Jury </str>
    <float name="score">0.22085238</float>
  </doc>
  <doc>
    <int name="number">21</int>
    <str name="title">Other Defects
    of the Present Confederation </str>
    <float name="score">0.19242279</float>
  </doc>
  </result>
</lst>
```

To get the term query constructed from Paper 33 we set debugQuery=true:

```
<str name="rawMLTQuery">
  text:laws text:which text:power text:clause
  text:powers text:supreme text:law text:would
  text:constitution text:its text:have text:taxation
  text:taxes text:upon text:what text:been text:laying
  text:societies text:may text:necessary text:declares
  text:land text:state text:tax text:from
</str>
```

The top five documents like Federalist Paper 81, *The Judiciary Continued, and the Distribution of the Judicial Authority*, are Papers 82, 83, 80, 47, and 65. The term query constructed from Paper 81 is:

```
<str name="rawMLTQuery">
  text:courts text:court text:supreme
  text:jurisdiction text:which text:law
  text:jury text:fact text:inferior text:judicial
  text:causes text:state text:may text:cognizance
  text:have text:been text:would text:power text:from
  text:tribunals text:legislature text:states
  text:appeals text:trial text:upon
</str>
```

The top five documents like Federalist Paper 42, *The Powers Conferred by the Constitution Further Considered*, are Papers 80, 44, 22, 53, and 69. The term query constructed from Paper 42 is:

```
<str name="rawMLTQuery">
  text:states text:consuls text:which text:confederation
```

```
    text:commerce text:articles text:power text:state
    text:have text:foreign text:law text:been
    text:privileges text:regulate text:may text:trade
    text:term text:other text:within text:would text:offenses
    text:has text:treaties text:nations text:public
  </str>
```

Invoking the MLT component adds significant processing time. Almost all processing time is spent processing the MLT queries. To run three MLT queries over a small index takes 47 milliseconds, using the default MLT parameters. Increasing the number of documents returned by the search query to 10 increases performance time to 178 milliseconds.

The Solr wiki provides documentation on the MoreLikeThis component and the MoreLikeThis Handler.

Highlighting Component

The `HighlightingComponent` retrieves a query term and its context, called a *snippet*, from a document and returns it as part of the search response. Highlighting is turned on by the request parameter `hl=true`. As an example, we run a search with highlighting over the `core_fedpapers` index, searching the text field for the token *judge*. The HTTP request is:

```
http://localhost:8983/solr/core_fedpapers/select?
q=judge&hl=true&debugQuery=true
```

Default values are used for all unspecified parameters. The search query uses the default field `text` and returns the top five results. The default response writer is the `XMLResponseWriter`. The HTTP response consists of four elements:

```
<response>
  <lst name="responseHeader"></lst>
  <result name="response" numFound="18"
          start="0" maxScore="0.16902463"></result>
  <lst name="highlighting"></lst>
  <lst name="debug"></lst>
</response>
```

The five top-scoring documents are Paper 79, *The Judiciary Continued*; Papers 33, 34, and 35, all of which are titled *The Same Subject Continued (Concerning the General Power of Taxation)*; and Paper 47, *The Particular Structure of the New Government and the Distribution of Power Among Its Different Parts*.

The highlighting `lst` element contains a series of `lst` elements, one per document in the `result` section. Highlighted words are surrounded by `<em>` tags.

```
<lst name="highlighting">
  <lst name="79">
    <arr name="text">
      <str> <em>judge</em> comes into office, in
      respect to him. It will be observed that a
      difference has been made</str>
    </arr>
  </lst>
  <lst name="33">
    <arr name="text">
      <str>This simple train of inquiry furnishes us
      at once with a test by which to <em>judge</em>
      of the true nature</str>
    </arr>
  </lst>
  <lst name="35">
    <arr name="text">
      <str>One which, if we may <em>judge</em> from
      the frequency of its repetition, seems most to
      be relied</str>
    </arr>
  </lst>
  <lst name="34">
    <arr name="text">
      <str> and exhausted as they both were, would so
      soon have looked with so hostile an aspect upon
      each other? To <em>judge</em></str>
    </arr>
  </lst>
  <lst name="47">
    <arr name="text">
      <str>, the life and liberty of the subject
      would be exposed to arbitrary control, for
      THE <em>JUDGE</em> would</str>
    </arr>
  </lst>
</lst>
```

In this example there is only one snippet per example and all snippets are roughly 100 characters long. The number of snippets returned per document is controlled by the parameter `hl.snippets` and it defaults to 1. Snippet size is controlled by the parameter `hl.fragsize`. The request parameters that control the highlighting component are documented in the Solr wiki, page `http://wiki.apache.org/solr/HighlightingParameters`.

Statistics

The stats component returns simple statistics for indexed numeric, date, and string fields within the set of result documents. It is used to provide information such as the minimum and maximum values in a field. The stats component is invoked by the request parameter `stats=true`. The parameter `stats.field` specifies the field for which statistics are generated. This parameter may be invoked multiple times in a query in order to request statistics on multiple fields.

This particular feature is not particularly useful for *The Federalist Papers* case study dataset nonetheless, to see how this works, we provide two example queries: one that matches exactly one document in the index and a second query that matches all documents in the index. For each query we get statistics for the `number` and `pubDate` fields.

The name *Pericles* is mentioned in only one document, Paper 6. The HTTP request is:

```
http://localhost:8983/solr/core_fedpapers/select?q=pericles
&stats=true&stats.field=number&stats.field=pubDate
```

The HTTP response includes a top-level `lst` element named `stats` that contains a `lst` element named `stats_fields` that contains a list of stats for each `stats.field` parameter in the search request.

```
<lst name="stats">
  <lst name="stats_fields">
    <lst name="number">
      <double name="min">6.0</double>
      <double name="max">6.0</double>
      <long name="count">1</long>
      <long name="missing">0</long>
      <double name="sum">6.0</double>
      <double name="sumOfSquares">36.0</double>
      <double name="mean">6.0</double>
      <double name="stddev">0.0</double>
      <lst name="facets"/>
    </lst>
    <lst name="pubDate">
      <date name="min">1787-11-14T05:00:00Z</date>
      <date name="max">1787-11-14T05:00:00Z</date>
      <long name="count">1</long>
      <long name="missing">0</long>
      <lst name="facets"/>
    </lst>
  </lst>
</lst>
```

```
</lst>
```

The count value gives the number of non-null values found in the results set while the missing value gives the number of null values. Since the results set contains only one document, the min and max values are the same. Only the min, max, count, and missing fields are computed over date fields.

To create a document set that contains all 85 documents in the core_fedpapers index, we use the word which as the query term. The HTTP response is:

```
<lst name="stats">
  <lst name="stats_fields">
    <lst name="number">
      <double name="min">1.0</double>
      <double name="max">85.0</double>
      <long name="count">85</long>
      <long name="missing">0</long>
      <double name="sum">3655.0</double>
      <double name="sumOfSquares">208335.0</double>
      <double name="mean">43.0</double>
      <double name="stddev">24.681301964577692</double>
    <lst name="facets"/></lst>
    <lst name="pubDate">
      <date name="min">1787-10-27T05:00:00Z</date>
      <date name="max">1788-12-22T05:00:00Z</date>
      <long name="count">85</long>
      <long name="missing">0</long>
    <lst name="facets"/></lst>
  </lst>
</lst>
```

Further documentation is available on the Solr wiki page, http://wiki.apache.org/solr/StatsComponent.

8.9.3 Using the Solr Admin UI for query tuning

The Solr Admin UI provides a query tool that is quite useful for query development and tuning. We use it to search the Solr index core_fedpapers for the query string *Powers of the Judiciary*.

Figure 8.4 is a screenshot of using the query tool in the Solr Admin UI to execute this query on core_fedpapers. The controls on the left side of the query screen are used to construct a query over the index. The Execute Query button at the bottom of this query constructs and runs the query.

We use the controls on the left side of the query screen to construct the query. In the textbox labeled q we enter the Powers of the Judiciary. In

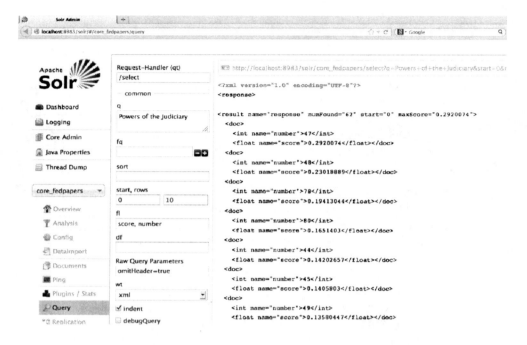

Fig. 8.4: *The Solr 4 Admin UI, Query tool.*

the textbox labeled fl we enter the field names score,number. We use the
Raw Query Parameters to add the additional parameter omitHeader=true.
The pulldown menu labeled wt (writer type) controls the format of the query
response. We select format xml and check the indent checkbox. The Execute
Query button at the bottom of this query constructs and runs the query.

The right side of the query tool displays the results. At the top is the query
URL and beneath it is the response. Note that the query displayed at the top of
the results section is URL encoded:

```
http://localhost:8983/solr/core_fedpapers/select?
q=Powers+of+the+Judiciary&fl=score%2C+number&df=text
&wt=xml&indent=true&omitHeaders=true
```

A URL-encoded string is restricted to alphanumeric ASCII characters plus the
characters hyphen, underscore, period, and asterisk. The percent character is
used as a special character. Spaces are converted to '+' and all other characters
are represented as a sequence *%xy*, where *xy* correspond to the two-digit hex
value of each byte of the byte value of the character. The percent character
is syntactically meaningful therefore, if it occurs in the string, it will be URL
encoded as %25. See section 5.2.1 for further details.[4] We note that in the query

---

[4] The HTTP requests in the Solr logfiles show up as URL-encoded strings, exactly as received by

used in this example is the same query as was used in section 7.8.1, where we used the program `LuceneSearch` to run the query. The results shown in the screenshot in Figure 8.4 are identical to the results obtained by `LuceneSearch` in section 7.8.1.

8.10   Beyond Search

The information in the Lucene index can be used for language-specific tasks such as spell-checking and autocomplete as well as general machine-learning tasks such as clustering and classification. As discussed in chapter 7, a Lucene index is an inverted index that provides a mapping from terms to documents, where a term is a pairing of field names and field values (see section 7.1, Figure 7.1).

A text field is indexed by breaking the text into a stream of tokens and producing terms from the token stream. A term may contain token position and token offset information. The term index can be used to compute term frequency across all documents. This aggregated information can be used to identify likely and unlikely terms and can be used for spell checking and autocomplete.

8.10.1   Suggesting Query Terms: Spell Checking

Spell checking is the technique of adding new terms to a search query that are similar to the terms in the original query. This is not the same as spelling correction, since terms are not removed from the search query. The suggested terms can be supplied from a file or other word list or they can be taken from directly from the index.

The Solr `SpellCheckComponent` performs this operation. It must be included in the list of search components in the search request handler configuration in `solrconfig.xml`. In the configuration file we specify a threshold called `maxResultsForSuggest`. The `SpellCheckComponent` is invoked automatically when the number of hits for a query is at or below this threshold. This avoids sending two separate requests to Solr: one for the original query and a second one to get suggestions. If the `SpellCheckComponent` is invoked, the query response includes a list of spell-check suggestions in addition to the query result.

The goal of spell checking is to mitigate typing and spelling errors by adding the intended terms to the search query. Since intention is highly context-dependent, the spell-checking component must be configured and tuned on an application-specific basis.

---

the Solr server.

Edit Distance

String similarity is based on *edit distance*. Edit distance is a metric based on the kind and number of changes required to transform one string into another, one letter at a time. Changes include transformation of one letter to another, insertion, deletion, and transpositions. Different weights can be assigned to each operation so that insertions or deletions can have a higher penalty than changing one letter to another or the cost of changing an *a* to a *k* can be higher than that of changing an *a* to an *e*.

The default metric used by Lucene is the *Levenshtein distance*, which is the minimum number of single-character edits (insertion, deletion, substitution) required to change one word into the other, with all edits having a cost of 1.[5] For example, to change the string *cat* into the string *dog* requires at least 3 substitutions, so the these strings have a Levenshtein distance of 3, whereas *cat* and *cab* have a distance of 1 and *cat* and *cat* have a distance of 0.

The *Jaro-Winkler distance* measure was developed for name comparison in the U.S. Census. It is designed to compare surnames to surnames and given names to given names. It is best suited for comparing short strings. Another similarity metric is the *n-gram distance*, which computes word similarity based on shared substrings.

Suggested Word List

Spelling correction operates over a suggested word list by computing the edit distance between the terms in the query and the terms in this list. The word list can be supplied as a data file or it can be taken from the term dictionary of the index itself. Using the terms in the index guarantees that there will be documents in the index that match the suggested query terms. Prior to Solr 4, the class IndexBasedSpellChecker would build a parallel index to be used for spell checking. As of Solr 4, the class DirectSolrSpellChecker allows use of the index directly.

Example Configuration

We have added the spell-check example configuration from the Solr CNET example `solrconfig.xml` file to the config for the `core_fedpapers` index. Here is the configuration for the spell-check component:

```
<searchComponent name="spellcheck"
                 class="solr.SpellCheckComponent">
  <str name="queryAnalyzerFieldType">text_std_analyzer</str>

  <lst name="spellchecker">
```

---

[5]In this implementation, transposition counts as two edits.

```
    <str name="name">direct</str>
    <str name="classname">solr.DirectSolrSpellChecker</str>
    <str name="field">text</str>
    <str name="distanceMeasure">internal</str>
    <float name="accuracy">0.5</float>
    <int name="maxEdits">2</int>
    <int name="minPrefix">1</int>
    <int name="maxInspections">5</int>
    <int name="minQueryLength">4</int>
    <float name="maxQueryFrequency">0.01</float>
  </lst>

  <lst name="spellchecker">
    <str name="name">wordbreak</str>
    <str name="classname">solr.WordBreakSolrSpellChecker</str>
    <str name="field">text</str>
    <str name="combineWords">true</str>
    <str name="breakWords">true</str>
    <int name="maxChanges">10</int>
  </lst>
</searchComponent>
```

The first element of the spell-check `searchComponent` definition specifies the analyzer used to process the query string, indirectly, by specifying a field type. The analyzer specified for that field type will be used by the spell-check component. The Solr wiki recommends using an analyzer which performs minimal tokenization and stemming in order to get relevant spelling suggestions, e.g., to avoid stemming changes such as *made* to *mad*. In this example the field `text`, defined in the `schema.xml` file, tokenizes with the Solr Standard-Tokenizer, removes stop words, converts all tokens to lowercase, and adds synonyms to the query.

A spell-check component can have several `lst` elements with attribute name, value `spellchecker`. The spell-checker name is used as the name of the dictionary of suggestions. Parameters to the spell-checker are specified as a list of name, value pairs. Each `lst` element contains a set of `str` elements that specify the parameters used to construct this dictionary. The `classname` parameter specifies the class of the spell-checker instance and this determines what other parameters must or can be specified.

The abstract class `SolrSpellChecker` in package `oas.spelling` has several concrete subclasses. Of these, the classes `DirectSolrSpellChecker`, `FileBasedSolrSpellChecker`, and `IndexBasedSolrSpellChecker` provide spelling suggestions on a per-token basis, using the tokenization of the query string produced by the spell-checker's tokenizer. The class `WordBreakSpellChecker` generates suggestions by combining adjacent words as well as breaking single words apart. It is designed to be used in conjunction with one of the per-token spellcheckers.

The named spell-check component and the names of the spell-checker dictionaries are plugged into the definitions for request handlers that include the spell-check component as part of the search components pipeline. We define a search request handler /spell that uses both the default and wordbreak spell-checkers in conjunction. Here is the configuration for the /spell request handler:

```
<requestHandler name="/spell" class="solr.SearchHandler"
                startup="lazy">
  <lst name="defaults">
    <str name="df">text</str>
    <str name="spellcheck">on</str>
    <str name="spellcheck.dictionary">direct</str>
    <str name="spellcheck.dictionary">wordbreak</str>
    <str name="spellcheck.count">10</str>
    <str name="spellcheck.alternativeTermCount">5</str>
    <str name="spellcheck.maxResultsForSuggest">5</str>
    <str name="spellcheck.extendedResults">true</str>
  </lst>
  <arr name="last-components">
    <str>spellcheck</str>
  </arr>
</requestHandler>
```

The spell-check component named spellcheck is added as the last component in the tokenizer/filter chain used to process the search query. The spell-check component parameters are specified as part of the default parameter list. These parameter names are prefixed by spellcheck. There is a rich set of configuration options that are documented on the Solr wiki page http://wiki.apache.org/solr/SpellCheckComponent.

We set the parameter spellcheck to on in order to invoke the spell-check component by default. We specify both spell-checker dictionaries default. When no dictionary is specified, Solr will try to use a dictionary named *default* and the request returns an error message. The parameter spellcheck.count specifies the maximum number of suggestions to return for terms that aren't in the index, and the parameter spellcheck.alternativeTermCount is the maximum number of suggestions for terms in the index.

If the query results in a low number of hits, then the spell-check component will be invoked as part of the request. Queries that contain typos and misspellings may still return many results. If the query results are greater than the value of parameter spellcheck.maxResultsForSuggest, then the search will be deemed successful and the handler will return the search results without invoking the spell-check component.

To see this in action, we search the `core_fedpapers` index using the `/spell` request handler instead of the `/select` request handler. The search query is *america* and the HTTP request is:

```
http://localhost:8983/solr/core_fedpapers/spell?q=america
```

The response is:

```
<response>
  <result name="response" numFound="46" start="0">
    ...
  </result>
  <lst name="spellcheck">
    <lst name="suggestions"/>
  </lst>
</response>
```

As the term *america* occurs in 46 documents, well above the `maxResultsForSuggest` limit of five, this search returns a set of results (contents omitted) and an empty list of suggested spelling corrections.

If instead of typing *america* we type *amerias*, the search returns zero results and contains a list of spell-check suggestions:

```
http://localhost:8983/solr/core_fedpapers/spell?q=amerias
<response>
  <result name="response" numFound="0" start="0"/>
  <lst name="spellcheck">
    <lst name="suggestions">
      <lst name="amerias">
        <int name="numFound">3</int>
        <int name="startOffset">0</int>
        <int name="endOffset">7</int>
        <int name="origFreq">0</int>
        <arr name="suggestion">
          <lst>
            <str name="word">america</str>
            <int name="freq">46</int>
          </lst>
          <lst>
            <str name="word">american</str>
            <int name="freq">17</int>
          </lst>
          <lst>
            <str name="word">americans</str>
```

```
            <int name="freq">3</int>
          </lst>
        </arr>
      </lst>
      <bool name="correctlySpelled">false</bool>
    </lst>
  </lst>
</response>
```

The wordbreak spell-checker looks for ways to combine or break apart words. The query *judi cial* returns no results. The spell-check component returns suggestions for each of *judi, cial,* and *judi cial.* For *judi* the suggestions are *just, judge, jury, july,* and *juris.* For *cial* the suggestions are *civil, call, city, cabal, cool, calm, chap,* and *cite.* For *judi cial* the suggestion is *judicial.*

Searches that result in one to five hits return both results and suggestions as well. The name *Pericles* is mentioned exactly once, in Federalist Paper 6, which is larded with examples from antiquity. A search for *pericles* returns Paper 6 as a result as well as suggestions *perils* and *prices.*

8.10.2 Document Clustering

Document clustering is the task of grouping a set of documents into subsets, possibly overlapping, based on some measure of document similarity. There are many document clustering algorithms as well as many similarity metrics. Clustering is computationally expensive, and clustering large sets of documents easily becomes extremely computationally expensive therefore, in online and other real-time applications, clustering can be carried out only over small numbers of documents.

Solr can be configured to dynamically cluster search results as part of the search request by defining a search request handler that includes a `ClusteringComponent` as the last component in the processing chain. As of Solr 4, the `ClusteringComponent` can be configured with a `searchComponent` that uses the Carrot2 framework to dynamically cluster the set of documents in a query result. Carrot2 is an open-source clustering engine that can find thematic clusters in a small set of text documents. Carrot2 clusters either on snippets from the `HighlightingComponent` or on entire stored fields. The Solr wiki page `http://wiki.apache.org/solr/ClusteringComponent` provides documentation and examples.

Appendix A

Java Basics

In this appendix, we go over some of the basics of Java that are particularly relevant for text and numerical processing. The programs for this appendix are in the example source code distribution subdirectory:

    javabook/src/basics

This directory contains an Ant `build.xml` file that has targets to compile and run the examples. The programs belong to package `com.colloquial.basics`. The subdirectory `javabook/src/basics/src` contains the Java source files.

A.1   Numbers

In this section, we explain different numerical bases, including decimal, octal, hexadecimal, and binary.

A.1.1   Digits and Decimal Numbers

Typically, we write numbers in the Arabic form (as opposed to, say, the Roman form), using decimal notation. That is, we employ sequences of the ten digits 0, 1, 2, 3, 4, 5, 6, 7, 8, 9.

A number such as 23 may be decomposed into a 2 in the "tens place" and a 3 in the "ones place." What that means is that $23 = (2 \times 10) + (3 \times 1)$; similarly, $4,700 = (4 \times 1,000) + (7 \times 100)$. We can write these equivalently as $23 = 2 \times 10^1 + 3 \times 10^0$ and $4,700 = (4 \times 10^3) + (7 \times 10^2)$. Because of the base of the exponent, decimal notation is also called "base 10."

The number 0 is special. It's the additive identity, meaning that for any number x, $0 + x = x + 0 = x$.

We also conventionally use negative numbers and negation. For instance, -22 is read as "negative 22." We have to add 22 to it to get back to zero. That is, negation is the additive inverse, so that $x + (-x) = (-x) + x = 0$.

The number 1 is also special. 1 is the multiplicative identity, so that $1 \times x = x \times 1 = x$. Division is multiplicative inverse, so that for all numbers x other than 0, $\frac{x}{x} = 1$.

We also use fractions, written after the decimal place. Fractions are defined using negative exponents. For instance $.2 = 2 \times 10^{-1} = \frac{2}{10^1}$, and $.85 = .8 \times 10^{-1} + .5 \times 10^{-2}$.

For really large or really small numbers, we use scientific notation, which decomposes a value into a number times an exponent of 10. For instance, we write 4,700 as 4.7×10^3 and 0.0047 as 4.7×10^{-3}. In computer languages, 4,700 and 0.0047 are typically written as `4.7E+3` and `4.7E-3`. Java's floating point numbers may be input and output in scientific notation.

A.1.2   Bits and Binary Numbers

Rather than the decimal system, computers work in the binary system, where there are only two values. In binary arithmetic, bits play the role that digits play in the decimal system. A *bit* can have the value 0 or 1.

A number in *binary notation* consists of a sequence of bits (0s and 1s). Bits in binary numbers play the same role as digits in decimal numbers; the only difference is that the base is 2 rather than 10. For instance, in binary, $101 = (1 \times 2^3) + (0 \times 2^2) + (1 \times 2^0)$, which is 7 in decimal notation. Fractions can be handled the same way as in decimal numbers. Scientific notation is not generally used for binary numbers.

A.1.3   Octal Notation

Two other schemes for representing numbers are common in computer languages: octal and hexadecimal. As may be gathered from its name, *octal* is base 8, conventionally written using the digits 0–7. Numbers are read in the usual way, so that octal 43 is expanded as $(4 \times 8^1) + (3 \times 8^0)$, or 35 in decimal notation.

In Java (and many other computer languages), octal notation is very confusing. Prefixing a numeric literal with a 0 (that's a zero, not a capital o) leads to it being interpreted as octal. For instance, the Java literal 043 is interpreted as the decimal 35.

A.1.4   Hexadecimal Notation

Hexadecimal is base 16, and thus we need some additional symbols. The first 16 numbers in hex are conventionally written

0, 1, 2, 3, 4, 5, 6, 7, 8, 9, A, B, C, D, E, F.

In hexadecimal, the value of A is what we'd write as 10 in decimal notation. Similarly, C has the value 12 and F the value 15. We read off compound numbers in the usual way, so that in hex, $93 = (9 \times 16^1) + (3 \times 16^0)$, or 138 in decimal notation. Similarly, in hex, the number $B2F = (11 \times 16^2) + (2 \times 16^1) + (15 \times 16^0)$, or 2,863 in decimal notation.

In Java (and other languages), hexadecimal numbers are distinguished by prefixing them with 0x. For example, 0xB2F is the hexadecimal equivalent of the decimal 2863.

A.1.5 Bytes

The basic unit of organization in contemporary computing systems is the byte. By this we mean it's the smallest chunk of data that may be accessed programmatically, though in point of fact, hardware often groups bytes together into larger groups that it operates on all at once. For instance, 32-bit architectures often operate on a sequence of 4 bytes at once and 64-bit architectures on 8 bytes at once. The term "word" is ambiguously applied to a sequence of 2 bytes, or to the size of the sequence of bytes at which a particular piece of hardware operates.

A *byte* is a sequence of 8 bits and is sometimes called an octet for that reason. Thus, there are 256 distinct bytes, ranging from 00000000 to 11111111. The bits are read from the high (left) end to the low (right) end.

In Java, the byte primitive type is signed. Bytes between 00000000 and 01111111 are interpreted as a binary number with a decimal value between 0 and 127 (inclusive). If the high-order bit is 1, the value is interpreted as negative. The negative value is the value of the least significant 7 bits minus 128. For instance, 10000011 is interpreted as $3 - 128 = -125$, because 00000011 (the result of setting the high bit to 0) is interpreted as 3.

The unsigned value of a byte b is returned by (b < 0 ? (b + 256) : b).

The primitive data type for computers is a sequence of bytes. For instance, the contents of a file are a sequence of bytes, as is the response from a web server to an HTTP request for a web page. Most importantly for text processing, sequences of characters are represented by sequences of bytes.

A.1.6 Code Example: Integral Number Bases

The program ByteTable.java displays bytes values in decimal followed by their corresponding unsigned value and the conversion of the unsigned value to octal, hexadecimal, and binary notations. The work is done by the loop:

```
for (int i = 0; i < 256; ++i) {
    byte b = (byte) i; // overflows if i > 127
```

```
int k = b < 0 ? (b + 256) : b;
System.out.printf("%3d  %5d  %3s  %2s  %8s\n",
        k, b, Integer.toOctalString(k),
        Integer.toHexString(k),
        Integer.toBinaryString(k));
```
}

This code may be run from Ant by invoking the `byte-table` target:

> *ant byte-table*

The output, after trimming the filler generated by Ant, looks like:

```
BASES
 10    -10     8  16          2

  0      0     0   0          0
  1      1     1   1          1
  2      2     2   2         10
. . .
  9      9    11   9       1001
 10     10    12   a       1010
 11     11    13   b       1011
. . .
127    127   177  7f    1111111
128   -128   200  80   10000000
129   -127   201  81   10000001
. . .
254     -2   376  fe   11111110
255     -1   377  ff   11111111
```

A.1.7   Other Primitive Numbers

In addition to bytes, Java provides three other primitive integer types. Each has a fixed width in bytes. Values of type `short` occupy 2 bytes, `int` 4 bytes, and `long` 8 bytes. All of them use the same signed notation as `byte`, only with more bits.

A.1.8   Floating Point

Java has two floating point types, `float` and `double`. A `float` is represented with 4 bytes and said to be single precision, whereas a `double` is represented with 8 bytes and said to be double precision.

In addition to finite values, Java follows the IEEE 754 floating point standard in providing three additional values. There is positive infinity, conventionally

∞ in mathematical notation, and referenced for floating point values by the static constant `Float.POSITIVE_INFINITY` in Java. There is also negative infinity, $-\infty$, referenced by the constant `Float.NEGATIVE_INFINITY`. There is also an "undefined" value, picked out by the constant `Float.NaN`. There are corresponding constants in `Double` with the same names.

If any value in an expression is `NaN`, the result is `NaN`. A `NaN` result is also returned if you try to divide 0 by 0, subtract an infinite number from itself (or equivalently add a positive and negative infinite number), divide one infinite number by another, or multiple an infinite number by 0.

Both `n/Double.POSITIVE_INFINITY` and `n/Double.NEGATIVE_INFINITY` evaluate to 0 if n is finite and non-negative. Conversely, n/0 evaluates to ∞ if n is positive and $-\infty$ if n is negative. The result of multiplying two infinite number is ∞ if they are both positive or both negative and $-\infty$ otherwise. If `Double.POSITIVE_INFINITY` is added to itself, the result is itself, and the same for `Double.NEGATIVE_INFINITY`. If one is added to the other, the result is `NaN`. The negation of an infinite number is the infinite number of the opposite sign.

Monotonic transcendental operations such as exponentiation and logarithms also play nicely with infinite numbers. In particular, the log of a negative number is `NaN`, the log of 0 is negative infinity, and the log of positive infinity is positive infinity. The exponent of positive infinity is positive infinity and the exponent of negative infinity is zero.

A.2 Objects

Every object in Java inherits from the base class `Object`. There are several kinds of methods defined for `Object`, which are thus defined on every Java object.

A.2.1 Equality

Java distinguishes reference equality, written ==, from object equality. Reference equality requires that the two variables refer to the exact same object. Some objects may be equal, even if they are not identical. To handle this possibility, the `Object` class defines a method `equals(Object)` returning a `boolean` result.

In the `Object` class itself, the equality method delegates to reference equality. Thus, subclasses that do not override `Object`'s implementation of equality will have their equality conditions defined by reference equality.

Subclasses that define their own notion of equality, such as `String`, should do so consistently. Specifically, equality should form an equivalence relation. First, equality should be reflexive, so that every object is equal to itself;

`x.equals(x)` is always true for non-null x. Second, equality should be symmetric, so if x is equal to y, y is equal to x; `x.equals(y)` is true if and only if `y.equals(x)` is true. Third, equality should be transitive, so that if x is equal to y and y is equal to z, then x is equal to z; `x.equals(y)` and `y.equals(z)` both being true imply `x.equals(z)` is true.

A.2.2   Hash Codes

The `Object` class also defines a `hashCode()` method, returning an `int` value. This value is typically used in collections as a first approximation to equality. Thus, the specification requires consistency with equality in that if two objects are equal as defined by `equals()`, they must have the same hash code.

In order for collections and other hash-code dependent objects to function properly, hash codes should be defined.

Although the implementation of `hashCode()` is not determined for `Object` by the language specification, it is required to be consistent with equality. Thus, any two objects that are reference equal must have the same hash code.

A.2.3   String Representations

The `Object` class defines a `toString()` method returning a `String`. The default behavior is to return the name of the class followed by a hexadecimal representation of its hash code. This method should be overridden in subclasses primarily to help with debugging. Some subclasses use `toString()` for real work, too, as we will see with `StringBuilder`.

A.2.4   Other Object Methods

Determining an Object's Class

The runtime class of an object is returned by the `getClass()` method. This is particularly useful for deserialized objects and other objects passed in whose class might not be known. It is neither very clear nor very efficient to exploit `getClass()` for branching logic. Note that because generics are erased at runtime, there is no generic information in the return.

Finalization

At some point after there are no more references to an object left alive in a program, it will be finalized by a call to `finalize()` by the garbage collector. Using finalization is tricky, and we will not have cause to do so in this book. For some reason, it was defined to throw arbitrary throwables (the superinterface of exceptions).

Threading

Java supports multithreaded applications as part of its language specification. The primitives for synchronization are built on top of the `Object` class. Each object may be used as a lock to synchronize arbitrary blocks of code using the `synchronized` keyword. Methods may also be marked with `synchronized`, which is equivalent to explicitly marking their code block as synchronized.

In addition, there are three `wait()` methods that cause the current thread to pause and wait for a notification and two `notify()` methods that wake up (one or all) threads waiting for this object.

Rather than dealing with Java concurrency directly, we strongly recommend the `java.util.concurrent` library for handling threading of any complexity beyond exclusive synchronization.

A.2.5   Object Size

There's no getting around it–Java objects are heavy. The lack of a C-like `struct` type presents a serious obstacle to even medium-performance computing. To get around this problem, in places where you might declare an array of `struct` type in C, we often employ parallel arrays rather than arrays of objects.

The language specification does not describe how objects are represented on disk, and different JVMs may handle things differently. We'll discuss how the 32-bit and 64-bit Sun/Oracle JVMs work.

Header

Objects consist of a header and the values of their member variables. The header itself consists of two references. The first establishes the object's identity. This identity reference is used for reference equality (==) and thus for locking. It is also used as the return value for the `hashCode()` implementation in `Object`. Even if an object is relocated in memory, its reference identity and locking properties remain fixed. The second piece of information is a reference to the class definition.

A reference-sized chunk of memory is used for each piece of information. In a 32-bit architecture, references are 4 bytes. In 64-bit architectures, they are 8 bytes by default.

As of build 14 of Java SE 6, the `-XX:+UseCompressedOops` option may be used as an argument to `java` on 64-bit JVMs to instruct them to compress their ordinary object pointers (OOP) to 32-bit representations. This saves an enormous amount of space, cutting the size of a simple `Object` in half. It does limit the heap size to 32 gigabytes (around four billion objects), which should be sufficient for most applications. As of build 18 of Java SE 6, this flag is on by default based on the maximum heap size (option `-Xmx`).

Member Values

Additional storage is required for member variables. Each primitive member variable requires at least the amount of storage required for the primitive (e.g., 1 byte for `byte`, 2 bytes for `short`, and 8 bytes for `double`). References will be 4 bytes in a 32-bit JVM and a 64-bit JVM using compressed pointers and 8 bytes in the default 64-bit JVM.

To help with word alignment, values are ordered in decreasing order of size, with doubles and longs coming first, then references, then ints and floats, down to bytes.

Finally, the object size is rounded up so that its overall size is a multiple of 8 bytes. This is so all the internal 8-byte objects inside of an object line up on 8-byte word boundaries.

Static variables are stored at the class level, not at the individual object level.

Subclasses

Subclasses reference their own class definition, which will in turn reference the superclass definition. They lay out their superclass member variables the same way as their superclass does. They then lay out their own member variables. If the superclass needed to be padded, some space is recoverable by reordering the subclass member variables slightly.

A.2.6 Number Objects

For each of the primitive number types, there is a corresponding class for representing the object. Specifically, the number classes for integers are `Byte`, `Short`, `Integer`, and `Long`. For floating point, there is `Float` and `Double`. These objects are all in the base package `java.lang`, so they do not need to be explicitly imported before they are used. Objects are useful because many of the underlying Java libraries, in particular the Java Collections Framework (JCF) classes in `java.util`, operate over objects, rather than over primitives.[1]

Each of these wrapper classes holds an immutable reference to an object of the underlying type. Thus, the class is said to "box" the underlying primitive (as in "put in a box"). Each object has a corresponding method to return the underlying object. For instance, to get the underlying byte from a `Byte` object, use `byteValue()`.

Two numerical objects are equal if and only if they are of the same type and refer to the same primitive value. Each of the numerical object classes is both serializable and comparable, with comparison being defined numerically.

---

[1] Open-source libraries are available for primitive collections. The Jakarta Commons Primitives and Carrot Search's High Performance Primitive Collections are released under the Apache license and GNU Trove under the Lessger GNU Public License (LGPL).

Constructing Numerical Objects

Number objects may be created using one-argument constructors. For instance, we can construct an object for the integer 42 using new `Integer(42)`.

The problem with construction is that a fresh object is allocated for each call to new. Because the underlying references are immutable, we need only a single instance of each object for each underlying primitive value. The current JVM implementations are smart enough to save and reuse numerical objects rather than creating new ones. The preferred way to acquire a reference to a numerical object is to use the `valueOf()` static factory method from the appropriate class. For example, `Integer.valueOf(42)` returns an object that is equal to the result of new `Integer(42)` but is not guaranteed to be a fresh instance and thus may be reference equal (==) to other `Integer` objects.

Autoboxing

Autoboxing automatically provides an object wrapper for a primitive type when a primitive expression is used where an object is expected. For instance, it is legal to write

```
Integer i = 7;
```

Here we require an `Integer` object to assign, but the expression 7 returns an `int` primitive. The compiler automatically boxes the primitive, rendering the above code equivalent to

```
Integer i = Integer.valueOf(7);
```

Autoboxing also applies in other contexts, such as loops, where we may write

```
int[] ns = new int[] { 1, 2, 3 };
for (Integer n : ns) { ... }
```

Each member of the array visited in the loop body is autoboxed. Boxing is relatively expensive in time and memory and should be avoided where possible.

The Java compiler also carries out auto-unboxing, which allows things like

```
int n = Integer.valueOf(15);
```

This is equivalent to using the `intValue()` method,

```
Integer nI = Integer.valueOf(15);
int n = nI.intValue();
```

Number Base Class

Conveniently, all of the numerical classes extend the abstract class `Number`. The class `Number` simply defines all of the get-value methods, `byteValue()`, `shortValue()`, ..., `doubleValue()`, returning the corresponding primitive type. Thus, we can call `doubleValue()` on an `Integer` object; the return value is equivalent to casting the `int` returned by `intValue()` to a `double`.

A.3   Arrays

Arrays in Java are objects. They have a fixed size that is determined when they are constructed. Attempts to set or get objects out of range raise an `IndexOutOfBoundsException`. This is much better behaved than C, where out-of-bounds indexes may point into some other part of memory that may then be inadvertently read or corrupted.

In addition to the usual object header, arrays also store an integer length in 4 bytes. After that, they store the elements one after the other. If the values are `double` or `long` values or uncompressed references, there are an additional 4 bytes of padding after the length so that they start on 8-byte boundaries.

A.4   Synchronization

In the next two section we describe two fairly simple approaches to synchronization. For more information on synchronization, see Goetz et al.'s definitive book *Java Concurrency in Practice*.

A.4.1   Immutable Objects

Wherever possible, make objects immutable. After they are constructed, immutable objects are completely thread safe in the sense of allowing arbitrary concurrent calls to their methods.

(Effectively) Final Member Variables

In immutable objects, almost all member variables are declared to be final or implemented to behave as if they are declared to be final.

Final objects can never change. Once they are set in the constructor, they always have the same value.

Effectively final variables never change value. In this way, they display the same behavior as the hash code variable in the implementation of Java's `String`. In the source code for `java.lang.String` in Java Standard Edition version 1.6.18, authored by Lee Boynton and Arthur van Hoff, we have the following four member variables:

```
private final char value[];
private final int offset;
private final int count;
private int hash;
```

The final member variables `value`, `offset`, and `count` represent the character slice on which the string is based. This is not enough to guarantee true immutability, because the values in the value array may change. The design of the `String` class guarantees that they don't. Whenever a string is constructed, its value array is derived from another string or is copied. Thus, no references to `value` ever escape to client code.

The `hash` variable is not final. It is initialized lazily when the `hashCode()` method is called if it has not already been set.

```
public int hashCode() {
    int h = hash;
    if (h == 0) {
        int off = offset;
        char val[] = value;
        int len = count;
        for (int i = 0; i < len; i++) {
            h = 31*h + val[off++];
        }
        hash = h;
    }
    return h;
}
```

Note that there is no synchronization. The lack of synchronization and the public nature of `hashCode()` expose a race condition. Specifically, two threads may concurrently call `hashCode()` and each see the hash code variable `hash` with value 0. They would then both enter the loop to compute and set the variable. This is safe because the value computed for `hash` depends on only the truly final variables `offset`, `value`, and `count`.

Safe Construction

The immutable objects follow the safe-construction practice of not releasing references to the object being constructed to escape during construction. Specifically, we do not supply the `this` variable to other objects within constructors. Not only must we avoid sending a direct reference through `this` but also we can't let inner classes or other data structures containing implicit or explicit references to `this` escape.

296   APPENDIX A. JAVA BASICS

A.4.2 Read-Write Synchronization

Objects that are not immutable should have read-write synchronization. A read method is one that does not change the underlying state of an object. In an immutable object, all methods are read methods. A write method may change the state of an object.

Read-write synchronization allows concurrent read operations but ensures that writes do not execute concurrently with reads or other writes.

Java's Concurrency Utilities

Java's built-in `synchronized` keyword and block declarations use objects for simple mutex-like locks. Non-static methods declared to be synchronized use their object instance for synchronization, whereas static methods use the object for the class.

In the built-in `java.util.concurrent` library, there are a number of lock interfaces and implementations in the subpackage `locks`.

The `util.concurrent` base interface `Lock` generalizes Java's built-in `synchronized` blocks to support more fine-grained forms of lock acquisition and release, allowing operations like acquisitions that time out.

The subinterface `ReentrantLock` adds reentrancy to the basic lock mechanism, allowing the same thread to acquire the same lock more than once without blocking.

The `util.concurrent` library also supplies an interface `ReadWriteLock` for read-write locks. It contains two methods, `readLock()` and `writeLock()`, which return instances of the interface `Lock`.

There is only a single implementation of `ReadWriteLock`, in the class `ReentrantReadWriteLock`. Both of the locks in the implementation are declared to be reentrant (recall that a subclass may declare more specific return types than its superclass or the interfaces it implements). More specifically, they are declared to return instances of the static classes `ReadLock` and `WriteLock`, which are nested in ReentrantReadWriteLock.

The basic usage of a read-write lock is straightforward, though configuring and tuning its behavior are more involved. We illustrate the basic usage with the simplest possible case, the implementation of a paired integer data structure. The class has two methods, a paired set and a paired get, that deal with two values at once.

Construction simply stores a new read write lock, which itself never changes, so may be declared final.

```
private final ReadWriteLock mRwLock;
private int mX, mY;

public SynchedPair(boolean isFair) {
```

```
        mRwLock = new ReentrantReadWriteLock(isFair);
    }
```

The set method acquires the write lock before setting both values.

```
    public void set(int x, int y) {
        try {
            mRwLock.writeLock().lock();
            mX = x;
            mY = y;
        } finally {
            mRwLock.writeLock().unlock();
        }
    }
```

Note that it releases the lock in a `finally` block. This is the only way to guarantee, in general, that locks are released even if the work done by the method raises an exception.

The get method is implemented with the same idiom, but using the read lock.

```
    public int[] xy() {
        try {
            mRwLock.readLock().lock();
            return new int[] { mX, mY };
        } finally {
            mRwLock.readLock().unlock();
        }
    }
```

Note that it, too, does all of its work after the lock is acquired, returning an array consisting of both values. If we'd tried to have two separate methods, one returning the first integer and one returning the second, there would be no way to actually get both values at once in a synchronized way without exposing the read-write lock itself. If we'd had two set and two get methods, one for each component, we'd have to use the read-write lock on the outside to guarantee the two operations always happened together.

We can test the method with the example program `SynchedPair.java`:

```
    public static void main(String[] args) throws
        InterruptedException {
        final SynchedPair pair = new SynchedPair(true);
        Thread[] threads = new Thread[32];
        for (int i = 0; i < threads.length; ++i)
            threads[i] = new Thread(new Runnable() {
                    public void run() {
```

```
            for (int i = 0; i < 2000; ++i) {
                int[] xy = pair.xy();
                if (xy[0] != xy[1])
                    System.out.println("error");
                pair.set(i,i);
                Thread.yield();
            }
        }
    });
    for (int i = 0; i < threads.length; ++i)
        threads[i].start();
    for (int i = 0; i < threads.length; ++i)
        threads[i].join();
    System.out.println("OK");
}
```

It constructs a SynchedPair and assigns it to the variable pair, which is declared to be final so as to allow its usage in the anonymous inner class runnable. It then creates an array of threads, setting each one's runnable to do a sequence of paired sets where the two values are the same. It tests first that the values it reads are coherent and writes out an error message if they are not. The runnables all yield after their operations to allow more interleaving of the threads in the test. After constructing the threads with anonymous inner-class Runnable implementations, we start each of the threads and join them so the message won't print and JVM won't exit until they're all done. The Ant target synched-pair runs the demo.

```
> ant synched-pair
OK
```

The program takes about two seconds to run on a MacBook Air.

Appendix B

Troubleshooting Text

When a text-processing application produces garbled or unreadable outputs, pinpointing the source of error can be surprisingly difficult. In this appendix we go over common sources of errors and how to correct them, using many of the example programs from the first part of this book as diagnostic tools. Additional programs are in the example source code distribution subdirectory:

```
javabook/src/diags/
```

This directory contains an Ant `build.xml` file that has targets to compile and run the examples. The programs belong to package `com.colloquial.diags`. The subdirectory `javabook/src/diags/src` contains the Java source files.

B.1 Validating and Verifying Text Data

To establish that a Java program is getting the right input data and producing well-formed text, we need to check the Java environment variables as well as the program's inputs and outputs. At the system level, data are streams of bytes sent to and from applications. Therefore, proving program correctness requires checking the conversion of inputs from bytes to characters and reverse conversion of characters to bytes for the outputs.

Character encodings are covered in chapter 2 and the process of converting byte streams to character data and back again is covered in chapter 3. Several of the example programs from these chapters provide useful diagnostics. In section 2.13.2 we discussed methods that can (sometimes) detect the character encoding. These can be used when the character encoding is unknown or there appears to be a mismatch between the actual encoding and the advertised encoding.

B.1.1   Check Java Character Encodings

One source of error is the mismatch between Java's default character encoding and the character encoding of the input file. Every instance of the Java virtual machine has a default charset, which may or may not be one of the standard charsets. The default charset is determined during virtual-machine startup and typically depends upon the locale and charset being used by the underlying operating system.

When a program doesn't specify the character encoding of an input or output stream, the Java environment variable `file.encoding` is used to get the `CharSet` name. We use the demo class `GetDefaults` to report the value of this variable.

```
System.out.println("encoding: "
                + System.getProperty("file.encoding"));
```

`GetDefaults` calls `System.getProperty(String)`, which returns the value of the system variable. The Ant target `get-encoding` compiles and runs this program.

```
> ant get-encoding
encoding: US-ASCII
```

On a Windows machine running XP the output is `cp1257`, which is the Windows version of Latin1 that includes ASCII as well as more punctuation characters and some common accented European characters. Both of these charsets are too limited to handle a large range of multi-lingual texts.

To avoid this problem, programs should always overtly specify the charset used when creating `Reader` and `Writer` objects for `InputStream` and `OutputStream` objects (in package `java.io`). Beware of using convenience classes `FileReader` and `FileWriter`, which use the platform's default character encoding. Instead use an `InputStreamReader` on a `FileInputStream` and an `OutputStreamWriter` on a `FileOutputStream` using the constructor methods that take a charset argument.

B.1.2   Validating Strings

Since it's possible to create strings that aren't a legal UTF-16 sequence, in section 2.9.10 we created the example class `ValidateUtf16` which checks that a `CharSequence` consists of a valid sequence of UTF-16 byte pairs. This program contains the public static method `isValidUtf16(CharSequence)`, which can be used to check that a `String` object is well formed.

B.1.3 Verifying Strings

We can inspect the contents of a String by printing the hex value of each char, as we did in section 2.9.14 in the demo program ByteToString, and then comparing the hex value to the corresponding Unicode code point for that char (or surrogate pair, for characters from the Supplementary planes, see section 2.3.1). We use the demo class VerifyChars to show how this works.

```
public static void main(String[] args) {
    System.out.println("a string of question marks");
    hexForChars("???");
    System.out.println("a string of japanese characters");
    hexForChars("\u4eca\u65e5\u306f");
}

static void hexForChars(String s) {
    for (char c : s.toCharArray())
        System.out.printf("%4s  ",Integer.toHexString(c));
    System.out.println();
}
```

The method hexForChars(String) prints the formatted hex values of each char of its String argument. In this example we call this method twice, first with a string consisting of three question marks and then with a string consisting of three Japanese characters. The Ant target verify-chars compiles and runs this program.

```
> ant verify-chars
a string of question marks
   3f    3f    3f
a string of japanese characters
4eca  65e5  306f
```

We use the question mark character in this example because this character is typically the default replacement string used by a charset decoder when it encounters a sequence of bytes that are outside of the allowed byte codes for that charset. When constructing a string from bytes, a character encoding is used to convert the bytes into char values (see section 2.9.1). At the point where the contents of a string are only question marks, it is necessary to look upstream in the processing chain to check the encoding and contents of the input data.

B.2 Escaping Text

One of the challenges for developers of text-processing applications is that almost every text-processing component allows strings to contain meta and control characters. To allow text data to be treated merely as data and not as special instructions, these characters must be either escaped or otherwise recoded.

For instance, Java string literals cannot span multiple lines. In order to create a string literal that includes a newline character, we write "\n" instead. In XML, we cannot have use the less-than character (<) as part of a text value, so we use the sequence < instead. We often have to deal with data generated in comma-separated value (CSV) format or in XML, or in Penn Treebank format, all of which have their own way of escaping special characters. Often such transformations are context specific. For instance, quoting a field is optional in CSV if it doesn't contain any quote characters or newlines. In the context of a quoted field, newlines do not separate rows but act as characters in the field's value. In XML, the pair of elements <![CDATA[and]]> act like quotes in CSV, and all characters between those boundaries are interpreted literally. Unlike CSV, there is no way to escape the close CDATA sequence]]>, so if this sequence occurs in the text itself, it must be placed outside of the CDATA section, and if more text follows, then a new CDATA section is opened, (see section 5.3.1).

When we wrap or chain together programs, input texts may go through a series of parsers. It's necessary to identify each point in the pipeline where text data will encounter a parser and to know which symbols are syntactically significant for that parser and how those symbols are escaped.

B.2.1   Escapes for Java Programs

In a Java program it is possible to write any Unicode character by using the escape format \u*xxxx*, where *xxxx* is the hexadecimal encoded value of the Unicode code point of that character padded to four characters with leading zeroes (see section 2.5.1).

String Objects

Several characters may not be used directly within character (or string) literals: newlines, returns, form feeds, backslash, or a single quote character. We can't just drop in a Unicode escape such as \u000A for a newline, because that behaves just like a newline itself. To get around this problem, Java provides special escape sequences that may be used in character and string literals including: \n (newline a.k.a. line feed), \t (tab), \' (single quote), \" (double quote), and \\ (backslash). See section 2.6 for full details.

Escapes for java.util.regex Regular Expressions

The backslash character is used to escape metacharacters in the regex language. The syntax of the regular expression language used by the `java.util.regex` package is covered in chapter 4. Further information can be found in the javadoc for the `Pattern` class in this package.

The regex language uses two-character sequence backslash followed by an alphabetic character as an escaped construct. Examples of these escaped constructs include: \xhh (hexadecimal values), \uhhhh (Unicode code points in hex), \t (tab), and \n (newline). Otherwise the backslash character is used to escape the following (non-alphabetic) metacharacter.

The set of metacharacters in the regex language differ slightly depending on whether or not they occur inside a character class specification. A character class specification is a set of character alternatives enclosed in brackets. Within a character class the singe period (.) character is not treated as the wildcard character but the hyphen (-) is treated as the range-forming metacharacter. Outside of a character class specification the characters used for grouping and quantification must be escaped.

To escape the backslash itself, it must be preceded by another backslash. Since Java also uses the backslash character as an escape character, in order to set up a `Matcher` that matches against a backslash character, this character must be twice escaped. To create the regex \\ (the regex that matches a backslash character), we need to use two backslash escapes in our string literal, writing `Pattern.compile("\\\\")`.

B.2.2 Escapes for XML

The reserved characters in XML are the open and close tags symbols and the single quote, double quote, and ampersand characters. These are escaped by using the named entity references: < for < (open tag), > for > (close tag), & for &, ' for ' (single quote), and &quot for " (double quote). Some Unicode characters are not legal XML characters, in particular, some ASCII control characters and some characters in the surrogate code blocks. See section 5.3 for complete details.

By default, XML processors parse all text in an XML document in order to find markup and entity references. CDATA is unparsed character data within an XML element. A CDATA section starts with <![CDATA[and ends with]]>. Nested CDATA sections are not allowed. The sequence]]> is always interpreted as the close of a CDATA section. If this sequence occurs in the text itself, it must be placed outside of the CDATA section and if more text follows, then a new CDATA section is opened.

CDATA sections are useful for documents that contain fragments of XML or HTML. This aids readability as well as the cost of converting all open and close tag symbols to their named entity reference. However, CDATA sections are restricted to only the legal XML characters in the declared encoding for that document. Problems can arise when writing programs that use CDATA sections to embed data in some legacy encoding in an XML document if those data contain illegal characters or characters not in the document's declared encoding.

B.2.3   Escapes for HTML

As in XML, the characters that are syntax markers cannot be used directly in text and the entity references must be used instead. HTML lacks the equivalent of the CDATA section. While the safest way to insure that character data always render correctly is to use entity references for all non-ASCII characters, this approach has several drawbacks: the web page is all but unreadable outside of a browser, a numeric character reference uses five characters to encode a single character, and the browser has to do more work to render a page. See section 5.4 for complete details.

B.2.4   Escapes for JSON

JSON consists of Unicode characters, and the default encoding is UTF-8. JSON has six *structural characters*:

   : , [ ] { }

When a string contains double quotes or structural characters, these are escaped by the backslash \, as is the backslash character itself. Unicode characters may be written as is or as the hex value of the Unicode code point preceded by \u. Unicode characters outside of the Basic Multilingual Plane must be written out as the UTF-16 surrogate pair. For example, a string containing only the G clef character (U+1D11E) is written "\uD834\uDD1E". See section 5.5 for complete details.

B.2.5   Escapes for CSV

CSV is a common data-exchange format. CSV stands for *comma-separated values*. A CSV file is a plain-text file consisting of a series of records, one record per row, where each row contains the same number of variable-width fields in the same order. A comma is generally used as the field delimiter, hence the name however, other characters may be used instead.

    Any field may be enclosed in quotes. Text fields containing commas as part of the text must be enclosed in quotes. A newline is used as the record delimited, so there is usually one record per line however, some applications may produce text data that contain newlines, in which case the field must be enclosed in quotes. Generally double quotes are used as the quote character. To escape a double quote character itself, it is preceded by a double quote. This is an example of one record consisting of three fields:

```
1997,Ford,E350,"Super, luxurious truck"
```

This is an example of another record that contains a text field that contains quoted quotes:

```
1997,Ford,E350,"Super, ""luxurious"" truck"
```

B.2.6 Escapes for the Unix Shell

There are many flavors of Unix, but in all cases the shell's parser performs the following operations: first it substitutes the value of variables and command outputs, then it generates filenames from expressions, then splits on whitespace to break the input into an array of input arguments, and finally it removes the escape character or any enclosing quotes from these arguments.

The shell provides three escape mechanisms: the backslash can be used to escape individual characters including the backslash character itself, or a pair of single quotes can be used to enclose one or more characters to escape the entire sequence by blocking all parsing operations, or a pair of double quotes allows processing of shell variable references and execution of commands enclosed by backquotes but blocks filename expansion and splitting on blanks.

Outside of single and double quotes the backslash character can be used to escape any character including spaces and all special characters. The backslash character can also be used to block interpretation of the newline as the command termination character therefore, a backslash followed by a newline allows continuation of the command on the next line. Inside of double quotes the backslash character can be used to escape double quotes, the dollar sign ($), backquote, and the backslash itself. Inside of double quotes the backslash character followed by a newline will allow continuation of the command onto the following line but the backslash and newline will be removed from the input.

We use the echo command to see how this works. The environment variable $SHELL is replaced by its value:

```
> echo $SHELL
SHELL=/bin/bash
```

but the backslash blocks variable expansion:

```
> echo \$SHELL
\$SHELL
```

Backquotes control command expansion:

```
> echo `date`
Mon Sep 30 20:18:19 EDT 2013
```

The backslash blocks it:

```
> echo `date`
`date`
```

When enclosed in single quotes, all parsing is blocked:

```
> echo '\`date\`'
\`date\`
```

Note that the enclosing single quotes are removed from the output.

B.2.7   Escapes for the DOS Shell

If the following characters do not occur within quotes ("), they must be escaped by preceding them with a carat (^).

```
& | ( ) < > ^
```

B.2.8   Escapes for Multiple Stages of Parsing

We reprise an example search from section 7.8.1 where escapes are used to pass inputs through the parsing gauntlet. In that example, we wrote a program called LuceneSearch whose main method takes a string argument that is passed in to the Lucene query parser that parses the string into a query object. The Lucene query parser has its own syntax. In particular, a query string that is surrounded by double quotes is treated as a phrase query. The challenge here is to send the Lucene query parser a query string including the enclosing double quotes.

We use Ant to run this demo program from the shell command line. In the build.xml file we define the Ant target lucene-search, which uses Ant properties to specify the arguments to the program.

```
<target name="lucene-search"
        depends="jar">
  <java classname="com.colloquial.applucene.LuceneSearch"
        classpathref="classpath"
        fork="true">
    <arg value="${lucene.dir}"/>
    <arg value="${query}"/>
    <arg value="${max.hits}"/>
  </java>
</target>
```

To set the value of the Ant property ${query} we pass it in from the command line as an environment variable. The command looks like this:

```
> ant lucene-search -Dquery="\\\"Powers of the Judiciary\\\""
```

This command consists of the program name `ant` and two arguments: the name of the Ant target and a Java environment variable of the form -D<name>=<value>. We enclose the value in double quotes in order to prevent the shell from splitting the input on whitespace. The Unix shell strips off one set of backslash characters, taking the sequence \\\" to \".

Ant is running as a Java process. The Java executable sees the -D flag and parses the second argument into a name-value pair, stripping off the enclosing quotes around the value. At this point the value of the property `query` is:

```
\"Powers of the Judiciary\"
```

Ant, like the shell, treats the backslash as a quote mechanism that is removed from the input string by the Ant parser. Ant doesn't try to split the string on whitespace but treats the entire string as an argument to the target Java program, so that the string passed in as the second argument to the `main(String[])` method of `LuceneSearch` is:

```
"Powers of the Judiciary"
```

The Lucene query parser treats this argument as a phrase query, as seen in the output from Ant:

```
index=lucene
query="Powers of the Judiciary"
```

B.3 Displaying Text

The final consumer of text data is the display device, e.g., the terminal window, browser, or printer, which takes in a stream of bytes from an application or file and maps them to characters according to a specified character encoding and then uses sets of installed fonts to display these characters.

If the specified character encoding doesn't match the encoding used to produce these bytes, the result usually looks like a mix of question marks and random glyphs, such as ‡, foreign currency symbols (£) or the copyright symbol (©).

If the font is missing or a character isn't defined for the specified font, then the missing character glyph is displayed instead. If the display is set to UTF-8 and the European languages display correctly but not all of the Russian, Japanese, or Korean symbols display, then it is likely that the fonts needed to display these characters are missing.

Index

CPSIA information can be obtained at www.ICGtesting.com
Printed in the USA
BVOW01s1845050814

361780BV00006B/119/P